Thinking Through Jeremiah

L. A. Mott, Jr.

Thinking Through Jeremiah
© 2009 by DeWard Publishing Company, Ltd.
P.O. Box 6259, Chillicothe, Ohio 45601
800.300.9778
www.dewardpublishing.com

Unless otherwise noted, all Scripture quotations are from the American Standard Version of the Bible. Any emphasis to the Biblical text has been added by the author.

Reasonable care has been taken to trace original sources for any excerpts and quotations appearing in this book and to document such information in the footnotes. For material not in the public domain, fair-use standards and practices were followed. Should any attribution be found to be incorrect or incomplete, the publisher welcomes written documentation supporting correction for subsequent printings.

Printed in the United States of America.

ISBN: 978-0-9819703-6-3

CONTENTS

FOREWORD

Jeremiah is one of the most admirable characters appearing on the pages of God's book. Few others, especially in the Old Testament, were as Christ-like as Jeremiah. In fact, when Jesus came, some of his contemporaries thought that he was Jeremiah reincarnated (Matt 16.14). Yet many Bible students today know less about him than about a host of other Old Testament heroes.

One reason Jeremiah is so little known may be the fact that his life is not laid out in an easily read narrative. Reading just a few chapters from Genesis or the books of history will provide a fair knowledge of the lives of Abraham, Isaac, Jacob, Joseph, David, Solomon, Elijah, Elisha and other great servants of God. But to know Jeremiah, one must read through the books of Jeremiah and Lamentations and be familiar with the historical background found in Kings and Chronicles. This is a rather daunting task for the average Bible student. Complicating the undertaking is the fact that the book is not in chronological order.

One who turns to commentaries for help will find that many of them are filled with complex discussions of strange Hebrew words and consideration of technical critical questions with which most of us are totally unconcerned. Some draw questionable implications and fabricate unsound predictions of a future earthly kingdom which do not harmonize with truth. Wading through all of this tends to obscure the personality of the prophet.

A serious Bible student wishing to know Jeremiah and to understand his character, his preaching and his times will be grateful for L. A. Mott's *Thinking Through Jeremiah*. As in other of Mott's works, a logical outline provides a simple guide to the text itself, and brings to light what otherwise might be overlooked in a casual reading. In a previous edition, long out of print, his notes were not only useful to students but also to knowledgeable teachers who wished to present the message of the book as simply as possible in sermons and classes. We predict for this new edition a wider circulation and an even greater appreciation of its value. We also predict for those who use it in their study a new appreciation of one of God's greatest servants—Jeremiah.

Sewell Hall
September, 2009

PREFACE TO 2009 REPRINT

This book was originally printed in 1979, set up in double columns by means of an IBM Selectric typewriter. Only 1,000 copies were produced. A few others were printed and bound in another form by Darrell Hymel for use in a class. He provided me with 50 copies as I recall, which were advertised in my Memo and quickly sold. But other than that, the book has been out of print for a long time.

No great public demand for a reprint has emerged, but now and then someone asks for it, and certainly others share my enthusiasm for Jeremiah. So I am changing the title of my *Notebook on Jeremiah* to *Thinking Through Jeremiah,* and republishing it in the style of my *Thinking Through the Bible Series.* I always credit my son Rick for the improved styling of my later books. But now this role is being taken over by Nathan Ward of DeWard Publishing, and I am hopeful the relationship with DeWard will produce a lot of good work in future.

The preaching I have done on Jeremiah has mostly focused on the personal element. Jeremiah felt all that we feel in the way of discouragement, and his feelings come out in a number of passages. He had a tough job to do in Judah's darkest days. If the description of Jeremiah as "the weeping prophet" has caused you to think of Jeremiah as a weepy, effeminate figure, you have missed the point. Jeremiah was the toughest man God could find for a mission to Judah when the apostasy had reached such depth that the nation could not be saved. Jeremiah wanted to quit. He wanted to abandon the task and perhaps to retire to the wilderness, where he could set up a little motel or refreshment stand and serve those who passed through. But to get away and to be done with this treacherous people. But feeling all this, he went on and did his duty anyway. And so can we. That is why reflection on the experience of Jeremiah is so inspiring. I am not much inspired by those who can walk the hot coals without flinching. I am not like that. But someone like Jeremiah, who feels all that I often do, and yet goes ahead and does the job anyway, is an inspiration to many of us who share his feelings.

His times were like our own, dark days indeed. Francis Schaeffer sensed it, and one of his books written to inspire and challenge those who lived amidst the social and cultural developments toward the end of the twentieth century was based on the prophecy of Jeremiah.[1] The study of Jeremiah can continue to guide those who endeavor to speak the word of God into the twenty-first century. We must not neglect this book.

I have not done major restudy, and so the content of the book is almost the same as the original. A few minor changes in content have been made, but only the styling is substantially different.

Two books on Jeremiah should be added to the list of those recommended below, the commentaries of J. A. Thompson and John Humphrey. I have not found time to study them, but recommend the authors. The fact is, someone who mostly teaches classes only in local churches, and small ones at that, does not find occasion to repeat courses on major prophets very often.

L. A. Mott
Jacksonville, Florida 2008

---

[1] *Death in the City.*

PREFACE TO 1979 PRINTING

I think Homer Hailey is the one who made me want to study the whole Bible. I am sure he is the teacher who first introduced me to the book of Jeremiah. My class with Brother Hailey was in the late fifties. I did not teach Jeremiah until about the early seventies at Romulus, Michigan. Since then I have taught it several other times in various types of classes; some shorter, some longer; in Alabama, in Maine, in Indiana, in Michigan, in Florida.

"Notebook" is a good description of this work on Jeremiah.[2] It is a Bible class teacher's notebook. It began as a set of notes jotted down for my own use in class teaching. The second time I taught Jeremiah I wrote an outline on the book, copies of which were reproduced, along with brief notes, as an aid to my students. Finally, I have greatly expanded the outline and the notes, and am happy to make my notebook available to a wider audience.

I hope you get some good out of it.

L. A. Mott, Jr.
Silver Springs, Florida
Summer of 1979

[2]*Notebook on Jeremiah* was the original title of the book.

FOR FURTHER STUDY

I think the first book on Jeremiah I studied was the commentary of C. F. Keil. After studying a number of others, I keep recommending this starting point as the most helpful book I have read for the general analysis of the book of Jeremiah. The reader will have to look no further than my outline, in which I have tried very hard to make independent judgments both as to what the units are and as to the headings which most accurately reflect their contents,[3] in order to see how much I think of C. F. Keil.

Other commentaries of value for one reason or another are those of John Bright (Anchor Bible), S. R. Driver, R. K. Harrison (Tyndale series), E. Henderson, T. Laetsch, A. W. Streane (Cambridge Bible for Schools and Colleges), and C. von Orelli. Driver, Henderson and Streane are out of print, and will have to be found in libraries or used book stores; von Orelli was reprinted in 1977 by Klock and Klock.[4]

[3]I think Jeremiah is the first book to which I applied this study method. Since then it has been a main feature in my methodology, applied in every book of exposition, and I recommend it to every student of scripture. You will be surprised at how much good it will do you.

[4]Two other commentaries on Jeremiah have been published since mine appeared in 1979, which should be added to this list: one by J. A. Thompson, the other by John Humphrey.

OUTLINE

Headings Of Major Units Of Jeremiah

Prophecies from the Reign of Josiah
Jeremiah 1–20

Part One: Background, Call of Jeremiah, and the First Speech (Jer 1.1–3.5)

Part Two: The Rejection of Impenitent Israel (Jer 3.6–6.30)

Part Three: The Way of Salvation (Jer 7–10)

Part Four: Covenant Disloyalty and the Consequences (Jer 11–13)

Part Five: Revelation on the Occasion of Drought (Jer 14–17)

Part Six: Jeremiah's Message in Symbols and the Results of its Proclamation (Jer 18–20)

Part Seven: Jeremiah's Message Concerning the Kings and Leaders of Judah After Josiah (Jer 21–24)

Part Eight: Jeremiah's Prophecy of the Seventy Year Empire of Babylon (Jer 25–29)

Part Nine: Jehovah's "Good Word" Concerning the Future of His People (Jer 30–33)

Addendum to Chapters 30–33: The Jews and the Land

Part Ten: The Conquest and Destruction of the Kingdom of Judah: Prophecies and Events to the Fall of Jerusalem (Jer 34–39)

Part Eleven: The Conquest and Destruction of the Kingdom of Judah: Words and Experiences of Jeremiah After the Fall of Jerusalem (Jer 40–44) and a Special Message for Baruch (Jer 45)

Part Twelve: Jehovah's Word Concerning Foreign Nations: Egypt, Philistia, Moab, Ammon, Edom, Syria, Arabia, Elam (Jer 46–49)

Part Thirteen: Jehovah's Word Concerning Foreign Nations (2), and Historical Appendix (Jer 50–52)

In general, these thirteen units correspond to the thirteen one and one half hour sessions into which I prefer to organize my course on Jeremiah. Usually, however, I find it necessary to depart from this natural organization at one point. Part Four can be covered in less than an hour and a half. So, usually I go on into Part Five and conclude the session at Jeremiah 15.9. (Hopefully the notes will show the logic of making Jeremiah 15.9 a break point.) Then the next session covers Jeremiah 15.10–ch 20. That permits me to bring together material on Jeremiah's trial of faith in chapter 15 with similar material in chapter 20.

Another place where it is difficult to keep to schedule is at Part Nine. It is difficult to do all that I attempt at that point in one session.

For shorter classes, I recommend that Jeremiah be taught in twenty-six sessions (two quarters), and that the natural units of the book of Jeremiah be observed as much as possible.

The reader will discern that I am a believer in having an organized approach to Bible study. I have little use for the "Mark-Your-Bible-at-this-Place-Start-There-Next-Time" theory of teaching.

ABBREVIATIONS

ASV	American Standard Version
ISBE	International Standard Bible Encyclopedia
KJV	King James Version
Mg	Margin (usually written out in second printing)
NAB	New American Bible
NASB	New American Standard Bible
NBD	New Bible Dictionary
NBV	New Berkeley Version
NEB	New English Version
NIV	New International Version
RSV	Revised Standard Version
LXX	Septuagint: Greek translation of Hebrew Old Testament
SDB	Smith's Dictionary of the Bible (four volume edition)
WNCD	Webster's New Collegiate Dictionary (1961)
YAC	Young's Analytical Concordance to the Bible

The basic text on which my comments are written is the American Standard Version. But many other versions have also been used, as the notes will show. Unfortunately I did not have the New International Version until the notes were well advanced, but I did use it at the end.

Prophecies from the Reign of Josiah

Jeremiah 1–20

Background of the First Twenty Chapters

From all specific indications of date (1.2; 3.6), Chapters 1–20 (treated in Parts One through Six) consist of prophecies during the reign of Josiah. After 3.6 no specific indication of time is given until 21.1. Is not the logical presumption that everything up to 21.1 comes during the time of Josiah? Is there any statement in these chapters that could not be explained in the context and setting of Josiah's reign?[5]

[5]Recent reading of the first twenty chapters (2008) turned up only about two or three passages that made me wonder. But I am leaving the heading as it is and simply challenge readers to consider this question for themselves.

PART ONE

Background, Call of Jeremiah, and the First Speech

Jeremiah 1.1–3.5

I. Heading, Indicating the Historical Setting of the Book of Jeremiah (1.1–3)

Explanation of This Heading

Keil thinks these verses are intended as a heading for the whole book of Jeremiah. Some prophecies came after Zedekiah's eleventh year, but are ignored here as being "of but subordinate importance for the theocracy." However, verses 1–3 are a perfectly accurate heading for Chapters 1–39, and it may be that these verses are intended as a heading for only this section, while the later prophecies have a heading of their own (cf. 40.1).

Kings Important to the Background of Jeremiah

Manasseh	687/86–643/42
Amon	643/42–641/40
Josiah	641/40–609
Jehoahaz (Shallum in 22.11)	609
Jehoiakim	609–598
Jehoiachin (Coniah in 22.24)	598–597
Zedekiah	597 –586

Dates must often be given in the form 687/86 because the Hebrew year did not begin and end at the same time as ours. Jeremiah omits Jehoahaz following Josiah, and Jehoiachin after Jehoiakim, though these are mentioned in 22.11, 24 under other names. Each reigned only three months.

Background in Judah

Jeremiah began his work in the thirteenth year of Josiah's reign (v 2). The historical background relevant to Jeremiah's work is found at 2 Kings 21–25 and 2 Chronicles 33–36. After the death of the good king Hezekiah, *Manasseh* corrupted Judah to a point from which there would be no return (2 Kings 21; 2 Chron 33). His repentance and reformation at the end had no deep or permanent effect on the nation. (Probably for that reason it is not even mentioned in Kings.) *Amon*, his son, reigned for only two years and returned to idolatry. Even *Josiah*'s reforms (2 Kings 22–23; 2 Chron 34–35) could not save the nation. The reforms were superficial and the people were not really converted. Destruction was decreed in spite of the reforms because of the sins of Manasseh which remained in the hearts of the people and had not really been effectively eradicated from the nation (2 Kings 23.26; cf. 24.3–4; Jer 15.4). The first twenty chapters of Jeremiah report the preaching of Jeremiah during the time of Josiah and expose the weakness of Josiah's reformation (cf. esp. 3.6–10). When the evil *Jehoiakim* came to the throne the floodgates were opened and the apostasy which had been outwardly restrained under Josiah burst forth to fill the land. Judgment day was just ahead. Jeremiah was to be God's spokesman in Judah's darkest days.

Important Dates in the Reign of Josiah (2 Chron 34–35)

1. Eighth year: Began to seek Jehovah (2 Chron 34.3).
2. Twelfth year: Began purge of idolatry (2 Chron 34.3–7).
3. Thirteenth year: Jeremiah began his work (Jer 1.2).
4. Eighteenth year: Book of the law found and reformation pressed on even more thoroughly (2 Chron 34.8ff).

International Relations

Assyria experienced a rapid decline through the reign of Josiah. In 612 BC the Assyrian capital at Nineveh fell to a Medo-Babylonian coalition. The Assyrian king with the remnants of his army withdrew and attempted a last stand in northern Mesopotamia. Pharaoh-Neco of Egypt was trying to regain Palestine and Syria for Egypt. Evidently thinking it would be to Egypt's advantage to have the greatly weakened Assyria survive as a buffer between Egypt and Babylon, in 609 BC he took his armies into northern Mesopotamia to support Assyria against the Medes and Babylonians. (RSV's translation at 2 Kings 23.29—"*to* the king of Assyria"—is not only grammatically possible but agrees with the Babylonian Chronicle which indicates that Egypt was Assyria's ally, not its enemy.) Josiah, perhaps to keep Palestine out of Egyptian hands, attempted to head the Egyptians off at Megiddo. Josiah was killed, but Egypt was not able to prevent Assyria from being finally crushed at Haran by the Medo-Babylonian alliance. After the death of Josiah Judah was briefly dominated by Egypt (2 Kings 23.31–35). But in 605 BC Nebuchadnezzar of Babylon administered a crushing defeat to Egypt in the *Battle of Carchemish* (cf. Jer 46.2–12). That decisive battle determined that Babylon, not Egypt, would be the power dominating the ancient near eastern world for the next seventy years. Jeremiah understood the significance of Carchemish and advised Judah and the surrounding nations to submit to Babylon (Jer 25, 27). But Judah insisted upon wavering between Babylon and Egypt and wove a web of political intrigue which would be the immediate cause of its destruction.

1.1 Hilkiah. is not likely to be the high priest under Josiah mentioned in 2 Kings 22.3ff and 2 Chronicles 34.8ff. The high priest would likely live in Jerusalem rather than Anathoth.

1.1 Anathoth. A town about 2 1/2 or 3 miles northeast of Jerusalem; one of the towns assigned to the priests (Josh 21.18).

1.2 The thirteenth year of his reign. About 627 BC

1.3 The eleventh year of Zedekiah. 587 BC

II. Jeremiah's Call to the Prophetic Office (1.4–19)

A. Jeremiah's Call (1.4–10)

1.5 Before ever Jeremiah was born God had him in mind for this work as his spokesman. The work might be difficult and calculated to cause doubt. When some would say, "God hath not sent thee" (cf. 43.2), Jeremiah himself must have no doubt. He must speak with certainty. These words at the beginning of his commission would provide the assurance and the sense of destiny Jeremiah would need for such work.

A prophet. A spokesman; a mouth through which God would speak (cf. Exod 4.16 with 7.1; Deut 18.15–19 with Jer 1.4–10).

Unto the nations. Not just Judah. See verse 10; 27.1–11; chapters 46–51.

1.6 I am a child. Hebrew may refer to an infant (as in Exod 2.6 and 1 Sam 4.21), but also to a young man (as in Gen 14.24; 34.19). RSV's "youth" probably best represents the idea here. Jeremiah protests that he lacks the maturity and experience for such a work. But God "persuaded" him with the following words (cf. 20.7).

1.7 Jehovah provides encouragement to overcome Jeremiah's reluctance. "Don't worry about youth or inability. Just go where I tell you to go and say what I command you to say."

1.8 Jeremiah is not sent forth under an illusion. There will be opposition. But it will be nothing to fear, for Jehovah will be with him.

1.9 Touched my mouth. How is not explained. Undoubtedly in a vision. Cf. Isaiah 6; Ezekiel 2.8–3.3; Daniel 10.16.

1.10 I have this day set thee over the nations. Jeremiah was given a position of authority. The Hebrew word is rendered *made overseer* in Genesis 39.4–5 and *made governor* in Jeremiah 40.5, 7. Hence NEB: "I give you authority over nations and over kingdoms," and NBV: "I have appointed you as the overseer of nations and over kingdoms." "Jeremiah, so to say, is to be Yahweh's vice-gerent over the kingdoms of the earth, with authority to declare His purposes regarding them" (Driver). The nations boast of their power. But Jehovah is the real ruler. Jeremiah exercises this power over nations as God's representative through the word he would speak. That word would not be ineffective but would certainly be fulfilled; it would be powerful—like fire, like a hammer that smashes a rock (23.29; cf. Isa 55.10ff). Cf. 31.28 where the same expressions are used concerning God as are here used of God's spokesman.

B. Two Visions Providing Assurance and Confirmation Regarding the Mission Assigned to Jeremiah (1.11–16)

1. A branch of an almond-tree (1.11–12). The certainty that the word of Jehovah spoken by Jeremiah will come to pass … providing the assurance God's spokesman needs as he begins his work, enabling him to speak with conviction and certainty.

1.11 A rod of an almond-tree. Or put "shoot" or "branch" for rod (as in Gen 30.37–39). No reference to the rod used for punishment or the traveler's staff. Hebrew for *almond-tree* is *shaked* meaning to be awake, watchful, alert; hence the "awake" or the "watching" tree. The almond-tree was so called as being the first tree to awake from winter's sleep; the first to bud or blossom forth. Now watch the play on words in verse 12.

1.12 Thou hast well seen. "You are a close observer!" (NBV).

For I watch over my word to perform it. Hebrew for watch is *shoked.* The "awake" tree represents Jehovah in his attitude toward his word. He will not be found asleep, so that time goes on and his word is never fulfilled. He is awake and watching so as to bring his word to certain fulfillment. Every preacher who proclaims the word must keep in mind this characteristic of God, and let no shadow of doubt be seen in his preaching.

2. A boiling pot (1.13–16). Judgment to be poured out from the north. As the first vision indicated the certainty of Jeremiah's message, this one describes its content.

1.13 A boiling caldron. Or pot. A great pot, such as our old wash pots, is referred to. *Boiling* is literally *blown upon*—"i.e. made to boil by the flames being fanned under it" (Driver). NEB: "a cauldron on a fire, fanned by the wind."

And the face thereof. I.e. the top or surface. "It is tilted away from the north" (NEB). The scalding contents are about to be poured forth *from the north.* Not "toward the north," as KJV text. Rather *from,* KJV margin. The caldron represents the judgment to come "out of the north" (v 14).

1.14 Explanation of the vision. Evil means calamity or disaster. Cf. our "bad times."

1.15 They shall set every one his throne. Indicating the intention to establish their authority in all these places.

1.16 And I will utter my judgments against them. A judicial procedure in which Jehovah brings them into court, examines and sentences them. The means of it is the coming of enemy armies (v 15). Cf. 39.5 and 52.9 where Nebuchadnezzar pronounces judgment upon his disloyal vassal Zedekiah. But more than that is involved. The judgment against Judah is one executed by Jehovah upon his faithless people.

Have burned incense. It could also be "have offered sacrifices" (NASB, NBV, NEB). Hebrew refers to the sending up of odors or sweet smelling smoke whether from the burning of incense (Exod 30.7–8; 40.27) or the burning of sacrifices (Exod 29.13, 18, 25; Lev 1.9, 13, 15; etc.). In some passages (Jer 1.16; 7.9 for example) it is uncertain whether the reference is to incense or sacrifices.

C. Charge to Jeremiah and Assurance of Divine Aid and Protection in This Difficult and Dangerous Assignment (1.17–19)

1.17 Gird up thy loins. I.e., tie your robe about you. Elsewhere the girding of the loins is preparation for travel (Exod 12.11; 2 Kings 4.29; 9.1); running (1 Kings 18.46); doing battle (Job 38.3; 40.7; contrast 12.21). Jeremiah is told to get ready for action. It is no time to run and hide or to shrink from the task behind a wall of excuses. The times demand courageous action.

Speak unto them all that I command thee. Later Jehovah added, "Diminish not a word" (26.2). Whatever the reaction, whether they like it or not, whatever they might do, Jeremiah is forbidden to hold back anything that God has given him to say. Cf. Ezekiel 3.16–18; 33.1–9.

Be not dismayed ... lest I dismay thee. The ASV translation is an effort to preserve the play on words found in the original. As pointed out in KJV margin, the Hebrew root means *to break* or *to break down*. NEB: "do not let your spirit break at sight of them, or I will break you before their eyes." The first occurrence is perhaps comparable to our "nervous break-down" or "mental breakdown." Reference is to a break-down of nerve or loss of courage. Jeremiah faces ridicule and scorn, severe opposition and persecution, physical and mental suffering—a great trial! But he must not let the opposition weaken his resolve. Whatever the dangers, he must steadfastly do his duty without wavering. That is his only hope. He must face his task with absolute confidence in Jehovah and Jehovah's word, trusting God to be his protector. If he does he will be safe; otherwise he will meet with defeat, be "broken to pieces" (as KJV margin has it). He has no choice but to trust in Jehovah.

1.18 The promise of divine protection in three figures, assuring Jeremiah that God will give him strength to overcome if he will do his duty without flinching. Cf. 5.17 and 8.14 on *a fortified city*; Judges 16.29 on *an iron pillar.*

Brazen walls. *Brazen* means "made of brass or bronze," the latter being an alloy of copper and tin which had been known a long time in Jeremiah's day. This "brass" or "bronze," says Laetsch, "was the toughest metal known to the ancients." With Jehovah's protection Jeremiah would be a brass wall able to resist every attack and to stand triumphant at last. But it would mean disaster to him if he did not endure in that confidence (v 17b).

1.19 Jeremiah is not to labor under any delusion. He faces terrific opposition. He will be an embattled prophet. But his enemies will not win. He will win! So he is assured, and given the reason for the assurance. Observe: "they," "thee," "I."

III. First Speech: The Case Against Israel (2.2–3.5)

Introduction

Only compelling evidence can set aside the conclusion (to which 1.2 points) that this section contains Jeremiah's first speech, delivered in the thirteenth year of Josiah's reign. The call and commission of Chapter 1 is clearly dated in that year. Chapter 2 seems to continue with the message Jeremiah carried to Judah beginning that year. (The references to Egypt do not necessarily demand a later date. See notes on specific verses.)

As Jeremiah begins he faces a nation which denies its guilt (vv 23, 35) and complains against Jehovah about the chastisements brought upon it (vv 29–30). Jeremiah's job is to set forth Jehovah's indictment of the nation in an effort to bring conviction to such a people. That is the burden of this first speech, which, however, also reveals the hopelessness of the situation in the time of Jeremiah.

Driver's heading for 2.1–4.4, though this division of verses is questionable, is at least appropriate to the section 2.1–3.5. The speech does give *The Verdict on Israel's History*, setting forth a judgment concerning the history of the nation as a whole. Later the distinction between "Israel" and "Judah" becomes significant (3.6–7).

Josiah's reformation began in the twelfth year of his reign (2 Chron 34.3–7). Jeremiah's work began in the thirteenth year (Jer 1.2). Although Jeremiah is not mentioned in the historical books until his lamentation at Josiah's death (2 Chron 35.25), undoubtedly he was a supporter of Josiah. But the prophet saw that the reformation was superficial and external, and not bringing about the inward conversion of heart necessary to save the nation. His speeches continually demanded a real conversion of heart on the part of the people, without which the nation was doomed.

The speeches of Jeremiah were not, of course, delivered from manuscript. They were first delivered orally and only afterwards put in writing (36.2–4, 32).

A. The Devotion of Israel's Youth (2.1–3)

2.2 The kindness of thy youth. "The devotion of your youth" (RSV, NASB). Cf. Hosea 2.15; 11.1. Reference to the early history of the nation at the end of the Egyptian sojourn; the period of betrothal before the covenant was entered at Sinai. Although the people murmured repeatedly against Moses (Exod 14.11–12; 15.24; 16.2–3; 17.2–3), no apostasy from Jehovah took place until the incident of the golden calf at Sinai. See further in Keil.

The love of thine espousals, Or "betrothals" (NASB) or "bridal days" (Driver, NEB) or "as a bride" (RSV). Like Hosea before him, Jeremiah portrays Israel as a bride who becomes unfaithful to Jehovah her husband (v 20, 3.1, etc.).

2.3 Holiness unto Jehovah. As his own chosen people (Exod 19.5–6; Deut 7.6; 14.2).

The first-fruits of his increase. Hebrew for *increase* is literally "income" and refers to that which "comes in" as the produce of the fields. The first-fruits were not for common use but were to be given to God (Exod 23.19; Lev 23.10–14; Num 18.12–13). Anyone who took the first-fruits for common use would incur guilt and be liable to punishment. So of anyone who devoured Israel.

All that devour him etc. As the first-fruits of God. *Devour* = eat.

Evil shall come upon them. Cf. Exodus 17.8–16 for an example.

B. Israel's Ungrateful Defection From Its Divine Benefactor (2.4–8). Israel soon left its "first love" (cf. Rev 2.4).

2.4 All the families. Includes even the northern tribes in captivity.

2.5 What unrighteousness? Cf. Deuteronomy 31.14–30 re. the song of witness which is given in Deuteronomy 32. The song is a vindication of God, putting the blame for the calamities that the people would suffer upon their unfaithfulness. Cf. also Isaiah 5.3–4; Micah 6.3. No accusation could be leveled against God (cf. v 29). Israel's apostasy was without excuse, altogether unjustified and unreasonable.

Have walked after vanity. Referring to the worship of false gods, called "foreign vanities" in 8.19. Cf. the parallelism in Deuteronomy 32.21 between "that which is not God" and "their vanities." The Hebrew word is literally *a breath*; it gives emphasis to the nothingness, uselessness, futility of a thing; is perhaps defined by "things that do not profit" (vv 8, 11). Cf. the description of idols in Psalm 135.15–18 and especially the statement, "They that make them shall be like unto them." Those who devote themselves to that which is without real existence *become vain*, futile and useless themselves, powerless to reach goals or accomplish anything of value. Cf. 2 Kings 17.15; Romans. 1.21.

2.6 Neither said they, Where is Jehovah? Not only did they forsake Jehovah (v 5); they ceased to seek him—the one who had done so much for them.

2.8 Indictment of all classes of leaders—those who led the people into the attitude of verse 6. They that handle the law are the priests (Lev 10.11; Deut 33.10; Mic 3.11; Mal 2.7).

C. Israel's Apostasy Astonishing and Unprecedented (2.9–13). Such apostasy is unheard of; it is shocking.

2.9 Wherefore I will yet contend with you. *Yet* or "still" (RSV), since the present generation continues the apostasy of their fathers (vv 5ff). *Contend* is better than "plead" (KJV) for modern readers. "Plead" is used in the old sense of *to argue for or against a cause.* A matter of controversy is involved. Jehovah is presenting the case against Israel. For other uses of the same Hebrew word see Genesis 26.20; 31.36; Exodus 17.2; Judges 6.31; Isaiah 1.17; 3.13; 45.9; 49.25; 50.8; 51.22; 57.16; Jeremiah 50.34; 51. 36; Micah 7.9; et al. For the related noun see Deuteronomy 25.1; 2 Samuel 15.2, 4; Jeremiah 25.31; Hosea 4.1; Micah 6.2. See discussion in Driver.

2.10 The isles of Kittim. Or coastlands (NASB) or coasts (RSV). *Kittim* refers to the town of Kition on the island of Cyprus. "… The name seems to have come to apply to the whole island of Cyprus (Isa 23.1, 12), and then in a more general way to the coastlands of the Eastern Mediterranean (Jer 2.10; Ezek 27.6)" (NBD, 701–702). *Kedar* was "a nomadic tribe which inhabited the Syro-Arabian desert" (NBD, 688) and represents the peoples east of Palestine. Hence: Go east or go west—you will not find such a case. Israel's apostasy is unexampled.

2.12 "The conduct of the Israelites was so atrocious, that it was calculated to fill the very heavens that witnessed it with amazement and horror" (Henderson).

2.13 Living waters. An expression used in the Bible for flowing or running water, as from a spring, as opposed to water lying stagnant in a pool or cistern. Jehovah had not been "a wilderness unto Israel" (v 31) but "the fountain of living waters" from which comes life, health and refreshment.

Broken cisterns. The imaginary gods that had no life and of course could not give life.

D. The Bitter Consequences of Israel's Course (2.14–19). By this double sin (v 13) Israel has brought upon itself all its present trouble. But instead of correcting its error, it continues to rely upon human expedients certain to bring further calamity.

2.14 A slave is treated like a piece of property belonging to someone. Israel is not a slave. But other nations have overrun Israel and treated it as if it were a slave belonging to them. Verses 15–16 provide the details.

2.15 The main reference is probably to the destruction of the northern kingdom. But even Judah had often been overrun by enemies and suffered partial destruction. *Lions* is a figure for enemies preying upon a nation. Cf. 49.14; 50.44; Isaiah 5.29; Micah 5.8.

2.16 Memphis and Tahpanhes. Cities of Egypt. This verse does not demand a date after Josiah. It may refer to a past event. But some take it as a prophecy with the fulfillment given in 2 Kings 23.28–35. Laetsch thinks it has special reference to the death of Josiah at the hands of Pharaoh-neco.

2.17 Israel had brought all this trouble upon itself by forsaking Jehovah. Verse 17 answers the question raised in verse 14.

2.18 Israel reacted to the trouble that resulted from forsaking Jehovah not by returning to Jehovah ("the fountain of living waters," v 13) but by seeking the support of foreign nations—"to drink the waters of the Shihor" (= the Nile) or "the River" (= the Euphrates). Isaiah uses similar imagery. See 8.6–8.) This in spite of the evidence that both Assyria and Egypt were enemies out for their own gain! (vv 15–16).

The reference to Assyria fits the reign of Josiah, before Assyria's fall, rather than later. And the reference to Egypt does not demand a later date. As far back as Isaiah's time supporters of alliance with Egypt were found in Judah. "Verse 18 refers to overtures of a political nature, no doubt advocated by rival parties in Judah. Assyria and Egypt hold the balance of world power, a situation that did not obtain after the very beginning of Jeremiah's career" (Bright).

2.19 Thine own wickedness shall correct thee. Exactly what happened! Judah's political maneuvering failed to produce a security system and instead became a web in which the nation became entangled to its destruction. The destruction of the nation was not merely an arbitrary judgment decreed by Jehovah without relation to circumstances. It was the natural end of the course Judah was following. That end would show that the forsaking of Jehovah in favor of a policy of dependence upon human expedients was *an evil thing and a bitter*. Paul says a similar thing about sin in Romans 6.21.

Cf. 4.18 for the judgment brought upon Judah by its wickedness. The context there is a description of invasion and siege.

E. Israel's Incurable Passion for Idolatry (2.20–25)

2.20 The Correct Reading if *text* be followed in verse 20a it is a reference to the liberation from Egyptian bondage. But the margin preserves an alternative reading *(thou hast broken thy yoke)* which better fits the context. Cf. the parallel in 5.6. Further, the reading *I will not serve* in place of *transgress* is more appropriate to the context.

Thou didst bow thyself. "You bowed down as a harlot" (RSV) or "You have lain down as a harlot" (NASB) better preserves the imagery which refers to the depraved and promiscuous worship of the fertility gods and goddesses. NEB has "you sprawled n promiscuous vice." More than *spiritual* harlotry, even actual physical promiscuity, was involved in the apostasy from Jehovah.

The alternatives before Israel were the same as those which confront modern man—the spiritual and the fleshly. The apostasy from Jehovah involved the choice of the things of the flesh over the spiritual life. And it is the same today: Many are choosing the way of the flesh rather than that of the spirit, even in their worship! Can you think of examples?

2.21 Cf. Isaiah 5.1–7 for fuller development of this figure.

2.22 The deeply ingrained nature of Israel's wickedness. Even after the strongest measures have been taken and the strongest detergents known have been applied, the stain of Israel's guilt remains. Might there be some reference to Josiah's reformation? All his efforts failed to produce a real change of heart (cf. 3.6–10).

2.23 Israel denies its guilt, but the evidence is clear: *See thy way*, i.e., your way of doing, your behavior, *in the valley*, likely referring to the Valley of Hinnom running south of Jerusalem, where the most depraved idolatrous rites were performed (cf. 7.31).

A swift dromedary. Or young camel (margin). In its passion for idolatry Israel was like a young she-camel or *a wild ass* (v 24) in heat. She rushes about intertwining or entangling her ways, rushing first one way, then another in her feverish search for a mate.

2.24 That snuffeth up the wind. She sniffs at the wind trying to detect the male scent (Harrison).

In her occasion. I.e., "the time of her heat" (NASB), "the time of her mating" (NBV).

2.25 Withhold thy foot. I.e. "Do not run thy feet bare, and thy throat dry, in the eager pursuit of strange gods" (Driver).

But thou saidst. Not necessarily in so many words. But this is what the response to Jeremiah's preaching amounted to.

It is in vain. Hopeless. Such advice is to no avail. This verse reveals the hopelessness of the situation in Jeremiah's day. The nation was determined to persevere in its apostasy and would not listen to any plea to change its course.

Strangers. Perhaps including not only foreign gods (as in Deut 32.16) but also foreign peoples (v 36). But see 3.13.

F. The Foolishness of Idolatry, Which Only Puts to Shame And Is Of No Help In Time Of Trouble (2.26–28). The truth of these verses appears again and again in the history of Israel. Jeremiah lived to see it in the reign of Zedekiah.

G. Israel's Guilt, In Spite Of Its Denial (2.29–37)

2.29 Wherefore will ye contend with me? "Plead" (KJV) as explained on verse 9. Cf. Judges 21.22 on the present usage of the word; also Job 33.13 and Jeremiah 12.1. They disputed with God re. the chastisements brought on them (v 30).

Ye all have transgressed against me. And therefore have no ground for complaint.

2.30 They have not accepted discipline either by word (*prophets*) or act (*smitten*).

Devoured your prophets. Cf. re. Manasseh, 2 Kings 21.10–16.

2.31 Have I been a wilderness unto Israel? Barren and unfruitful. Or perhaps, as some suggest, inhospitable. Rather, he had richly blessed Israel (cf. vv 5–7).

Wherefore say my people...? Why are they so bent on being free of their Benefactor? It is inexcusable.

We are broken loose. We roam about free and unfettered; we will not bear the yoke (v 20).

2.32 The unnaturalness of forgetting God. The real glory of Israel was its relation to Jehovah. He was the nation's most precious possession and chief ornament. Their behavior toward God was as unnatural as a bride forgetting her attire.

2.33 How trimmest thou thy way. Hebrew verb means "'to make good,' here 'to study out,' and the whole phrase means 'to walk in an artificial manner,' 'like a courtesan'" (ISBE); hence *to walk in a studied, artificial manner, such as a prostitute might do.* Israel was an expert on finding lovers, capable of training prostitutes, as verse 33b points out.

2.34 Descriptive of a murderer with blood on his garments. The words likely point to the persecution of the prophets mentioned in verse 30 and the innocent blood with which Manasseh filled Jerusalem (2 Kings 21.16; 24.4).

2.34b is difficult. It is variously explained: **1.** As in ASV text: *thou didst not find them breaking in*, i.e. as a burglar, the killing of whom might have been excusable (Exod 22.1), but it is because of all these things, referring to the apostasy from Jehovah and the idolatry in which it was desired to continue. Manasseh, for example, sought to crush all opposition to his idolatry (2 Kings 21.16). **2.** As in KJV and ASV margin: *I have not found it by secret search*—i.e., it was not necessary to break into houses or to dig into some secret place to find the blood, *but upon all these things*, i.e., these garments or skirts; or as others explain, openly, all about in Jerusalem, the prophet pointing to various sites with this phrase. **3.** Driver translates *not at the place of breaking in have I found it,* again with allusion to Exodus 22.1–2, *but upon all these (garments).* **4.** Still others put a period after *breaking in*, and connect the last words with verse 35 thus: *Yet in spite of all these things, you say...* (RSV; cf. NBV, NASB).

2.35a Protestation of innocence. Manasseh's atrocities were in the past and Josiah's reforms brought a reprieve in the threatened judgment (2 Kings 22.18–20), and for the time the nation had peace. Perhaps that explains how the people could delude themselves into thinking they were innocent and Jehovah's anger gone. Still the protestation of innocence manifests a peculiar depravity and loss of conscience.

2.36 But in spite of the feeling of security expressed in verse 35a, Judah continued to protect itself from enemies by means of foreign alliances. They roamed about, relying now upon one nation, now upon another. Ahaz had formed an alliance with Assyria (2 Kings 16.7–9) which had brought disaster (2 Chron 28.16–21; 2 Kings 18–19), just as Isaiah had warned it would (chs 7–8). Now the tendency was to ally with Egypt. But that move would be just as foolish.

2.37 With thy hands upon thy head. Sign of deep humiliation and sorrow as in 2 Samuel 13.19.

H. Conclusion of the Discourse: Jehovah's Call to Repentance and Israel's Response (3.1–5). Verse 6 is a new heading, evidently beginning another speech.

3.1 An allusion to Deuteronomy 24.1–4.

Yet return again to me. In spite of such faithlessness, with infinite grace, Jehovah pleads with his people to return (cf. Book of Hosea). That explanation has the support of ASV and KJV, although almost all others (e.g. RSV, NASB, NEB, NBV) give it a different slant, either making it a question (with the meaning, Is it possible or imaginable that you could return to me under these conditions?) or a statement of fact: You return (hypocritically) to me. But it best suits the parallel passages to understand Jehovah as inviting Israel to return and as being willing to receive her, provided she truly repents (cf. vv 7, 12–15, 22; 4.1–2). Even after the bill of divorcement (v 8) Israel is invited to return (v 12). This explanation is defended in Nagelsbach (in Lange), Henderson, and Laetsch. Keil, Driver, Bright and Streane take the other view.

3.2 The evidence of harlotry and justification of the call to "return." The bare heights refers to the places of idolatrous worship (cf. Hos 4.13).

By the ways hast thou sat for them. in the manner of a harlot (cf. Gen 38.14, 21; Prov 7.12). RSV: "you have sat awaiting lovers." Perhaps alluding to idolatrous altars erected along the way at street corners and gates (2 Kings 23.8; Ezek 16.25).

As an Arabian. Referring to the Arabian freebooter waiting in the wilderness to rob travellers passing by. Just as eagerly the Israelite watched for every opportunity to commit whoredom.

3.3 The showers have been withholden. Disciplinary action designed to correct (cf. Amos 4.6–11), but without effect—Judah cannot be brought to shame.

3.4 Wilt thou not from this time...? Bright explains: the time of the drought (v 3). Others: the time of Josiah's reformation begun in his twelfth year and completed in his eighteenth (2 Chron 34). Israel responds to the call for a return (v 1) with a return in appearance only; it is superficial and hypocritical. The calling upon Jehovah is only a lipservice, for it is not an expression of real repentance. Cf. the way verse 5c is managed in ASV margin. Another way of achieving the same result would be to use some mark of punctuation after *spoken*, a comma or semi-colon. Thus RSV: "Behold, you have spoken, but you have done all the evil that you could." You have spoken in the manner described (vv 4–5), all the while persevering in your evil ways, without the change of life which would signify genuine repentance. The next speech begins with renewed call for a return to God and elaboration of the meaning of repentance and return to God.

PART TWO

The Rejection of Impenitent Israel

Jeremiah 3.6–6.30

Introduction

At the end of the first speech in which the indictment of Israel was set forth, it was shown that God's call for repentance was met by superficiality and hypocrisy. The next section begins by explaining and defining the real repentance demanded by Jehovah.

I. The Change of Heart Necessary to the Salvation of the Nation and the Fulfillment of Its Destiny (3.6–4.4)

A. The Lesson of Israel's Rejection Not Heeded by Judah Whose Return to Jehovah Was Hypocritical (3.6–10)

3.6 In the days of Josiah the king. No other date is given until 21.1. Is not the natural assumption that all the material up to 21.1 dates from Josiah's reign? Observe also that later prophecies are dated.

Israel as here distinguished from Judah, refers to the northern kingdom, which had been in exile for a century.

3.8 Israel's rejection should have been a warning to Judah. But Judah ignored the warning and played the harlot, evidently considering herself immune to judgment. This speech explodes Judah's delusion and false sense of security.

3.9 The lightness of her whoredom. She treated this whoredom lightly. It was simply nothing—not to be taken seriously. Does this explain the denials of guilt in chapter 2?

Adultery with stones and with stocks. Referring to idols made of stone or of wood. Some put "trees" for *stocks* (RSV, NASB).

3.10 Her treacherous sister Judah. Strange! Verse 9 seems to describe Judah. Yet verse 10 calls Judah the *sister* of the one described there. The Septuagint has simply *treacherous Judah* in verses 7, 8, 10—perhaps the original reading, esp. in verse 10.

Feignedly. Or "in pretense" (RSV, NBV, NEB) or "in deception" (NASB). This feigned return to God refers to Josiah's reforms. The people returned outwardly, but the return had no depth, was superficial. The outward appearance was a pretence. Idolatry was still in their hearts. Cf. the end of the first speech (vv 4–5).

B. Invitation to Israel to Return to God in True Repentance (3.11–18). Yet this message is addressed to Judah. The intent is evidently to humble Judah and to provoke it to jealousy in the manner of Romans 11.11–14.

3.11 More righteous than treacherous Judah. Cf. Ezekiel 16.51–52. Judah's guilt was increased by the warning example of Israel, which it had before its eyes to turn it from sin, and by superior privileges —the temple and its service, the Levitical priesthood, the Davidic kings. Henderson mentioned esp. the efforts of Josiah.

3.12–13 Toward the north. I.e., in the direction of Israel's captivity.

Return … Only acknowledge thine iniquity. The restoration of covenant relations between God and Israel was not guaranteed unconditionally.

Only acknowledge thine iniquity. Contrast 2.23, 35. Confession of guilt is an indispensable requirement. Jehovah cannot forgive them of sins they will not acknowledge.

The strangers. Strange gods (cf. Deut 32.16).

3.14 One of a city, and two of a family. The prospect is not of a great national turning to Jehovah, but of a few individuals coming to repentance. Even if so few as *one of a city*, and *two of a family* heed the call to *Return*, God will accept them. A spiritual kingdom composed of converted people is the prospect, unlike the former physical nation which was composed of believers and unbelievers. The numbers *one* and *two* show that family "is a larger community than the inhabitants of one town, i.e. that it indicates the great subdivisions into which the tribes of Israel were distributed" (Keil).

I will bring you to Zion. In accord with the promises of Deuteronomy

30.1–5. The "restoration" promises are discussed at more length in an appendix to chapters 30–33.

3.15 Shepherds. Rulers. Cf. 2.8 where *rulers* is literally *shepherds*; KJV has pastors.

According to my heart as 1 Samuel 13.14 and not as Hosea 8.4.

3.16 They shall say no more, The ark of the covenant of Jehovah. Remember that though the passage is about Israel it is addressed to Judah. And understand the ground of their feeling of security. The impenitent people depended upon sacrifice, the temple, the ritual (6.20; ch 7), thinking the perpetuation of these things secured them against judgment. On the ark of the covenant, which was the place where Jehovah was enthroned among the people (cf. Exod 25.22) and the symbol of his presence, see esp. the superstitious regard for the ark revealed in 1 Samuel 4.3–8 and the words of 1 Samuel 4.21–22. All that Judah depended upon would be of no significance in the restoration. The ark would not be present after the captivity. But that would be of no significance. Thus again a change in the form of the kingdom is indicated. Cf. John 4.20–24. Jeremiah knocks the props from under Judah.

3.17–18 The ark had been the place where God was enthroned. Now with the ark gone, Jerusalem is called the throne of Jehovah—a far cry from the days when idolatry filled the city. Not just Jews but *all the nations* would be gathered to this place where Jehovah had revealed himself (cf. Isa 2.2–4). Verse 18 assumes the future exile of Judah from which both they and Israel would return to the land together.

See the appendix to chapters 30–33 for fuller treatment of the issues raised in this whole passage. Hosea 1.10–2.1, 23 helps on this return of the Israelites. See Romans 9.25–27 and 1 Peter 2.9–10 for the Holy Spirit's own application. Compare also Isaiah 11.10–11, the fulfillment and application of which is indicated by Romans 15.12.

Re. what is said of Jerusalem in this text, observe the importance of Jerusalem in the early days of Christianity. But the Jerusalem that is important to the people of God in new covenant days is not the physical city but that heavenly city foreshadowed by the earthly. See Galatians 4.25–26; Hebrews 12.22; 13.12–14.

Summary on the Restoration

1. Return of a remnant (v 14). 2. Godly rulers (v 15). 3. Passing of O. T.

forms (v 16). 4. Jerusalem the religious center to which all nations gather (v 17). 5. Restoration of unity between Judah and Israel (v 18). No special advantage for Judah.

Much of this prospect, clearly, only becomes a reality in gospel terms in the Messianic Age.

C. The Repentance Necessary to Restoration Depicted (3.19–25)

1. God's Original Purpose for Israel (v 19). *But I said, etc.* means *to myself*; i.e. "I thought" (RSV). Verse 19 describes God's thought or intention at the beginning in choosing Israel. *How I will put thee etc.* is an exclamation (ASV) rather than a question (KJV), expressing the divine purpose for Israel. *Ye shall call me My Father, etc.* is the response that would have been appropriate on Israel's part and the one intended by Jehovah.

2. Israel's Treachery, Causing the Need of Repentance (v 20). God's intention and expectation was not fulfilled. His high hopes for Israel were disappointed. Israel's response to the high and holy destiny held out before her was nothing less than treacherous. This treachery and faithlessness is what now makes repentance absolutely necessary to her ever attaining her destiny.

3. Israel's Brokenhearted Cry as She Sees the End to Which Idolatry Has Led (v 21). *The bare heights* (ASV; KJV, high places) is the scene of the idolatry (vv 2, 6). In a dramatic portrayal, Jeremiah imagines the people finally coming to understand the stupidity and the futility of idolatry and weeping with broken heart at the place where the idolatry had been practiced.

4. God's Invitation and the Manner of Israel's Return (vv 22–25)

3.22a The merciful Jehovah extends an invitation to his wayward people to come back and be healed of apostasy and the misery it had brought.

3.22b Israel's response, renewing the covenant with Jehovah. Cf. Deuteronomy 26.16–19; 27.9; 29.10–13 on this language.

3.23–25 Israel comes to recognize that salvation can be found only in Jehovah. The idols bring only shame.

3.23a RSV and NBV have, "Truly the hills are a delusion, the orgies on the mountains." NASB is similar. KJV's *the multitude of mountains,* though a possible translation (see Keil), does not fit the situation as well as ASV's *the tumult on the mountains.* ASV margin has *noisy throng* for *tumult.* "The allusion is to the noisy orgies accompanying the idolatrous cults celebrated on the mountains" (Driver). Cf. 1 Kings 18.26–29; Hosea 4.13–14.

The shameful thing, Literally as KJV, "shame," perhaps to be spelled with a capital "s." The reference is to "Baal, god of shame" (NEB), as the parallelism of 11.13 makes clear; cf. Hosea 9.10. Jehovah was their glory (2.11); Baal, the god of shame.

Hath devoured the labor of our fathers. Keil thinks reference is not to the *flocks, etc.* sacrificed to Baal, since sheep and cattle were also offered to Jehovah, but to the judgments brought down upon the people through enemy invasions due to idolatry. See 5.17 and cf. Deuteronomy 28.30, 33.

3.25a is the words of a people who realize that they are getting what they deserve and who are reconciled to it.

Let us lie down. The action of one brought low, humbled, suffering anguish. Cf. 2 Samuel 12.16; 13.31; 1 Kings 21.4. "So deep was their sense of shame that they were quite overwhelmed by it" (Henderson).

3.25bc They are described as also coming to understand the reason for their humiliation.

D. The Condition Indispensable to Israel's Salvation and to the Attaining of its Destiny (4.1–4)

1. Jehovah's Answer, Concluding the Section Dealing With the Northern Kingdom and Summarizing the Conditions Necessary to its Restoration (4.1–2)

4.1 Thine abominations. I.e., the idols (1 Kings 11.5, 7); "your loathsome idols" (NEB).

Then shalt thou not be removed. Rather than being a promise of permanence in the land, perhaps better explained as simply adding another condition or strengthening the previous one: "and do not waver" (RSV); "and will not waver" (NASB); "and cease wandering" (NBV); "and stray no more" (NEB)—referring to the straying from Jehovah, wandering off after the idols (cf. 2.23; 3.13).

4.2 And thou shalt swear. Some explain this as a kind of oath of loyalty to Jehovah, a renewal of the covenant (in the manner of Deut 26.17; 29.12). But the contrast with Jeremiah 5.2 suggests that the emphasis may be upon *in truth, etc.* Whatever swearing was done was to be *by Jehovah* rather than other gods (cf. Deut 6.13–15; 10.20; Amos 8.14) and it was to be done *in truth, etc.* rather than *falsely* (cf. Jer 5.2).

And the nations shall bless themselves in him. The consequence of Israel's faithfulness to Jehovah; with allusion to the promises to Abraham, Isaac and Jacob (Gen 12.3; 18.18; 22.18; 26.4; 28.14). Jeremiah has explained the terms on which Israel can reach the destiny intended for it by Jehovah. Yet Jehovah's purposes will not be blocked even if Israel is not faithful, as we see from Romans 11.11–14. God is prepared for any contingency.

2. Application to Judah (4.3–4). Important! All of this about Israel is really addressed to Judah and intended to destroy the false security she felt. Israel had forsaken Jerusalem, the temple and the rule of the house of David. In addition, Israel had now been in exile far from the land for a century. (Cf. Ezek 11.15 for the kind of false conclusions that could arise from that situation.) Judah's trust was in the fact that she had these things (cf. 6.20 in this section and 7.1–15 in the next). Judah completely missed it on why Israel went into exile. And that explains why Judah took no warning from the destruction of Israel (3.6–10). Jeremiah shows the reason for Israel's exile but also indicates the possibility of its recovery; he shows that the absence of the covenant forms would be no hindrance to the restoration of Israel (3.16). The northern kingdom, together with Judah (3.18), could yet attain the destiny God intended (3.19; 4.2) *if they would repent*. But that is the key. Israel must experience a genuine conversion of heart in order to be restored. And Judah must do the same in order to avoid a fate like that Israel had already experienced (4.4b). Without that change of heart, neither Jerusalem nor the temple nor the sacrifices could save Judah.

4.3 Break up your fallow ground. *Fallow ground* is new land, ground that has been left uncultivated. The figure of plowing new ground is used in a call to repentance and a change of life. Cf. Hosea 10.12–13. Another figure is used in verse 4.

4.4 Circumcise yourselves. All Jewish men were circumcised physically. But their hearts (= the thinking, reasoning part of a person, 3.17; 4.9, 14, 19; 5.23; 7.24, 31; etc.) were insensitive to the will and word of God, as though covered by a foreskin keeping God's word from reaching it. (In 6.10 the *ear* is so described. Other passages referring to this spiritual circumcision are 9.25–26; Deut 10.16; 30.6; Rom 2.28–29; and Col 2.11.) So again we have a call to repentance under another figure. Circumcision was a token of the covenant between God and Israel (Gen 17.9–14). The advantage of it was access to the law and the covenant blessings. But if a

Jew made no use of these he was no better than any pagan without the covenant sign (Rom 2.25–29).

II. The Judgment Coming Upon Judah in the Absence of the Repentance Demanded by Jehovah (4.5–31)

(Or, taking our cue from verse 4b: The Burning Wrath of God Which Will Consume Judah in the Absence of the Repentance Demanded by Jehovah.)

Jeremiah's plea for repentance is based upon the certainty of the judgment which will otherwise come upon the nation.

A. Destruction From the North (4.5–9). With dramatic effect the invasion is portrayed as already set in motion.

4.5 Blow ye the trumpet in the land. Sounding the warning; calling the people to take refuge within walled cities.

4.6 Set up a standard toward Zion. *Zion* was the stronghold. A flag was to be put up as a signal directing the people into the place of safety.

Evil from the north. Cf. 1.14–15; 6.1, 22; referring to the Babylonians (25.9).

4.7 The enemy is represented as already on the way; the lion has left his lair.

4.8 For this gird you with sackcloth. Nothing is left to do but raise a lamentation and put on sackcloth, the coarse cloth which was the usual accompaniment of mourning.

For the fierce anger of Jehovah is not turned back from us. Referring to "the burning wrath on account of the sins of Manasseh, with which the people has been threatened by the prophets (Keil). See 2 Kings 21.10–15. Josiah's reformation, perhaps, deluded the people into thinking, "Surely his anger is turned away from me" (Jer 2.35). But not so! In spite of Josiah's reforms the wrath due to Manasseh's sins remained (2 Kings 23.26–27; 24.3; 15.4), for the people had not truly repented of these sins and they had not returned unto Jehovah with their whole heart but only with pretense (Jer 3.10).

4.9 The collapse of all leadership at the invasion; the perplexity and helplessness of all classes of leaders. Nobody among the leaders knows what to do; all are left at a loss. Morale is shattered.

B. Exclamation of the Prophet (4.10). A sign bursts forth from Jeremiah in reaction to the revelation of judgment in verses 5–9, expressing deep feeling. The words *Ye shall have peace* are clearly those of the false prophets (6.14; 14.13; 23.17). Yet the words are ascribed to Jehovah: *Surely thou hast greatly deceived this people and Jerusalem, sayings, etc.* The verse is to be explained in the light of 1 Kings 22.19–23, Ezekiel 14.1–11, and 2 Thessalonians 2.8–12. The message of peace was not Jeremiah's message. He had shown the people they could expect anything but peace. The false prophets were indicted as liars. (See context of above passages.) That was Jehovah's message. But the people hardened their hearts against it and refused to repent (cf. 5.12–13). Thereupon Jehovah punished that attitude toward his words by using the false prophets who would tell the people what they wanted to hear. God did not put their message into their hearts directly. It was their message, not God's. But Jehovah controls all things as the Sovereign Lord of the whole creation. He is able to use even bad men and false prophets to accomplish his purposes—in this case, to punish a bad attitude toward truth. Thus the deception of the people was the first stage of their punishment. Is there a warning here for us?

C. Continuation of the Description of the Impending Invasion, From Which Only Swift Repentance Can Save (4.11–18)

4.11 A hot wind etc. Refers to the *sirocco,* the scorching wind which blows in from across the eastern desert, withering the vegetation and making life almost unbearable; here a figure for the invader.

The daughter of my people. Hebrew has *daughter* and *people* in apposition—*my daughter people.* Personification of the people of Jerusalem, treating the population as if one person.

Not to winnow, etc. Referring to the process of throwing wheat into the wind to separate the chaff from the good grain. Not a gentle breeze suitable for winnowing was to be expected, but *a wind too strong for these* (v 12, margin; also RSV, NASB, NBV, NEB). The work of Jeremiah would show that what was required at this stage in the history of Israel was not a gentle breeze to separate the good from the bad but a strong wind that would sweep away the entire people into exile.

4.12 Utter judgments against them. So ASV and KJV margin. See the note on 1.16.

4.14 Plea for repentance, the only hope of deliverance. External reform would not do. They must wash the heart from wickedness and the evil thoughts which they had entertained all too long. This verse illustrates the conditional nature of such prophecies of doom. Judah could still repent and be saved.

4.15 The *urgency* of the repentance called for in verse 14. The approach of the invaders is already reported from *Dan* at the northern boundary of Palestine and from *the hills of Ephraim* just a few miles north of Jerusalem.

4.16 Make ye mention to the nations. The warning concerns not just Jerusalem but the surrounding nations as well.

Watchers. "Besiegers" (RSV, NASB, NBV).

4.17 As keepers of a field. Enemy tents will be scattered round the cities "like the shelters or booths erected by shepherds and gardeners to protect their produce or flocks" (Harrison).

4.18 Fixes the responsibility for the calamity. Sin brings its own bitter end. Cf. the note on 2.19 where the context is more specific about the *way* and the *doings* of Judah which brought such a bitter end, while this context is fuller in describing the nature of the end.

D. Outcry of the People Caught Up in the Invasion (4.19–21)

The vision of invasion has been so graphic, so real for Jeremiah, that he feels all the emotion of one caught up on the actual siege. Compare the effect of a dramatic motion picture in which the audience becomes so involved and caught up in the story as even to cry out. But Jeremiah is not speaking only for himself. Jerusalem has been directly addressed in verse 18. The bitterness of her wickedness at the end has been described. Now Jeremiah speaks for the personified mother city, expressing the anguish she will feel at the end. The painful feelings Jeremiah has at the vision are the feelings the people will have when the vision is translated into reality. The plural "tents" and "curtains" (in v 20) suggest more than one person. And the suggestion is confirmed by 10.19ff where the community is clearly speaking.

4.19 My anguish. Literally as KJV: "My bowels." NBD, 164, says the term "refers primarily to the intestines," but "may sometimes refer collectively to all the internal organs." Perhaps "innards" is the best translation. "NASB puts "inward parts" in the margin as a literal translation. Reference is clearly to the seat of the deepest feelings and emotions.

My very heart. Hebrew *the walls of my heart.* The sensation was as it were a pounding against the walls of the heart.

My heart is disquieted in me. "My heart is beating wildly" (RSV). "My heart is pounding in me" (NASB).

I cannot hold my peace. I.e., I must cry out, giving vent to the emotion that fills me upon hearing the blasting forth of the trumpet.

4.20 Destruction upon destruction is cried. As the fall of one city after another is reported, *the whole land* being *laid waste.*

4.21 Cry of despair. No end is in sight.

E. Reason of the Horrors Described: The Guilty Folly of the People (4.22). Jehovah breaks in imperceptibly, assigning the reason for the judgment. Observe what such passages indicate re. the inspiration of the prophet. He moves imperceptibly from what he announces Jehovah as saying, to what he himself says, to what Jehovah is saying, without any special introductory "Thus saith Jehovah." Such is the prophet's relationship with Jehovah that he moves from one form to another without fear that the failure always carefully to distinguish one from another will be misleading. In fact it is all inspired of Jehovah.

4.22 Sottish. "Stupid" (RSV, NASB, NBV), "silly" (NEB). Sottish suggests behaving as stupidly as one under the influence of liquor.

They are wise to do evil. "They are experts in doing evil" (NBV); "skilled in doing evil" (RSV).

F. Jeremiah's Vision of the Devastation Effected by the Enemy (4.23–26). The completeness of the desolation is set forth in bold poetical imagery.

4.23 Waste and void. Perhaps better: "formless and empty" (NBV, after Driver). The land is portrayed as reduced to primeval conditions. Cf. Genesis 1.2; Isaiah 24.19; 34.11.

4.24 The mountains. The most solid and stable things of earth. But they quiver before the judgment of God.

4.25–26 "All is represented as one complete scene of solitude and desolation; no vestige of the human or of the feathered creation is to be seen. City and field are alike laid waste" (Henderson).

The fruitful field. "The garden land" (NBV, after Driver). Hebrew is the proper name *Carmel*, the lower slopes of which were famed for fruitfulness, and here stand as representative of all the fruitful areas of the land (Keil).

G. Judah's Doom Decreed and Not to be Prevented by Human Expedients (4.27–31)

4.27 Not … a full end. One of the recurring expressions in Jeremiah (5.10, 18; 30.11; 46.28; cf. Ezekiel 11.13). Not a complete annihilation. A remnant to be spared (cf. Isa 6.13; 10.20–23; 11.11, 16; Amos 9.8–10; Mic 2.12; 5.7–8; Zeph 3.13; etc.).

4.28a Poetic imagery. "The whole of nature is clad in gloom at the awful catastrophe" (Henderson).

4.30 Thou that clothest thyself with scarlet. Judah tries various expedients in order to avoid calamity. The nation is personified and compared to a prostitute trying to make herself attractive to her lovers. Some think of Judah's efforts to gain the favor of her enemy and avoid disaster; others, of the effort to court and win the support of Egypt. The former seems most consistent with verse 30c. Cf. 2 Kings 9.30.

Enlargest thine eyes with paint. I.e., blackening above and below the eyes in order to make the eyes appear larger.

Lovers. Political friends or allies. Cf. 2.33, 36; Ezekiel 23.5, 7, 9, 12, 16, 20.

4.31 The daughter of Zion. "I.e. the personified population of Zion" (Driver). Cf. verse 11; 6.2; 8.11, 19; and often.

That spreadeth her hands. Better, "stretching out her hands" (RSV, NASB). I.e., pleading, "begging for help" (tr. in NBV).

III. The Moral Necessity of Punishment Upon "Such a Nation as This" (Ch 5)

Observe the refrain in verses 9 and 29—the key to the section; also the indication of verses 1 and 7 that Jehovah desires to pardon. But he cannot pardon "such a nation as this." The total corruption of the people makes judgment a moral necessity.

A. The Total Corruption and Obstinacy of Judah Which Demands Judgment and Makes Pardon Impossible (5.1–9)

1. Corruption and Rebellion in All Classes (5.1–5)

5.1 "Jeremiah anticipates Diogenes of Greece in his quest for an honest man" (Harrison).

If ye can find a man. The verse intends to illustrate the vast extent of the corruption. A search of the streets would not be likely to reveal a good man. Not that absolutely none were present in Judah, for think of Josiah, Zephaniah, Jeremiah himself and his scribe Baruch. But the corruption was so extensive these were exceptions not to be taken into account. "… The little good that was left in the land was driven out of sight by the prevailing wickedness, and exercised no appreciable effect upon it" (Streane).

That seeketh truth. Hebrew *emunah* is very often rendered *faithfulness*; hence truth not merely in the intellectual sense, but as an attribute of a person; characteristic of a *reliable* person. Observe context.

And I will pardon her. As Genesis 18.22–33.

5.2 The law set forth two principles on oaths: (1) They were to swear by the name of Jehovah rather than other gods (Deut 6.13–15; 10.20), and (2) they were not to swear falsely by his name, which would profane his name (Lev 19.12). Judah violated both principles. They swore by false gods (v 7) and they swore falsely by the name of Jehovah. NEB tr.: "Men may swear by the life of the Lord, but they only perjure themselves." They used the name of Jehovah to support a lie. They had no regard for either truth or God's name.

5.3 Do not thine eyes look upon truth? Faithfulness is the chief attribute Jehovah looks for in men. But it was not to be found in Judah.

5.3bc, God had chastised them, but the chastisement made no impression on them. They *refused to learn* (NEB).

5.4 Surely these are poor. "These are only the poor; they have no sense" (RSV). Cf. John 7.47–49, "this multitude that knoweth not the law."

5.5 The disregard of truth and law was in all classes.

2. The Necessary Punishment of "Such a Nation as This" (5.6–9)

5.6 Cf. Lev 26.22; 2 Kings 17.25; Ezekiel 14.15; contrast Hosea 2.18.

A wolf of the evenings, Most modern versions agree with ASV and KJV margin: "deserts." See RSV, NASB, NBV and NEB.

A leopard shall watch. Tristram says a leopard "will conceal itself near a village or wateringplace, and await for hours its opportunity of pouncing upon the cattle" (quoted in Driver), evidently also upon people (v 6b).

5.7 How can I pardon thee? It was simply impossible to do so consistently with his own regard for truth and right (cf. v 3a). He wanted to. He had chastised them, trying to teach, to correct and to bring them back. But they would not return and he could not pardon.

When I had fed them to the full, "I.e. I supplied them abundantly with all needful good" (Henderson). But another reading, which differs only "to the slightest possible extent in the Hebrew" (Streane), is given in ASV margin and accepted by Keil and others: *when I had made them swear,* referring to the oath or vow by which they were brought into relation to Jehovah as his spouse, first given at Sinai (Exod 24) and then repeated in various renewals of the covenant (Deut 26.16–19; 29.10–13; Josh 24; 2 Kings 23.1–3). That oath and covenant were violated by their *adultery.*

They committed adultery. The spiritual whoredom of idolatry is likely included, but idol worship often included harlotry in a quite literal sense. Hosea deals with this subject and shows also a relationship between the immoral worship and the breakdown in homes (4.11–14).

5.9 Such abandoned behavior demands punishment.

B. Judgment to Come by Means of a Powerful Enemy in Spite of the False Feeling of Security Characteristic of Judah and Supported by False Prophets (5.10–18)

1. The Order to the Enemy (5.10)

5.10 Go ye up upon her walls. Most modern versions, because of the context, follow the explanation given in Driver and render, "Go up through her vine rows" (RSV; NASB; cf. NEB; NBV). Judah is of course being described under the figure of a vineyard [*branches*] (cf. Isa 5). But *walls* could refer to the walls of a vineyard rather than of a city (Keil). The walls are scaled and the vineyard destroyed.

But make not a full end. Cf. verse 18 and 4.27 with note.

Take away her branches. As in Isaiah 6.13, the branches are stripped away and the stock remains.

For they are not Jehovah's. Cf. 2.21.

2. The Reason for Judgment—the Treacherous Denial of Jehovah and His Word (5.11–13)

5.11 It is not he. This is the treachery of Israel and Judah. It is not an outright denial of Jehovah's existence in so many words. But, the following words suggest, they claimed that Jeremiah and such prophets of judgment to come were misrepresenting Jehovah (cf. 43.2); that it ws not Jehovah who sent prophets to say such things. But of course God did send these prophets and it was his word which they spoke. Therefore the denial of their message was in effect a denial of Jehovah.

The prophets. "The prophets who, like Jeremiah, foretold disaster" (Driver). The reference to *Israel* and *Judah* shows that the thought covers a great deal of the past, so that not just Jeremiah and his contemporaries but the many prophets of doom sent through the years would be included.

5.13 Shall become wind. Evidently meaning: The future will show them to be mere "windbags."

Thus shall it be done unto them. As in RSV and NASB (unlike NBV), continuing the words of the people, expressing their prediction or wish either (1) that the prophets may become wind (Keil) or (2) that the disaster predicted by the prophets may be fulfilled in themselves (Henderson).

3. Fulfillment of the Prophetic Word (5.14–18)

5.14 Vindication of the prophet. Jeremiah's message would be proved true by its fulfillment. It would not return void (cf. Isa 55.10–11). *Because ye speak this word* refers to what was said in verses 12–13. How Jeremiah's message would be fulfilled is explained in verses 15–18, which also explain the figure used in verse 14. The description is based on Deuteronomy 28.49–53.

5.15 A mighty nation. ASV margin, *an enduring nation*, a rendering transferred to the text in RSV and NASB. "Lit. *ever-full, never-failing*" (Driver)—properly used of streams which do not dry up. Cf. ASV margin at Psalm 74.15 and Amos 5.24.

5.16 An open sepulcher. Or tomb (RSV) or grave (NASB). *Their quiver*, filled with deadly arrows, had death in it.

5.17 Which thy sons and thy daughters should eat. But most all modern versions put "they shall eat up your sons and daughters" (RSV, NASB, NBV, NEB), which is perhaps explained not merely by the killing of these in war but also by the basic passage Deuteronomy 28.53.

C. The Reason for the Judgment Made Perfectly Clear (5.19–31)

1. A Just Recompense (5.19). The punishment matches the crime. "Because Judah in its own land serves the gods of foreigners, so it must serve strangers in a foreign land" (Keil).

2. A Stupid and Rebellious People (5.20–25). Not using their powers of perception, they had become so hardened and insensible that they did not even fear the God who is so powerful as to set the bounds of the sea (v 22) and so good as to provide rain and harvests (v 24), therefore cutting themselves off from the latter (v 25). Neither God's power nor his goodness moved them.

5.21 Foolish ... without understanding. Spiritually they were stupid, "foolish and senseless" (RSV, NASB, NEB). Hebrew for *without understanding* is literally *without heart*; hence NBV has *heartless*, but not in the sense of cruel. The heart is the seat of understanding. They did not have any sense. Perhaps the reason the people are addressed in so cutting a manner is that, if possible, they might yet be brought to their senses.

That have eyes ... ears. It is not that they did not have the powers of perception, but that they would not use the faculties they had; they closed their eyes and ears. Consequently they were afflicted with a spiritual blindness and deafness, and did not recognize God's hand at work in nature and in various disciplinary measures (vv 3, 22, 24) and did not hear the voice of God in his word.

5.22 One who could set bounds for the sea is certainly to be feared and will be feared by anyone who will use his head. God has made a mere sand beach the boundary beyond which the sea cannot pass. With all its raging the mighty ocean cannot pass beyond the boundary God set for it. That would certainly seem to indicate that God can stop a person or thing any time or place he chooses. Once cannot be successful in any rebellion against him. But Judah did not have the sense to read the lesson of the sea (v 23).

5.24 Another thing that should inspire man to reverence God is the divine goodness out of which he has made wonderful provisions to fill all man's needs. For *the former and the latter rain*, many versions give an interpretive rendering: *the autumn rain and the spring rain* (RSV, NASB, NEB). *The appointed weeks of the harvest*, i.e. "the weeks appointed for the harvest" (RSV,

NBV), are the seven weeks between Passover and Pentecost (also called the feast of harvest or of weeks). See Exodus 23.16; 34.22; Deuteronomy 16.9–10; cf. also Genesis 8.22.

5.25 But Judah did not recognize God's hand in these blessings. They did not respond with reverence and gratitude. Consequently their sins kept the blessings of verse 24 from coming.

3. The Wickedness Found Among the People (mentioned in v 25) Detailed (5.26–28)

5.26 As fowlers lie in wait. I.e., as bird catchers crouched down, waiting to spring the trap on the birds.

5.27 Full of deceit. Referring to the ill gotten gains obtained through deceit and heaped up in their houses. Henderson calls it "a metonymy of the cause for the effect"; reference is to "treasures acquired by fraud."

5.28 "They have grown fat and sleek" (RSV, NASB). NEB interprets "rich and grand."

They overpass. "They know no bounds in deeds of wickedness" (RSV; cf. NBV). "They also excel in deeds of wickedness" (NASB).

5.28cd Breakdown of social justice. The weak and helpless can never get the legal protection they need. The needy cannot get their case heard in the courts.

4. The Consequence: Such Corruption Demands Punishment (5.29)

5. A Final Summary (5.30–31)

5.30 "An appalling and horrible thing has happened in the land" (RSV, NASB). NEB has "an appalling thing, an outrage"; NBV puts "astounding" for *wonderful.*

5.31 What hope is there when those who should be giving moral and spiritual guidance to the nation are false and corrupt; when the people yield willingly to such leadership?

The prophets prophesy falsely. Instead of speaking the word of God they speak out of their own hearts (cf. the treatment in ch 23), simply telling the people what they want to hear. Cf. 6.13–14.

The priests bear rule by their means. As teachers and interpreters of the law, the priests were to decide various matters of controversy brought to them (Deut 17.8–13). But instead of deciding such matters on the basis of the law, the priests ruled *by their means*—literally *at* or *according to their hands* (Driver), meaning either *under the direction of the prophets* (Keil, comparing 1 Chronicles 25.2 and 2 Chronicles 23.18; see ASV margin; cf. RSV, NEB), or *on their own authority* (NASB; cf. NBV). Probably the former.

My people love to have it so. The guidance they received from prophets and priests was according to the lusts of their heart. They were being told what they wanted to hear.

And what will ye do in the end thereof? The only end such a course could lead to is judgment, and there will be nothing they can do to escape it. But they were not considering the *end* of their course. Jeremiah was trying to awaken them to consider the end of it and to turn from their way.

IV. The Outcome of the Period of Testing: The Rejection of a Worthless People (Ch 6)[6]

A. Graphic Portrayal of the Coming Attack on Jerusalem as a Warning to the People (6.1–8)

1. Description of the Attack (6.1–5).

6.1 Ye children of Benjamin. Jerusalem was in Benjamin.

Out of the midst of Jerusalem. Greater safety could be found by fleeing to the hill country than in the fortified city which was to be destroyed.

Blow the trumpet in Tekoa. The home of the prophet Amos (Amos 1.1), located in the hill country of Judah about twelve miles south of Jerusalem. The enemy is coming from the north. So the signals are given so as to direct flight toward the south.

Raise up a signal. NEB renders "fire the beacon"; KJV, "a sign of fire"; and many scholars think the reference is to some kind of fire signal. The Hebrew word "denotes a fire (or smoke) signal in the Lachish Letters (iv: 10); cf. Judges 20.38, 40" (Bright). (The Lachish Letters date from the time of the Babylonian invasion of Judah during the reign of Zedekiah.) The reference to the Lachish Letters reads thus: "And (my lord) will know that we are watching for the signals of Lachish, according to all the signs which my lord hath given, for we cannot see Azekah." D. Winton Thomas adds a comment: "This ostracon supplies important external evidence for the use of fire signals in ancient Israel. The Hebrew word used here

[6] I am taking a hint from the description of Jeremiah's work in verses 27–30.

is the same as that used in Jeremiah 6.1 (cf. Jdg 20.38, 40), namely, *maseth*. At Mari (Tell el-Hariri) on the middle Euphrates, fire signals were used as early as 2000 BC at times of military and political crisis, and on important occasions. The number of the signs and their movement, combination and direction together made up a code. It may be that at Lachish *maseth* was used of the signal system as a whole, whereas the *signs* (Hebrew *'othoth*) constituted the code or key to the system" (*Documents From Old Testament Times*, 216). This explanation seems probable, though see Keil who questions it.

Evil looketh forth. "Looms" (RSV, NBV, NEB).

6.2 Jerusalem is "personified as a beautiful and delicately reared woman" (Keil).

6.3 Shepherds with their flocks. NBV margin explains as "Bedouin invaders," but more likely shepherds is to be explained as a figure for rulers, as in 2.8 and elsewhere; reference to princes and their "flocks of soldiers." Cf. 1.15; 12.10.

6.4 We are placed right on the scene. We hear the enemy shout to each other—first a call to begin the attack; then the lament that day is ending and the city still untaken; finally a call to renew the attack in the night.

Prepare ye war. Hebrew as the margin: *Sanctify war.* "The expression no doubt arose either out of the custom of opening a campaign with sacrifices, or from the idea that war was a sacred service, undertaken in the name of the national God" (Driver). Cf. 1 Samuel 7.8–10; 25.28; Ezekiel 21.21–22. See also the Assyrian documents in which various kings claim to be acting under orders of their god (Pritchard's collection; Thomas, *Documents from Old Testament Times*; other collections). All of which gives a religious aspect to war.

Let us go up. I.e., launch the attack. RSV, NASB, NBV and NEB translate: "attack."

2. Reason for the Attack—It is Ordered by Jehovah Because of the Sins of Jerusalem (6.6–7)

6.6 Hew ye down trees. Cf. Deut 20.20.

Cast up a mound. "A siege mound" (RSV, NBV); "siege-ramps" (NEB); described in ISBE, IV, 2787: "The mound, or earthworks, (were) built up to the height of the walls, so as to command the streets of the city, and strike terror into the besieged. From the mound thus erected the besiegers were able to batter the upper and weaker part of the city wall (2 Sam 20.15; Isa 37.33; Jeremiah 6.6; Ezek 4.2; Dnl. 11.15; Lam 4.18). If, however, the town, or fortress, was built upon an eminence, an inclined plane reaching to the height of the eminence might be formed of earth or stones, or trees, and the besiegers would be able to bring their engines to the foot of the walls." These mounds permitted the enemy to bring to the wall a battering-ram which could be used to breach the wall or to batter open the gates (cf. Ezek 4.2; 21.22).

Visited. "Punished" (RSV, NASB, NBV).

She is wholly oppression. "There is nothing but oppression within her" (RSV, NBV).

6.7a "As water-springs maintain the water in a well at a constant level, so evil is springing up continually in Jerusalem" (Harrison). It keeps coming forth, as a continual stream of cool water from a well that never dries up.

2. Appeal to Jerusalem to Take This Warning to Heart—God Does Not Want Her Destroyed (6.8). Cf. Chapter 18. This is the verse that shows the intention of such a dramatic portrayal of the invasion and siege. If the approaching judgment can be made vivid and real enough, perhaps the people can be awakened to consider the certain doom that threatens them if they do not repent, and be persuaded to turn from their evil way.

6.8 Be thou instructed. "Be warned" (RSV, NASB). "Learn your lesson" (NEB).

Alienated. KJV, "depart," with margin, "be loosed or disjointed." Hebrew is literally *be torn* or *torn away*.

B. Such Warnings Going Unheeded by an Impenitent People, the Wrath of God Must Be Poured Out (6.9–15)

6.9 Reference to the repeated blows struck by the enemy. As in Isaiah 5, Israel is portrayed as a vineyard. After picking the grapes the enemy goes over the vine again. The vine is left stripped; one would find a few grapes only with difficulty (but see 4.27; 5.10, 18).

Turn again thy hand. The idea of 9a is repeated in the form of an order to the enemy (as 5.10). Hebrew is bettered rendered *shoots* (as ASV margin) than *branches*. Translate as RSV: "like a grape-gatherer pass your hand again over its branches." So NASB, NBV, NEB. The enemy will be like a grape-gatherer going over the vines again and again. Reference is to the repeated deportations (52.28–30; cf. 2 Kings 24.14; 25.11).

6.10 The prophet speaks. He has warned (v 8), but the warning goes unheeded. He is willing to speak again, but where can he find someone who will listen? What is the use?

Their ear is uncircumcised. Covered, as it were, with a foreskin, so that God's word cannot enter.

A reproach. Cf. 20.7–8.

6.11 This attitude toward the word of God which he speaks causes Jeremiah to be filled with the wrath of God. It threatens to burst forth, like hot air under pressure.

Pour it out. Command of God to the prophet. He is ordered to pour God's wrath out upon all classes of the people, which involves more than speaking, for the word spoken by the prophet will be effective, certain of fulfillment, not returning void (cf. 1.9–10; Isa 55.10–11).

The assembly of young men together. "The gatherings of young men" (RSV).

The aged with him that is full of days. The old and the very old; "the old folk and the very aged" (RSV); "the greybeard and the very old" (NEB).

6.12 Their houses … their fields and their wives. Compare the items listed with the commandment in Exodus 20.17 and Deuteronomy 5.21. The people have been covetous (v 13). Therefore they must suffer the loss of all possessions. Punishment matches crime.

6.13 Given to covetousness. "Greedy for gain" (NASB); "greedy for unjust gain" (RSV).

Every one dealeth falsely. Instead of seeking the good of the nation each is out to feather his own nest.

6.14 They have healed … slightly. Or *lightly* (RSV). Instead of taking stern measures to clean out and repair a grievous wound, they do not treat the matter seriously. It is as if a doctor prescribed a bandaid and an aspirin to treat a cancer, then told his patient, "Everything will be all right." Cf. Ezekiel 13.10.

6.15 Neither could they blush. In our age every kind of filth is offered on stage and screen for "mature" or "adult" audiences. But this ability to sit through such filth without the reddening of the cheeks, Jeremiah indicates, is not a mark of maturity but rather of ripeness … for judgment. It is the mark of a hardened and insensitive conscience. It was the characteristic of Judah just prior to her destruction.

C. The Fruit of Such Stubbornness and Hardness of Heart—A Judgment Which Cannot Be Averted By Sacrifice Without Repentance (6.16–21)

6.16–17 Jehovah had not left the people without direction. He sent various messengers to direct the people back to the old paths. Then when they rejected that way he sent prophets to sound a warning. But they remain heedless of all efforts to help.

6.16 Stand ye in the ways. I.e., the place where different roads come together. "Stop at the cross-roads" (NEB). "Stand at the crossroads" (NBV).

And ask for the old paths. "The ancient paths" (RSV, NASB, NBV, NEB). The way of the Mosaic tradition—the paths that had been marked out so long ago. They had forsaken "the ancient paths" and the "bypaths" which they had taken were leading to disaster (cf. 18.15–17).

Where is the good way. The way of the good, literally—the way that leads to good. Cf. Moses' appeals to Israel to walk in the way marked out by Jehovah in order that they might live and prosper in the land (Deut 5.33; 8.6; 10.12–13; 11.22–25; 19.9; 26.17; 28.9 in context of verses 1–14; 30.16); and the crossroads at which the people stood in Moab (Deut 11.26–27; 30.15–20).

Ye shall find rest. Not just in a spiritual sense, but peace, security and prosperity in the terms of the Deuteronomy passages above.

But they said. They refused; they preferred another way.

6.17 Prophets were sent to warn them of the disaster to which they were headed. *Watchmen* = the prophets (cf. Ezek 3.17; 33.1–16; Amos 3.6; Hab 2.1).

6.18 Therefore hear, ye nations. "Judah being thus hardened, the Lord makes known to the nations what He has determined regarding it" (Keil).

What is among them. Explained in the light of verse 19 as "what will happen to them" (RSV, NBV). NEB: "take note ... of the plight of this people." But reference may be to "their thoughts" (v 19).

6.19 The fruit of their thoughts. The catastrophe comes as the fruit of their stubborn resistance to the message of God. Cf. 2.19; 4.18.

6.20 Sacrifice and the temple service is to no purpose at all and completely unavailing when the heart is in rebellion against God. Cf. 1 Samuel 15.22; Isaiah 1.11; Hosea 6.6; Amos 5.21ff.

Frankincense from Sheba. *Sheba* was a country of South Arabia, celebrated in ancient times as the producer of *frankincense*, a fragrant resin used as one ingredient in the preparation of the sacred perfume called incense (Exod 30.34) and as an addition to the meal-offerings (Lev 2.1–2, 15; 6.15).

The sweet cane from a far country. Used for making a perfume; identified by Keil and others with the "sweet calamus" used in the preparation of the holy anointing oil (Exod 30.23). The *far country* is probably India. But it makes no difference how far it came from nor how expensive it may be; if the heart is not right, there is no use offering it to Jehovah.

6.21 Stumblingblocks. Explained in the following verses as referring to "the enemy against whom the people will stumble to their ruin" (Driver). Cf. v 15, ASV margin.

D. Description of the Cruel and Powerful Enemy to Come Down Upon Judah, the Prospect of Which Calls for Bitter Lamentation (6.22–26). Cf. 5.15–17.

1. Announcement of the Coming and Description of the Enemy (6.22–23)

6.23 Their voice. The sound of their approach is like the roar of the sea.

2. The Terror Spread Through the Land by the Appearance of the Enemy (6.24–26)

6.24 As one of the people Jeremiah gives voice to their feelings.

Our hands wax feeble. "Heb. *sink down* (Isa 5.24), or *drop down slackly*" (Driver); "are limp" (NASB); "hang limp" (NEB); "fall helpless" (RSV); "hang slack"—according to footnote, indicating "helplessness" (Isa 5.24)" (NBV). All the strength seems to go out of the hands; "all power to resist vanishes" (Keil).

6.26 Sackcloth … ashes. The ordinary accompaniments of mourning.

Wallow thyself in ashes. RSV, NASB, and NBV: "roll in ashes"; but Keil, NEB, and Driver have "sprinkle thyself with ashes," the latter stating that the exact meaning of the Hebrew is uncertain. Cf. Ezekiel 27.30; Micah 1.10.

As for an only son. Cf. Amos 8.10; Zechariah 12.10.

E. The Outcome of Judah's Time of Trial, A Rejected People (6.27–30). These verses (1) provide a basis for understanding the work of Jeremiah, and (2) explain the reason the destroyer is brought down upon Judah.

6.27 A trier. KJV and ASV margin, "tower." That is one meaning of the Hebrew word, but does not fit this context in which the language of metallurgy is so prominent as well as "trier" or "assayer" (RSV, NASB, NBV, NEB), which is also a meaning. This figure of a testing which is used all through verses 27–30 reveals the way in which Jeremiah's work in Judah is to be understood.

A fortress. Keil explains: "To be a trier have I set thee amid my people 'as a strong tower.'" Others differ, Driver omitting the word as an incorrect gloss, others translating "tester" (RSV, NASB) or "examiner" (NBV).

6.28 The character of the people revealed through the testing work of Jeremiah.

Grievous revolters. "Stubbornly rebellious" (RSV, NASB). Literally "revolters of revolters," a way of expressing a superlative. Hence "the most refractory of the refractory" (Driver); "arch-rebels" (NEB).

Brass and iron. Base, inferior metals when compared with silver (v 30).

6.29 "The trial of the people has brought about no purification, no separation of the wicked ones. The trial is viewed under the figure of a long continued but resultless process of smelting" (Keil). Driver calls verse 29 "a figurative description of the vain efforts made by the prophet to remove the evil elements from his people. In refining, the alloy containing the gold or silver is mixed with lead, and fused in a furnace on a vessel of earth or bone-ash; a current of air is turned upon the molten mass (not upon the *fire*); the lead then oxidizes, and acting as a flux, carries away the alloy, leaving the gold or silver pure (J. Napier, *The Ancient Workers in Metal*, 1856, pp. 20, 23). In the case here imagined by the prophet, so inextricably is the alloy mixed with the silver, that, though the bellows blow, and the lead is oxidized in the heat, no purification is effected: only impure silver remains." Or as Keil describes what has happened: "The smelting has been carried on so perseveringly, that the bellows have been scorched by the heat of the fire, and the lead added in order to get the ore into fusion is used up; but they have gone on smelting quite in vain." Driver's description of the smelting process is also quoted in NBV margin without crediting it to Driver.

Plucked away. Better, to suit the figure: "removed" (RSV, NBV), "separated," margin: "drawn off" (NASB), or "separated out" (NEB).

6.30 Refuse … rejected. Involves a "subtle wordplay … both terms coming from the same root" (Harrison). NASB brings out the wordplay by putting "rejected silver," which Henderson explains: "silver which is so completely mixed with alloy as to be utterly worthless." So the refining process concludes without revealing any good silver.

PART THREE

The Way of Salvation

Jeremiah 7–10

Introduction

1. *Date:* A comparison of Chapter 7 with 26.1–9 has led most scholars, even very conservative men, to date the prophecy early in the reign of Jehoiakim. The references to idolatry have also doubtless influenced this judgment. But no certain indication of a time later than Josiah is given after 3.6 until 21.1. Since the last indication of date was "in the days of Josiah the king" (3.6), since also the later prophecies show that it was usual for Jeremiah to assign a date to his prophecies, I am inclined to think that the prophecies up to 21.1 came during the time of Josiah.

As for some of the content of this section, references to idolatry for example, I would say that perhaps the historical books do not tell us as much as we would like to know about the times of Josiah. We do know from Jeremiah 25.1–7 that the message proclaimed by Jeremiah in the fourth year of Jehoiakim was one he had been offering continuously since Josiah's thirteenth year. Verses 30–31 seem to describe Manasseh's sins, which had evidently not been renounced by the people.

The comparison with Chapter 26 does not demand a date later than Josiah. The so-called "Temple Address" is probably not a speech delivered at only one time, but a written summary of preaching done by Jeremiah at the temple on several occasions.

2. *Message:* In Chapters 7–10 Jeremiah provides an exposition of the way of salvation. He begins by stripping away the false confidence in the temple and the sacrifices that afflicted the people. Harrison calls it the "Temple

Theology" taught by the false prophets. Hence the first section is negative—a false way; the way in which salvation is not to be found.

The only way to salvation, says Jeremiah, is through the knowledge of Jehovah, and that knowledge will be reflected in the lives of the people. The attitude toward the temple expressed in 7.1–11 shows a complete misapprehension of the nature of Jehovah. But the people refused to know Jehovah. They refused to repent, they would not listen to God's messengers, and therefore judgment must come. They had refused the knowledge of Jehovah and their ignorance was reflected in their conduct (9.2–6). Judgment would teach them what they refused to learn in any other way. Chapter 10.23 indicates the truth Judah would arrive at only through judgment and experience of the disastrous end to which they have come through following false and foolish paths. So we see that salvation can only come through judgment, with its chastening and instructive effects.

I. Warning Against a False Trust in the Temple and the Sacrificial Service (7.1–8.3)

A. The Vanity of Trusting in the Temple (7.1–15)

1. Amendment of Life Necessary to Continued Dwelling in the Land, Without Which the Presence of the Temple Will Not Preserve (7.1–7)

7.4 The idea is clarified by (1) the fuller development in verses 8–10, and (2) Micah 3.11, in which the false prophets are quoted as arguing, "Is not Jehovah in the midst of us? no evil shall come upon us." They argued that the temple as the sanctuary of God and the place of his presence would surely not be destroyed. The presence of the temple, therefore, was regarded as the guarantee of their safety. They had a superstitious regard for the temple, treating it as a kind of charm to ward off calamity. Cf. the attitude toward the ark in 1 Samuel 4.

Are these. The plural referring to the sanctuary itself and the complex of buildings connected with it.

7.5–7 Such trust is groundless, a delusion. The only way to safety is right living.

2. The Delusion of False Trust in the Temple (7.8–11)

7.10 I.e., "Ye appear in my temple to sacrifice and worship, thinking thus to appease my wrath and turn aside all punishment, that so ye may go on doing all these abominations." When they came to the temple they had no intention of quitting their sins. Rather: "By frequenting the temple, they thought to procure an indulgence for their wicked ongoings, not merely for what they had already done, but for what they do from day to day" (Keil). We can become guilty of the identical error today if we trust in the forms of religion—wearing "the right name," eating the Lord's supper every Sunday, giving money to the church—without making personal application of the Lord's will to the whole of life and without manifesting the humble and penitent spirit that is supposed to be reflected in the forms of religion.

7.11 A den of robbers. They regarded the temple as "a robbers' cave" (literally, as NEB). They could rob, murder, commit adultery; then run to the temple, offer the sacrifice, and be safe. Driver says the word *den* meant *a cave* in Old English. "There are many caves in the limestone strata of Palestine which in ancient times were often the homes of robbers."

I, even I, have seen it. I.e., I have seen you treat the temple as a robbers' cave. There is no use denying that you so regard it.

3. The Delusion Exposed by a Reference to Shiloh (7.12–15)

7.12 Where I caused my name to dwell at the first. *Shiloh* is where the tabernacle was erected after the conquest of the land (Josh 18.1; Jdg 18.31; 21.12, 19; 1 Sam 1.3, 9, 24; 2.14; 3.21; 4.3–4).

See what I did to it. The destruction of Shiloh is alluded to also in 26.6 and in Psalm 78.60, but the historical books do not record the event. Most likely the Philistines overran Shiloh after their victory in 1 Samuel 4. In any case the ark of the covenant was not returned to the tabernacle at Shiloh after its recovery from the Philistines, who had taken possession of it in the war. The tabernacle was at Nob during the reign of Saul (1 Sam 21). The present text implies that Shiloh was in ruins at the time of Jeremiah. A pilgrimage to Shiloh would explode the delusion about the temple. From Shiloh they could learn that the sacredness of a place does not save it from destruction if it has been defiled by sin.

Archaeological Footnote: In the 1920s Danish scholars excavated the site of Shiloh and found evidence of a destruction about 1050 BC, supporting what is said above about the time of its destruction. See G. Frederick Owen, *Archaeology and the Bible*, 314–315; Price, Sellers and Carlson, *The Monuments and the Old Testament*, 395; Joseph P. Free, *Archaeology and*

Bible History, 149; Merrill F. Unger, *Archaeology and the Old Testament*, 22; G. Ernest Wright, *Biblical Archaeology*, 89; Millar Burrows, *What Mean These Stones?*, 63, 80.

7.13 I spake unto you. Through the prophets (v 25).

7.15 The whole seed of Ephraim. *Ephraim* was the leading tribe of the northern kingdom and its name is often used to designate the kingdom as a whole. See Isaiah 7.1–2, 8–9 and many other such passages.

B. Destruction Not to be Averted by Prayer and Intercession From Jeremiah So Long as the People Continue in Sin (7.16–20). Prayer and intercession for an impenitent people would not save them any more than the temple would.

7.18 To make cakes to the queen of heaven. *The queen of heaven*, only mentioned in the Old Testament by Jeremiah (here and at 44.17–19, 25), is usually identified with Ishtar, the Assyrian goddess of war and love, who bore the title "queen of heaven" among others; who corresponded to Astarte (or Ashtoreth) in Phoenician or Canaanite mythology; the worship of whom "was of a grossly immoral and debasing character" (ISBE). She is also usually explained as a deification of the month (although SDB remarks: "It is so difficult to separate the worship of the moon-goddess from that of the planet Venus in the Assyrian mythology when introduced among the western nations, that the two are frequently confused"). Some light on the *cakes* made to the queen of heaven may be derived from 44.19. Where ASV text has *cakes to worship her* the margin has *to portray her.* RSV translates, "cakes for her bearing her image," evidently meaning cakes in the shape of the moon (undoubtedly the explanation behind the NEB rendering at 7.18, "crescent-cakes in honour of the queen of heaven"), or possibly with its image sketched upon them. YAC explains the Hebrew *kavvanim* as "cakes (with marks on them)."

Another reading, which is preserved in several manuscripts (SDB, III, 2651), is given in KJV margin: *frame*, or *workmanship of heaven.* Despite some uncertainties, what is undoubtedly true is that the worship of the heavenly bodies is somehow involved (cf. 8.2). Manasseh especially led Judah into the worship of "all the host of heaven" (2 Kings 21.3, 5).

For further reading see especially the Bible dictionaries: ISBE, IV, 2514; SDB, III, 2652; NBD, 1068 (which contains a picture of Ishtar from an Assyrian seal).

C. Nor will sacrifices avail to turn away the punishment. Sacrifice Not a Substitute for the Obedience Demanded by God (7.21–28)

7.21 Add your burnt-offerings unto your sacrifices. The law demanded that the whole of the *burnt-offerings* be burnt on the altar (Lev 1). None of the meat was to be eaten. *Sacrifices* refers to those of which the people could eat portions. But God tells the people that in the present condition of their hearts they might as well add their burnt-offerings to their sacrifices and eat them too. None of it meant anything to him. They might as well eat it all up. All of it was just meat (*flesh*) to be eaten. There was nothing sacred about any of their offerings.

7.22–23 These verses have often been interpreted as a contradiction of the Pentateuch as it now stands. But Jeremiah is not denying that sacrifice was a part of the legislation given at Sinai. Jeremiah was not opposed to sacrifice in itself, but to the abuses current in the nation. **1.** The condemnation of the temple service in verses 9–10 does not rest upon its lack of authority but upon its abuse by a morally indifferent people. **2.** The temple is called "this house, which is called by my name" (v 11). **3.** God refers to Shiloh as the place "where I caused my name to dwell at the first" (v 12). **4.** It was destroyed not because of God's rejection of the tabernacle service but because of the wickedness of the people. **5.** Sacrifice is a part of Jeremiah's vision of the happy future enjoyed by an obedient people (17.26; 31.14; 33.11, 18). **6.** Most modern commentators date this speech early in Jehoiakim's reign, and therefore after the finding of the book of the law during Josiah's reign (2 Kings 22). The critics make Jeremiah look so stupid as to undermine the authority of the book of the law which was the basis of all his prophetic work. Who can believe it?

Perhaps Oswald T. Allis has pointed the way to the necessary alternative explanation in *The Five Books of Moses*, pp. 170–173. Allis calls attention to the ambiguity of the Hebrew for *concerning*. The literal meaning of the preposition is *upon*, but for contextual reasons it often has the meaning and is rendered *because of* or *for the sake of*. Among the passages listed by Allis are Genesis 12.17 ("because of Sarai"), 20.11 ("for my wife's sake"), 20.18 ("because of Sarah"), 26.7 ("for Rebekah" = "for the sake of"; cf. 20.11), Deuteronomy 4.21 ("for your sakes"), and Psalm 45.4 ("because of truth").

So in Jeremiah 7.22. Jehovah does not mean that he had said or commanded nothing *concerning* sacrifices, although that is a possible meaning of the Hebrew—the word is ambiguous. But as soon as the people recalled all the instruction of the law on sacrifice they would understand what was intended—i.e., that Jehovah did not speak to the fathers *for the sake of* sacrifices, as if that were something he needed (cf. Psa 50.7–15).

Observe now how that explanation fits the context. Jews were treating the sacrifices as if they were the principal thing in the covenant with Jehovah. They continued in immoral conduct, but felt secure against judgment because they kept up the temple ritual. But Jehovah answers that they might as well make a common meal out of all their sacrifices and eat even the burnt-offerings, which were ordinarily to be entirely burned unto God (v 21). For, he continues, the revelation at Sinai was not made for the sake of sacrifices (v 22); God had no need of their sacrifices (cf. Psa 50.7–15); that was not the thing he wanted when he entered into covenant relation with Israel. He wanted their obedience (v 23). The sacrifices were related to their failures to perfect the obedience which was God's primary desire. Now Judah was treating covenant faithfulness and obedience as if they were of no importance and the sacrifices as if they were the primary condition of the covenant relationship.

Verse 23 contains the language of the covenant relation and indicates the essential ingredients of the compact between God and Israel. Cf. Exodus 6.6–8; 15.26; 19.5–6; 26.12; and the language of covenant renewal in Deuteronomy 26.16–19; 27.9–10; 29.1, 10–13. Then notice especially Deuteronomy 5.33, which follows the ten commandments and contains the only other occurrence of the expression used in Jeremiah 7.23, *to walk in all the way which God commanded.* So the compact between Jehovah and Israel was this: Jehovah would be their God and would provide many wonderful blessings. They would be his people and their covenant obligation was obedience to him. Sacrifice had its place in the covenant, as indicated above, but it is clear that it was not sacrifice that God was after but obedience. That is the meaning of the text. Israel's attitude toward the sacrifices and the temple ritual was a complete perversion of the covenant.

Other references: In addition to Allis' work, see also the commentary of Laetsch and F. F. Bruce's *The Book and the Parchments*, p. 47. Bruce comments thus on Hosea 6.6 and Jeremiah 7.22–23: "God did not want sacrifice for its own sake; what he wanted was obedient men and women, receptive of His self-revelation and loyal to the covenant which He had established with them. They were making the mistake of thinking that God wanted sacrifices and burnt offerings in themselves, whereas God wanted these only in so far as they expressed the inward and practical holiness of the worshippers. It was the same thing that God emphasized when speaking through Jeremiah—that it was not for the sake of burnt offerings and sacrifice that He gave them His law when He brought them out of Egypt, but in order that He might have a people responsive to His revealed character and will." In a footnote Bruce adds some other references: "It is possible that the words rendered 'concerning', in Jeremiah 7.22, might be rendered 'for the sake of': so L. Elliott Binns, *The Book of Jeremiah* (1919), pp. 75–77; also O. T. Allis, *The Five Books of Moses* (1943), pp. 168–171, approved in a review by W. F. Albright, *Journal of Biblical Literature*, 62 (1943), p. 360, where C. von Orelli's commentary on Jeremiah is cited to the same effect.

7.25 Indicates the persistence of Jehovah and his strong desire to turn the people from the path of destuction—a point much emphasized in Jeremiah (7.13; 25.3–6; 29.29; 35.14–15; 44.4).

7.27–28 They will no more listen to Jeremiah than to the prophets before him. Therefore, he must deliver the pronouncement of verse 28.

D. Call to Lamentation in View of the Shameful and Horrible Ruin to Come Upon the Disobedient People (7.29–8.3)

7.29 Cut off thy hair. The pronouns in this passage are feminine, showing that Jerusalem, personified as a woman, is being addressed. That is the reason for the supplying of *O Jerusalem* in KJV and ASV. Hebrew for *hair* is literally *crown*. Keil explains the use of the term *crown* for the *hair* by referring to the Nazarites on whom the uncut hair was a mark of special separation unto Jehovah (Num 6.5–7). "Cutting off this hair is not only in token of mourning, as in Job 1.20, Micah 1.16, but in token of the loss of the consecrated character." So NEB, adding the explanation, "the symbol of your dedication." But with Jerusalem here portrayed as a woman, perhaps 1 Corinthians 11.6, 15 gives the most help. So great is her grief that she cuts off her "crown" and her "glory"; she thus expresses her feeling of "shame." For baldness as a sign of shame and sorrow see, in addition to Job 1.20 and Micah 1.16, Isaiah 15.2 and Ezekiel 7.18.

7.30 They have set their abominations. The supreme gesture of contempt for the things of God. See 2 Kings 21.2–7 on Manasseh; 23.4; and Ezekiel 8 for later times. Jeremiah (in vv 30–31) is not necessarily describing practices of the present (time of Josiah). He has Manasseh's sins especially in view (cf. 15.4), sins, however, which had not been renounced by the people.

7.31 To burn their sons. Thus Manasseh (2 Kings 21.6).

Which I commanded not. In fact, had forbidden (Lev 18.21; 20.1–5; Deut 12.31).

7.32 The place of their sins becomes the scene of their judgment.

Till there be no place to bury. Topheth becomes a vast graveyard, until all burial space is used up and finally many are left unburied (v 33).

7.33b And none shall frighten them away. As Rizpah kept the birds and beasts from her sons (2 Sam 21.10). Cf. Deuteronomy 28.26 on the whole verse.

7.34 Will I cause to cease … the voice of mirth and the voice of gladness. I.e., "I will banish all sounds of joy and gladness" (NEB).

8.1 They shall bring out the bones. "Even sinners long dead must yet bear the shame of their sins" (Keil). The digging up of the bones was possibly a deliberate insult, but more likely aimed at getting the valuables which were often buried with the dead. The bones were dug up in the search for treasure and then scattered all about (v 2). Josephus provides an illustration: "David was buried by his son Solomon, in Jerusalem, with great magnificence, and with all the other funeral pomp which kings used to be buried with; moreover, he had great and immense wealth buried with him, the vastness of which may be easily conjectured at by what I shall now say; for a thousand and three hundred years afterwards Hyrcanus the high priest, when he was besieged by Antiochus, that was called the Pious, the son of Demetrius, and was desirous of giving him money to get him to raise the siege and draw off his army, and having no other method of compassing the money, opened one room of David's sepulchre, and took out three thousand talents, and gave part of that sum to Antiochus; and by this means caused the siege to be raised, as we have informed the reader elsewhere. Nay, after him, and that many years, Herod the king opened another room, and took away a great deal of money, and yet neither of them came at the coffins of the kings themselves, for their bodies were buried under the earth so artfully, that they did not appear to even those that entered into their monuments" (*Antiquities*, Book VII, Chapter xv, Paragraph).

8.2 And they shall spread them before the sun. Doubtless not in any orderly fashion but simply scattered all around. They are thus exposed to the action of the heavenly bodies upon them, so that they rot away and come to be so much manure scattered about to fertilize the earth. A fitting end! They have *loved* the heavenly bodies, *served* them, *walked after* them, *sought* them, and *worshipped* them. Now they lie out in the open before their gods, suffering the greatest indignity, and the gods are powerless to help.

All the host of heaven. Stars.

8.3 The condition of the survivors is worse than death. Cf. Lev 26.36–39; Deuteronomy 28.65–67.

II. The Stubborn and Stupid Commitment to Apostasy Which Brings Judah to Ruin (8.4–9.1)[7]

A. The Amazing and Unnatural Resistance to the Call for Repentance (8.4–7)

8.4 People often fall down. But they do not just lie there in the dirt—they get up. People often take wrong turns in their travel, but when they find themselves on the wrong road they go back and correct their error.

8.5 But the apostasy of this people is *perpetual.* They cling to their wickedness unnaturally. They cannot be persuaded to return to the right path.

8.6 The proof that "they hold fast deceit" and "refuse to return." Jehovah has given attention to what they say and do. He has heard "not one sinner crying remorsefully, 'Oh, what have I done?'" (NEB).

8.7 Her appointed times ... the time of their coming. The times set for the departure and arrival of migratory birds.

But my people know not. They do not have the sense of the birds. Attention is focused on the unnaturalness of this ignorance.

The law. Hebrew is *mishpat*, literally as the KJV, "*judgement* (properly a *decision* given by a judge), the term being used in an enlarged sense of *a prescribed system of observances*: so 8.7" (Driver, 344); "anything decreed by God, whether the instincts of the migratory birds or the directions given for human guidance" (Harrison). Not the same word as *law* in verse 8.

---

[7] 9.1 appears as 8.23 in the Hebrew text—probably a better arrangement.

B. The Rejection of Wisdom Followed by Judgment (8.8–13)

8.8 We are wise. Challenging the statement of verse 7c. They claim to be wise on the ground of the possession of the law. The people refused to return to God (vv 4–7) and now we see that they were supported by false prophets, priests and scribes who told them they had no need to return; they were all right as they were (vv 10b–11; cf. 18.18).

The false pen of the scribes hath wrought falsely. "Has made it into a lie" (RSV, NASB). KJV margin is correct. The *scribes* (lawyers, experts on the law) had "falsified" (NEB) the law. We are not told how—probably through false interpretation and application which misled the people regarding the demands of the law (cf. vv 10b–11). Thus they perverted the law into a lie. Laetsch reminds us that the lying pen of such scribes is still at work in our day.

8.9 And what manner of wisdom is in them? None. The word of Jehovah was Israel's wisdom and understanding (Deut 4.6). When that was rejected and perverted (cf. Deut 4.2) they had no wisdom.

8.10–12 An almost word for word repetition of 6.12–15.

8.10 Instead of giving moral and spiritual leadership to the nation, prophets and priests were out for their own gain—leaders in the false dealings that afflicted the nation.

8.11 Judah was afflicted with grievous wounds, but these spiritual doctors simply assured them that everything was all right; that they had no fear of any judgment to come.

8.12 The destruction of conscience, which is followed by judgment.

8.13 The verse has been explained in two ways. In either case Israel is thought of first as a vineyard (cf. Isa 5) and then as a fig-tree. But some translate with a future tense (*there shall be no grapes etc.*) and explain in accord with 6.9; others put a present tense (*there are no grapes etc.*, RSV) and explain in terms of the present fruitlessness of the nation. Cf. 17.5–8.

8.13c The Hebrew is difficult. Literally, according to Bright: *And I gave them they shall pass over them.* The ASV text and margin suggest variant attempts to explain this difficult language. The margin possibly has parallels in Isaiah 8.8 and 28.15, *pass over* (or *through*) *them*, meaning *as invaders.*

C. Horrors of the Coming Judgment (8.14–9.1)

1. Reaction of the People to the Approach of the Invader (8.14–17)

8.14 Let us be silent there. Or *perish* (margin, RSV, NASB).

Hath put us to silence. Or *caused us to perish* (margin), "has doomed us" (NASB), "has doomed us to perish" (RSV).

Water of gall. Hebrew for *gall* refers to a plant not certainly identified, but with extremely bitter fruit. Some render *poisonous water.* (Poison was likely to have a bitter taste.) In any case, *water of gall* is here a figure for bitter suffering.

8.15 We looked for peace. False hope excited by false prophets (v 11; cf. 4.10). The idea reappears in 14.19.

8.16 The snorting of his horses. *His* refers to the enemy.

Is heard from Dan. In northern Palestine. The enemy enters the land from the north (cf. 1.14; 4.6; 6.22).

8.17 Serpents. A new figure for the enemy.

2. Jeremiah's Sorrow (8.18–9.1). Jeremiah is cut to the heart at the prospect of the coming disaster to his country and gives vent to his deep grief in bitter lamentation.

8.19 From a land that is very far off. It is not absolutely certain that the people are imagined to be in exile, as most scholars seem to hold. The Hebrew form is only elsewhere at Isaiah 33.17 where ASV text reads *a land that reacheth afar*, while the margin gives an alternative (*a land that is very far off*) and explains the Hebrew as literally being *a land of far distances*. In our text the literal *from a land of far distances* can possibly be handled as RSV: "from the length and breadth of the land," or with Bright: "far and wide through the land."

Is not Jehovah in Zion? I.e., What is the explanation of the present misery and helplessness? Why does God not act? Why are we not rescued?

Why have they provoked me to anger? The question they should be considering. This is Jehovah's answer, which gives the real explanation of their trouble—not Jehovah's failure, but their apostasy.

8.20 Cry of despair from the people. *Summer* was the time of "ingathering of summer fruits" (ASV margin). Cf. "summer fruits" in 40.10, 12; 48.32. "If the harvest failed, the people might still look forward to the fruit season; but if the fruit, too, failed, famine stared them in the face" (NBV margin; cf. Streane). But there is no reference to a literal harvest. The language is figurative, something in the nature of a proverb. The reality is a giving up hope of rescue and deliverance. Think, for example, of the hope that Egypt would come to their rescue (cf. 34.21–22; 37.5–10).

8.21 The hopelessness of the case moves Jeremiah to cry out.

I mourn. Literally as KJV, *I am black*, which evidently "has reference to the dark and squalid attire and appearance of a mourner in the East (2 Sam 19.24; Est 4.1)" (Driver); i.e. I go about in mourning; I wear the garb of a mourner.

8.22 "Help is nowhere to be found" (Keil). *Balm* refers to some kind of medicine, evidently used for the healing of wounds, which was produced in *Gilead*, a region east of the Jordan. Cf. Genesis 37.25; Jeremiah 46.11; 51.8.

Hebrew for *health* is explained by YAC as meaning *lengthening* or *prolongation*. The connection with *recovered*, which literally means *gone up* (margin of both ASV and KJV), gives evidence for Driver's "fresh flesh," a translation he derives from a comparison of the Hebrew with an Arabic word meaning "the fresh flesh *lengthening itself*, i.e. gradually forming over a wound," an explanation also accepted by NEB: "Why has no new skin grown over their wound?" Bright says a literal translation is, "Why has the new flesh of My Daughter-My People not come up?" For this application of the Hebrew for *gone up* cf. Ezekiel 37.6, 8.

Others explain the Hebrew for *health* as referring to the *bandage* put upon a wound (ASV margin at 33.6; Keil).

9.1 Same as 8.23 in Hebrew A better division. The verse concludes the description of Jeremiah's sorrow over the calamity of the people, whereas 9.2 begins a new thought which is then treated at some length. "The calamity is so dreadful, that the prophet could weep about it day and night" (Keil). He expresses the wish that his head might be waters ("all water," NEB) and his eyes a continuously flowing fountain of tears, so that such weeping might be possible. Such is the depth of his grief.

III. Judah: A People Destroyed for Lack of Knowledge (9.2–11)

Judah does not know Jehovah (v 3); they refuse to know him (v 6). Therefore judgment must be brought against such a people (vv 7–11).

A. The Lack of Knowledge (9.2–6)

9.2 9.1 in Hebrew text. Jeremiah's lament over the coming destruction is followed by a lament over the wickedness which made the judgment necessary. Jeremiah yearns to "get away from it all" —to leave the wicked people.

A lodging-place of wayfaring men. A lodging place for travellers erected on a caravan route in the desert.

9.3 ***Their bow.*** The tongue a bow that shoots forth lies. Note change of figure in verse 8.

And they are grown strong in the land. The wicked, come to power in the land, abuse their position. They use their power and position for evil instead of good.

9.4 ***Take ye heed.*** "Let every one beware" (RSV). "Let every one be on guard against his neighbor" (NASB).

For every brother will utterly supplant. The word *supplant* is derived from a Latin root meaning "to trip up one's heels, throw down" (WNCD, 852). An allusion to Jacob's dealings with Esau (Gen 25.26; 27.36). The name Jacob is derived from a Hebrew root meaning *to be at the heel* or *to follow at the heel*; hence *to trip up, to cheat, deal in an underhanded way*. See Driver on Genesis 25.26; Speiser on Genesis 27.36.

9.5 ***They have taught their tongue.*** NEB puts "trained" for *taught*.

They weary themselves. I.e., "put themselves to great labour" (Keil), take great pains (Henderson).

9.6 Personal word from Jehovah to Jeremiah.

B. The Moral Necessity of Judgment Upon Such a People (9.7–9)

9.7 "By reason of this depravity, the Lord must purge His people by sore judgments" (Keil).

I will melt them. The same word is rendered "refine" in ASV at 6.29, "try" in Psalm 66.10 and other places, "purge away" in Isaiah 1.25, "refine" in Isaiah 48.10 and Zechariah 13.9. Some put "refine" here (RSV, NASB, NEB); others, "smelt" (Driver, NBV). The people must pass through "the furnace of affliction" (Isa 48.10) in order that the wicked may be separated. The refusal of the people to know Jehovah leaves him with no other alternative than to bring them through the purifying crucible of judgment. That is the only way the nation can be saved.

And try them. Or "assay" (NASB, NBV, NEB) "test" (RSV).
For how else should I do? The idea is that nothing else is left to be done.

9.8 Their tongue is a deadly weapon. I.e., killing, murderous.
Layeth wait. "Plans an ambush" (RSV), "sets an ambush" (NASB).

9.9 Refrain repeated from 5.9, 29.

C. Lamentation Over the Future Desolation of the Land (9.10–11). In vision Jeremiah sees the future desolation of the land and takes up a lamentation over it.

9.10 Neither can men hear. I.e., "the lowing of the cattle is not heard" (RSV, NASB).

9.11 Heaps. I.e. "a heap of ruins" (RSV, NASB, NEB, NBV).
Dwelling-place. "Lair" (RSV, NBV), "den" (Henderson, KJV), "haunt" (NASB, NEB).

IV. The Wisdom Attained Through Judgment (9.12–10.25)

A. The Reason for the Bitter Judgment Made Clear: It is Due to Judah's Abandonment of Jehovah (9.12–16). If I have not misunderstood this section, we must visualize Judah in ruins, the judgment having set in. The lesson of the judgment could be missed; it must not be misunderstood. It is not merely a case of a little nation being overrun by a great power. Nor is it a matter of Babylon's gods being stronger than Jehovah, the God of Israel. Compare and study Ezekiel 38.21–29 in the light of these issues.

9.12 The call for interpreters of the judgment. The reason for the judgment must be made perfectly clear. Jehovah must have his spokesmen who can explain the judgment and impress its lessons on the people that remain. *The wise man* is shown by the parallelism to be the man with prophetic inspiration who would be able to *understand* and to *declare* the reason for the judgment—men like Jeremiah whose message showed insight into the council of God, unlike the false prophets who spoke "a vision out of their own heart, and not out of the mouth of Jehovah"; who proclaimed a message of peace and thereby strengthened "the hands of evil-doers," thus demonstrating that they had no access to the council of Jehovah (23.14, 16–22).

9.13 Which I set before them. I.e., by means of the preaching of Jeremiah and others like him (26.4), just as Moses had set the law before Israel in the plains of Moab (Deut 4.8, 44). The real *wise man* would not be surprised by the judgment; nor would he have any trouble understanding it. Cf. 44.15–19 where the people even in the midst of the judgment showed themselves to be without understanding of it. They had followed stupid leaders and were hence themselves afflicted with stupidity.

9.14 Baalim. Plural; hence "the Baals" (RSV, NASB, etc.).

9.15 Wormwood. "Many species of wormwood grow in Palestine. ... All species have a strong, bitter taste, leading to the use of the plant as a symbol of bitterness, sorrow, and calamity" (NBD, 1340). With *water of gall* (explained at 8.14), it is symbolic of the bitter suffering to come upon Judah through destruction and exile.

9.16 And I will send the sword after them. No getting away. Not in Egypt (42.13–17; 44.26–28). Not anywhere.

B. The Call to Prepare for Mourning (9.17–22)

9.17 Consider ye. I.e., Give attention to the state of affairs now impending, the judgment that is just ahead, and call mourning women to raise a dirge for the dead.

The skilful women. I.e., "literally, *skilled in mourning for the dead*" (NASB margin). Cf. 2 Chronicles 35.25; Ecc 12.5; Amos 5.16; Matthew. 9.23; Mark 5.38. Reference to professional mourners who led in mourning for the dead and aided in giving expression to grief. (See further v 18.)

9.20 Wailing. RSV has "a lament"; for lamentation RSV and NASB have "a dirge," defined by WCD as "a lyrical or musical composition expressive of grief, as to accompany funeral or memorial rites."

Teach your daughters wailing. So many dead that additional mourners will be needed.

9.21 Death is personified; it enters the palaces; it stalks the streets. *From without* = "from the streets" (RSV, NASB). *From the streets* = "from the squares" (RSV), "from the town squares" (NASB).

9.22 As dung. Cf. 8.2; 16.4.

As the handful after the harvestman. Or "the sheaf after the reaper"

(NASB; cf. RSV). Hebrew for *handful* is defined in ISBE as "sheaf or bundle.' It signifies the quantity of grain a gleaner may gather in his hand." When the reaper forgot a sheaf in the field he was not to return for it but to leave it for the poor to glean (Deut 24.19). Dead bodies would fall and be left lying there like such sheaves.

C. The True Wisdom (9.23–10.16)

1. The Knowledge of Jehovah, The Only True Ground of Confidence (9.23–24). This is the great lesson that springs from Judah's disaster (described vv 17–22)—that in fact is practically forced upon one by it. Judah had put all its confidence in human wisdom, military power, and wealth. The judgment that befalls the nation is a certain demonstration that such things cannot save; that they are not worthy of confidence. The only object in which a person can place his confidence that will not let him down and leave him looking like a fool is Jehovah. The only true wisdom lies in the knowledge of Jehovah. In this alone can man find reason to glory (= boast, NASB).

9.24 Who exerciseth lovingkindness. The knowledge of Jehovah is defined as involving the character and nature of Jehovah. The knowledge of Jehovah as being of this character will of course have its impact upon the conduct of the one who knows Jehovah. One who knows Jehovah in this manner will not adopt Judah's "temple theology" expressed in 7.1–11.

2. Judgment to Fall Upon Circumcised and Uncircumcised Without Distinction (9.25–26). Circumcision can therefore be no ground of confidence or boasting. Circumcision was the token of the covenant relation with Jehovah (Gen 17.9–14). The advantage of it was that the circumcised man was among those to whom God had specially revealed himself. But if the circumcised man did not know Jehovah (v 24) and ignored Jehovah's revealed will (cf. Rom 2.25–27), then the advantage of circumcision was nullified. That was the case with Judah. They were no different from the uncircumcised heathen. And the outward sign would not save them.

9.25 All them that are circumcised in their uncircumcision. Literally, "all them that are circumcised with foreskin"—i.e., circumcised externally, but still with the foreskin covering the heart (v 26; cf. 4.4 with note). RSV: "circumcised but yet uncircumcised." NASB: "circumcised and yet uncircumcised."

9.26 Israel was uncircumcised in heart and that made them no different than the uncircumcised pagan nations. The outward sign was of no value without the spiritual condition symbolized by it.

All that have the corners of their hair cut off. So KJV in margin: "having the corners of their hair polled." *Of their hair* is italicized. These words are supplied by the translators on the basis of Lev 19.27 and 21.5. Herodotus mentions this Arabic practice: "The only gods the Arabs recognize are Dionysus and Urania; the way they cut their hair—all round in a circle, with the temples shaved—is, they say, in imitation of Dionysus" (iii. 8; Pelican edition, p. 177). It was a mark of consecration to a pagan god, which explains why the practice was forbidden to Israel.

3. The Folly of Idolatry: Jehovah, the One True and Living God, Alone to be Feared (10.1–16)

(a) Nothingness of the Idols (10.1–5)

10.2 The signs of heaven. Natural phenomena (eclipses, comets and such) taken by the heathen to be signs of extraordinary and disastrous events to come.

10.4 That it move not. NASB: "so that it will not totter." NEB: "so that they do not fall apart." Keil explains: tumble over. Cf. Isaiah 40.20; 41.7. Bright: "to keep them from wobbling."

10.5 A palm-tree, of turned work. Driver translates, "a pillar in a cumcumber-garden"—"i.e. what we would call a *scarecrow.*" So most modern translations: "scarecrows in a cucumber field" (RSV), "a scarecrow in a cucumber field" (NASB), "scarecrows in a cucumber garden" (NBV), "scarecrows in a cucumber patch" (Bright). "They can no more speak than a scarecrow in a plot of cucumbers" (NEB). Hebrew for *palm-tree* can evidently mean either *pillar* (margin) or *palm-tree* (which is like a pillar; cf. Jdg 4.5 for this usage). The other word involved (*miqshah*) is used for a cucumber garden in Isaiah 1.8. "That this was the sense in which the Jews themselves understood it at the time when the book of Baruch was written appears from the verse (Baruch 6.70) evidently based on this, 'as a scarecrow in a garden of cucumbers'" (Streane).

(b) Contrast The Incomparable Jehovah (10.6–10)

10.7 To thee doeth it appertain. The antecedent of *it* is *fear* (v 7a). The Hebrew verb means to be fitting, proper, becoming; as Henderson explains:

"... to be suitable to the nature or character of any object. To Jehovah alone it is fit and proper that religious reverence should be paid. Anything of the kind rendered to another is an infringement on his high and exclusive prerogative, besides being in itself in the highest degree unseemly and absurd." RSV: "for this is thy due." Similarly NASB. NEB: "for fear is thy fitting tribute."

There is none like unto thee. Including not merely *wise men* and royalty, but also that which is produced by skilful men—i.e., the idols.

10.8 Brutish. RSV and NASB: "stupid."

The instruction of idols! it is but a stock. RSV: "the instruction of idols is but wood!"—"i.e. is no better than the idol itself; idolatry is destitute of moral or spiritual force" (Driver). No wonder they remain "stupid and foolish"—they "learn their nonsense from a log of wood" (NEB).

10.9 However much expense and skill goes into the production of the idol it remains only *the work of skillful men*. Nothing can transform a block of wood into a god.

(c) Israel's Message to the Idolaters (10.11). This one verse is in Aramaic. It is difficult to explain. Perhaps it anticipates the time of the captivity when in Babylon the people would come to understand Aramaic (contrast 1 Kings 18.26 margin), and constitutes the message of Israel to worshippers of idols. Not only were the Jews not to fear the pagan gods (v 5), but also they were to speak this message to the idol worshipping world. But ???

(d) The Almighty Jehovah—the Only Wise, True and Living God (10.12–16). These verses are repeated in 51.15–19 in a context which may lend confirmation to the above explanation of verse 11.

10.12 The power and wisdom of Jehovah manifested in the creation.

10.13 God manifested in the storm. His voice refers to the thunder. The tumult of waters = "the roaring noise of rain driven by the wind in a heavy storm" (Driver).

Lightnings for the rain. "I.e. since the rain comes as a consequence of the lightning, for the lightning seems to rend the clouds and let them pour their water out on the earth" (Keil). The description is *phenomenal* (based on what is seen; what appears) and *poetic* rather than *scientific*. But it stresses the fact that God is behind the phenomena of nature.

10.14 The effect of such manifestations of the true God. Man with his idols is plain stupid, humiliated, in the presence of such phenomena.

10.15 The idols characterized. RSV, NASB and NBV put "worthless" for *vanity*. For *delusion* NASB and NBV put "mockery." Bright puts "nonentities" for *vanity* and "a ridiculous joke" for *a work of delusion*.

10.16 The one true and living God by contrast. NASB has "Maker" for *former*, with note in margin: "Lit., *fashioner*."

Additional Note: Compare my note at IV, A on 9.12–16 at the beginning of this section. If my analysis there is correct, 10.1–16 can be closely connected with the situation at the fall of Judah. The contrast between Jehovah and the idols will help prevent a misinterpretation of that disaster.

D. The Great Lesson of Judgment and Captivity (10.17–25). The judgment upon Judah teaches one great lesson which she had refused to learn in any other way—the lack of control that man has over the affairs of life; the foolishness of idolatry and of trust in men; the disastrous end to which human wisdom leads. When man acts independently of God he comes to ruin. Only in Jehovah is salvation to be found.

1. Call to Prepare for Exile (10.17–18)

10.17 Gather up thy wares out of the land. Margin, "thy bundle from the ground." The alternate renderings result from different derivations of the Hebrew (discussed in Driver). The derivation is uncertain. In any case, however, it is a call to prepare for departure into exile (cf. v 18).

O thou that abidest in the siege. Hebrew is literally, *O inhabitress of the fortress* (margin). Address directed to the population of the besieged city of Jerusalem, represented as a woman.

10.18 The reason for preparation for departure.

That they may feel it. Hebrew is literally *find*, without an object. (*It* is italicized.) Explanations vary. Can it refer to the new insights to be gained through the experience of exile? See verse 23.

2. The Response of the People to Their Fate (10.19–25). The speaker is the one addressed in verse 18, *the inhabitress of the fortress*. Jeremiah gives voice to the reaction of the people to the calamity that befalls them. Cf. 4.19–20.

(a) The Humbled People (10.19–22)

10.19 Truly this is my grief. Or sickness (margin). The words express resignation.

10.20 The population of Jerusalem has been represented as a woman (*inhabitress*, v 17 margin). The community bewails its fate, the desolation of Judah being "likened to a collapsed tent" (Harrison; so also Keil).

10.21 The main cause of the calamity. *Shepherds* = rulers (as 2.8 margin; 3.15; 23.1–4). *Brutish* = "stupid" (RSV, NASB).

Have not inquired of Jehovah. Source of their failure and cause of the nation's disastrous end: They relied upon human wisdom rather than upon God.

10.22 The sounds of invasion, bringing the calamity for which the people mourns (vv 19–21), are already heard. For *the voice of tidings* many substitute the exclamation "Hark, a rumor!" (RSV; Driver; cf. NEB and NBV).

(b) The Great Lesson (10.23). Jeremiah continues to speak for the people, giving expression to the great lesson which they have refused to learn for so long and which is forced upon them through the experience of destruction and exile. Only the experience of the disastrous end to which trust in human wisdom leads brings the people to acknowledge that control over the affairs of life is in other hands than man's. They had followed human leaders who had sought to rule independently of Jehovah (v 21), and the result was disaster. At last they perceive that man's only hope is in submission to and reliance upon Jehovah. For the language cf. verse 5, "neither is it in them to do good." I.e., they have not the power to do good. Cf. Psalm 37.23 and Proverbs 16.9 on the thought of the verse.

(c) Plea for Mitigation of Judah's Punishment and for God's Wrath to be Poured Out Upon Her Enemies (10.24–25)

10.24 But with judgment (KJV). So also ASV margin—a literal translation. "I.e. in a judicial spirit, not in anger (Psa 6.1, 38.1)" (Driver).

PART FOUR

Covenant Disloyalty and the Consequences

Jeremiah 11–13

I. Conspiracy in Judah and Consequences (Ch 11)

A. The Order to Proclaim the Covenant (11.1–5). This message is best explained as dating from the finding of the book of the law in the temple and as connected with Josiah's reform movement which followed (2 Kings 22–23). See on verse 2 below.

11.2 Hear ye. The plural would include Jeremiah (v 1) and others associated with him. But the identity of these "others" is uncertain. Keil thinks of "the prophets in general"; Henderson, of the priests as teachers of the law, of whom Jeremiah was one (1.1).

The words of this covenant. This expression (vv 2–3, 6, 8) treats the covenant as something that was then before the people. It is most understandable as coming in the aftermath of the finding of the book of the law (2 Kings 22.8–13) and its public reading (2 Kings 23.1–3) in Josiah's eighteenth year. With the covenant thus before the people Jeremiah was to support Josiah's effort by proclaiming loyalty to the covenant. I would guess that some time passed before the words of verses 9–13 in which the covenant is not spoken of as "this covenant" (= something before the people to which Jeremiah could point) but as "my covenant which I made with their fathers" (v 10). Remember that Jeremiah's speeches were not written immediately upon delivery but later (ch 36). Likely this chapter consists of pieces of material slightly separated in time but put together in the written version because they were related in subject.

11.3 Cursed be the man. Cf. Deuteronomy 27.26.

11.4 Out of the iron furnace. "I.e. the furnace in which iron is smelted; fig. of a place of severe suffering" (Driver); metaphor for the afflictions suffered in Egypt. Cf. Deuteronomy 4.20; 1 Kings 8.51.

Obey my voice. Cf. 7.21–23 and the notes on the covenant.

And do them. The pronoun has no proper antecedent in the immediate context. Some therefore follow the LXX reading: "and do according to all that I command you." So RSV, NASB, NBV, NEB. Henderson, however, finds an antecedent in verse 3: "the words of this covenant." Cf. verse 6.

So shall ye be my people. Expressing the covenant, compact or agreement between Jehovah and Israel. Cf. Deuteronomy 26.16–19; 27.9–10; 29.10–13. The occasion in 1 Kings 23.1–3 closely resembles, in a formal way, the occasion when Moses addressed Israel in the plains of Moab. Both were times of covenant renewal. And the preaching of Jeremiah resembles that of Moses.

11.5 Cf. Deuteronomy 1.8; 4.1; 6.10; 7.8, 12; etc.

Amen, O Jehovah. "So be it, Lord" (RSV). Expressing consent or agreement, adherence to the covenant, in the manner of Deuteronomy 27.15ff.

B. Warning From the Disloyalty of the Fathers and Its Consequences (11.6–8)

11.8 Yet they obeyed not. Referring to the fathers (v 7). Cf. 2 Kings 22.13.

Therefore I brought upon them. Referring to the curses threatened in the covenant for disloyalty to the covenant (cf. esp. Deut 28.15ff), including the extreme of exile in the case of the greater part of the people.

C. Disloyalty in the Present and the Threat of Inescapable Judgment (11.9–13). Evidently some time has passed. (See note on *the words of this covenant*, v 2.) If the first part of the chapter best fits the time of the finding of the book of the law and the public reading of the covenant, this part reflects a situation in which it has become clear that the commitment of the people to the covenant (2 Kings 23.1–3) was shallow and not lasting. They have gone back to the sins of their forefathers.

11.9 Conspiracy. Illustrated by 1 Samuel 22.8, 13 (accusations of Saul), 2 Samuel 15.12 (Absalom's conspiracy against David), 1 Kings 15.27; 16.9, 16, 20 (treason; Hebrew *qesher* as here); 2 Kings 11.14 (cf. 2 Chron

23.13; treason against Athaliah, Hebrew *qesher*); 15.10, 15, 25, 30; 17.4; many other occurrences. Here it refers to the apostasy, rebellion and revolt against Jehovah, defection from the covenant (v 10). With Keil and others, Harrison holds that "the conspiracy was not of a formal character," that the apostasy was "so widespread ... that it appeared as though the people had deliberately plotted to renounce their covenantal obligations and espouse apostasy." I am not so sure. Verses 18–23 give evidence of formal plotting among the men of Anathoth. Henderson and Streane think of secret measures, perhaps a compact entered into by those hostile to Josiah's reformation. Not unlikely at all.

11.11–13 Consequence of the faithlessness. Cf. 2.26–28.

11.13 The shameful thing. Hebrew *shame* (margin), as in 3.24; perhaps to be capitalized; refers to Baal.

D. Neither Prayer Nor Sacrifice Can Remove the Threat of Judgment From the Impenitent People (11.14–17)

11.14 Cf. 7.16.

11.15 What ... to do in my house? "What right has my beloved in my house...?" (RSV, NASB, NBV, NEB). But Keil explains: "What does it want there?" Perhaps: What could she possibly do there? What could she accomplish? Harrison suggests: "What business etc.?" Cf. 12.7 on *my beloved*, referring to the covenant people. *My house* = the temple as is clear from *holy flesh* (= sacrifices, Hag 2.12).

Lewdness. Hebrew *mezimmah* means *wicked thought or device*, and that is usually indicated in the translation. See Job 21.27; Psalm 10.2; 21.11; 37.7; Proverbs 12.2; 14.17; 24.8; Jeremiah 51.11. Harrison: "has perpetrated vile schemes."

With many, and the holy flesh. The Hebrew text is obscure. Just about all, even very conservative scholars, adopt, either wholly or in part, the reading preserved in the LXX: *Shall vows and holy flesh take away from thee thy wickednesses, or shalt thou escape by these?* RSV partly: "Can vows and sacrificial flesh avert your doom? Can you then exult?" So also NASB: "Can the sacrificial flesh take away from you your disaster, so (that) you can rejoice?" Note that *evil* is understood to mean calamity or disaster.

11.16 A green olive-tree. The name Jehovah had given her, showing his intention for her, indicating what he had made her—a flourishing, prosperous people. Cf. Psalm 52.8; 128.3; Hosea 14.6.

With the noise of a great tumult. The figure seems to be as explained in Driver and Harrison. A great storm arises. (Bright puts "with mighty thunder clap" for the above phrase.) The tree is struck by lightning and set ablaze, with branches broken.

11.17 Hath pronounced evil against thee. *Evil* in the sense of calamity, disaster.

E. A Plot Against Jeremiah's Life (11.18–23). Perhaps this plot is intended as evidence of the conspiracy mentioned in verse 9. Even people of Jeremiah's own town are found plotting against Jehovah's spokesman. Keil considers the plot as providing "evidence that Judah is unreclaimable, and that the sore judgments threatened cannot be averted ... a practical proof of the people's determination not to reform." The plot reveals how hopeless the situation is. The people are determined not to heed Jeremiah's message. Far from receiving the message and amending their lives, they determine to get rid of the messenger.

11.18 And Jehovah gave me knowledge of it. At first they plotted secretly. But Jehovah revealed the plan to Jeremiah. This statement will not seem so abrupt if it can be connected with verse 9 in the manner explained just above.

11.19 A gentle lamb. The Hebrew word rendered *ox* in KJV only has that meaning in Psalm 144.14 "as a poetical expression, *the domesticated ones*" (Streane). The literal meaning is *familiar* (Driver), and the word is here descriptive of *lamb.* It is the word rendered *friend* in Proverbs 16.28 and 17.9 and *guide* in Psalm 55.13 (ASV, *companion*), Proverbs 2.17 (ASV, *friend*), Jeremiah 3.4, and Micah 7.5 (ASV, *friend*, with *confidant* in the margin). (It has other applications elsewhere.) It describes a lamb that is "tame" (Driver, Henderson), "a pet lamb" (NBV), one like that in 2 Samuel 12.3, a friend of the family. Jeremiah had been like such a pet lamb, not at all suspecting he was about to be slaughtered.

The tree with the fruit thereof. Some understand the phrase as proverbial for complete destruction. Others explain *the fruit* as a reference to Jeremiah's prophecies (v 21). Others read "with its sap." (Bright thinks the explanation does not even require an emendation.) "The 'tree with its sap' is figurative for a person in the full strength and vigour of life" (Driver).

11.20 Who triest the reins and the heart (KJV). *Reins* = kidneys. Both terms together refer to the innermost "motives and thoughts" (Bright). "Jeremiah appeals to Yahweh, who can test the inmost feelings and purposes both of himself and of his foes, and knows therefore on which side the right lies" (Driver).

Revealed my cause. I.e., made it known, with the idea of confiding or committing his cause to God, turning it over to him, leaving it up to him.

11.21 Anathoth. Jeremiah's home (1.1).

II. Complaint Regarding the Prosperity of the Wicked (Ch 12)

A. Jeremiah's Complaint (12.1–4). The plot against Jeremiah's life (11.18–23) is undoubtedly what causes his mind to focus upon this problem. Jeremiah is perplexed to see the wicked prosper (vv 1–2) and to bring upon the land desolation which affects the innocent as well as the guilty (v 4).

12.1 Righteous art thou. Important! Jeremiah does not accuse Jehovah of injustice. The problem does not drive him from God but to God for an answer (cf. Psa 73.16–17). He does not question the justice of God. He has faith that in any controversy Jehovah will be found in the right. But he is perplexed with a problem—a situation that he cannot reconcile with God's righteousness. The wicked prosper while he suffers from their opposition. But he does not forsake God. Instead he takes the problem to God and lays it before him.

Yet would I reason the cause with thee. KJV better. Hebrew *speak of judgments*. NASB perhaps the clearest: "I would discuss matters of justice with thee."

12.2 Thou art near in their mouth. Prosperity (v 2a) in spite of such hypocrisy!

12.3 Jeremiah pleads that Jehovah knows his attitude towards him—that he has no faithlessness in his heart. It is that, Jeremiah feels, which demands that judgment be brought for him and against his opponents without delay. Cf. 11.20.

Prepare them. Hebrew is literally, *sanctify them for the day of slaughter*—i.e., Treat them as animals to be slaughtered as sacrifices.

12.4 I.e., How long will the whole land have to suffer due to the wickedness of sinners? The prophet would have God destroy the sinners and put an end to this injustice.

He shall not see our latter end. Most likely they refer to Jeremiah rather than to God. The prophet had said, "I shall see thy vengeance on them" (11.20), and Jehovah had predicted their *latter end* (11.21–23). But time goes on and Jeremiah's enemies continue to prosper. They begin to assert that Jeremiah will not live to see the fulfillment of his prophecies. Perhaps they even imply that they will do way with him (11.21). This saying of his enemies is what moves Jeremiah to break forth with his complaint. Mark 3.30 is perhaps a parallel, the *because* in each instance explaining the occasion for what was just said.

Others (e.g. NEB) follow the LXX: "God will not see what we are doing." Cf. Psalm 73.11.

B. Jehovah's Answer (12.5–17)

1. The Worst is Yet to Come (12.5–6). Jehovah delays the judgment out of longsuffering (cf. 2 Pet 3.9, 15). He gives every opportunity for repentance and only brings judgment when the case is absolutely hopeless. For that reason wickedness will get worse and worse in the land. Later Jeremiah pleads with God, "Take me not away in thy longsuffering" (15.15). The situation perhaps parallels that of Elijah (1 Kings 19).

12.5 "If you have raced with men on foot, and they have wearied you, how will you compete with horses?" (RSV). So the first part of God's answer is surprising: Things are going to get even worse. "What Jeremiah had to suffer from his countrymen at Anathoth was but a trifle compared with the malign assaults that yet awaited him in the discharge of his office" (Keil).

The pride of the Jordan. This expression appears here, 49.19, 50.44, and Zechariah 11.3. KJV has "the swelling of the Jordan" in all of these places except Zechariah 11.3 where it has "the pride of Jordan." The same word (*gaon*) is used in 13.9 (*the pride of Judah, and the great pride of Jerusalem*) and 48.29 (*the pride of Moab*). The literal sense is *rising*, but the word is nearly always used in the figurative sense of pride (19 times in KJV, according to YAC), arrogancy, majesty, etc. Instead of "the swelling of the Jordan" (cf. Josh 3.15), *the pride of the Jordan* more likely refers to the "dense thickets" (NEB) along the banks of the Jordan. RSV and NBV have "jungle." In Jeremiah 12.5 it refers to rough and dangerous country in contrast to "a land of peace"; in 49.19 and 50.44 it appears to be the lair of lions; and note especially Zechariah 11.3 where it is an area "laid waste" by fire, causing "a voice of the roaring of young lions."

12.6 A sample of what is to come. Even his family will turn against him. Hebrew for *fair words* is literally *good things*. NASB: "nice things."

2. Judah Given Up to Judgment (12.7–13). The passage points back to 11.14–17 (cf. "beloved" in 11.15 and 12.7) and contains an elaboration of the threat. It is probably intended as part of Jehovah's answer to Jeremiah. The judgment may be long delayed, for Jehovah is longsuffering and gives every opportunity for repentance, not acting before the case is hopeless (vv 5–6). Observe "the sorrow and reluctance with which Jehovah gives up His heritage" (Driver) as reflected in the passage. But judgment has been decreed and is only a matter of time. The verbs should be explained as "prophetic perfects," describing the future as though it were past. The judgment is seen from the standpoint of the divine purpose.

12.7 My house. Family, household. So the parallelism with "my heritage" (cf. v 8) and "the dearly beloved of my soul" would seem to indicate.

12.8 As a lion. Jehovah's heritage has acted toward him as a wild, ferocious animal. Verse 8 assigns the reason Jehovah abandons his people to her enemies.

12.9 The questions express amazement. Hebrew for *bird* is always used of a bird of prey. Hence the ASV: *a speckled bird of prey*, referring to a bird of strange and unusual appearance, which is for that reason attacked by the others. *Beasts of the field*, as *birds of prey*, is an emblem for enemies.

12.10 Many shepherds. Heathen rulers (as 6.3; cf. 2.8) that overrun the land with their armies.

12.13 They have sown wheat. Something in the nature of a proverbial saying. A fitting conclusion to verses 7–12. All the labors of the people have produced only a crop of thorns.

They have put themselves to pain. "They have tired themselves out but profit nothing" (RSV). "They have strained themselves to no profit" (NASB).

Your fruits. The products of their labors.

3. Jehovah's World-plan: Judgment Upon Judah and Its Neighbors Followed by Restoration (12.14–17). This outline of Jehovah's world-plan completes Jehovah's reply to Jeremiah's complaint. Judgment will fall upon the wicked Judah and its heathen neighbors. But judgment will be followed by restoration, with blessings extended to all. Thus Jehovah shows himself to be a God of grace, whose real and ultimate desire is to show mercy—to build rather than to tear down, to plant rather than to pluck up. That explains the long delay in bringing judgment. This passage is "a brief anticipation of the predictions contained in chapters 47, 48, 49" (Henderson).

12.14 All mine evil neighbors. Such neighboring heathen nations as mentioned in chapters 47–49: Philistines, Moabites, Ammonites, Edomites, Syrians. Jehovah is the real possessor of the land of Israel; he "dwells in Zion" (Psa 9.11; 74.2; 76.2). Such surrounding peoples are, therefore, his neighbors.

That touch the inheritance. I.e., in the manner of verses 10–12, violently, as an enemy.

12.14b, The heathen, as well as Judah, to be uprooted from their land.

12.15 At a later time they will be restored.

12.16 If they will diligently learn. Description of conversion to the true worship.

Then shall they be built up. They will be incorporated among the people of God and share their blessings. Thus the promises to Abraham will find fulfillment (cf. Gen 12.3; 22.18).

III. The Humiliation of Judah's Pride (Ch 13)

A. Jeremiah and the Linen Girdle: A Symbolic Action (13.1–7)

13.1 A linen girdle. Better as Driver, RSV and NBV: "waistcloth." The word *girdle* is used in English versions to cover several Hebrew terms and body-garments. Hebrew *ezor* "usually means 'waistcloth', 'loincloth'" (NBD, 470). This "loincloth" was not merely the girdle or belt which served to bind the outer garment about one. It "was always worn next to the skin. The figurative use made of it in Isaiah 11.5 and Jeremiah 13.11 will be lost unless this is remembered" (ISBE, II, 877). "The basic garment of the Israelite worker and soldier appears to have been a short wrap-around skirt or waistcloth (*ezor*) reaching down to about the middle of the thigh. The finest examples of it were made of linen, the more crude of leather" (G. Ernest Wright, *Biblical Archaeology*, 191). It was not a belt but a skirt (*Ibid*).

Wright has illustrations in Figures 49 and 64–65. Bright says the *ezor* (waistcloth) was "the usual undergarment; not a breechclout, but a short skirt worn wrapped about the hips, and reaching about halfway down the thighs. The translation 'girdle' (so older English versions) is inaccurate; this was a sort of waistband worn outside the skirt."

And put it not in water. Evidently meaning: Do not wash it. When it gets soiled, leave it that way. See on verse 10.

13.4 Go to the Euphrates. The place of the (future) captivity.

A cleft of the rock. Reference to the rocky soil near the Euphrates, as verse 7 shows.

13.7 Marred. "Spoiled" (RSV and NEB); "ruined" (NBV and NASB); perhaps decayed.

Profitable for nothing. "Good for nothing" (RSV and NBV); "totally worthless" (NASB).

B. Interpretation of the Symbolism (13.8–11)

13.9 The pride of Judah, Cf. "the pride of Moab" with the elaboration provided in 48.29. The pride of Judah is what made them so stubborn and kept them from submitting to Jehovah (v 10).

13.10 Shall even be as this girdle, Hebrew is literally *let it be* (Driver), NASB, NEB margin). The girdle represents the people; the wearing of the girdle, the close relation between Jehovah and the people (v 11). The people, like the girdle, gets soiled, but the dirt remains on it, not being washed off since the people remain impenitent (cf. v 1). The carrying of the girdle to the Euphrates is the captivity; the "many days" (v 6), the seventy years of captivity; the marring of the girdle, the physical ruin of Judah, its humiliation in exile.

13.11 That they may be. All this God intended them to be. All this they cast aside in their stupid pride.

C. Jehovah's Word to Judah, Clothed in a Proverbial Saying and a Second Symbol (13.12–14)

13.12 Bottle. Usage ("bottle of wine," 1 Sam 1.24; 10.3; 25.18; 2 Sam 16.1; cf. Jer 48.12) as well as the response of the people to the proverb would indicate that the Hebrew *nebel* was ordinarily used for wine.

13.13 I will fill … with drunkenness. Explaining the application of the proverb. To be understood in the light of Psalm 60.3; Isaiah 51.17; Jeremiah 25.15–16, 27; Obadiah 16; Rev 14.10. They will be made to reel and to stagger about as if drunk; they would be drunk on the wine of the wrath of Jehovah.

13.14 And I will dash them one against another. The effect of the drunkenness: "filled with drunken frenzy, they shall helplessly destroy one another" (Keil). Keil says it is "as jars are shivered when knocked together." But perhaps we are to think of drunk men stumbling and falling against each other.

D. Warning: Repent or Face Disaster (13.15–17). Even yet they may escape the impending ruin by humbling themselves before Jehovah, giving him the glory.

13.16 Give glory to Jehovah your God. Thus fulfilling the destiny appointed for them (v 11b).

E. Description of the State of Humiliation Which is the Consequence of Judah's Obstinate Devotion to Evil (13.18–27)

13.18 Unto the king and to the queen-mother. Whoever they might be at the time of the fall. Cf. the end of Jehoiachin and Nehushta (29.2; 2 Kings 24.8–17). This prophecy, however, was spoken during the time of Josiah, if I am not mistaken in my views of the date of the first twenty chapters (discussed elsewhere). Hebrew *gibirah* occurs six times in O. T.; in 1 Kings 11.19 refers to the wife of the (Egyptian) king; in 1 Kings 15.13 and 2 Chronicles 15.16, the mother of the king. In 2 Kings 10.13 the reference is not defined so clearly. Nor is it in Jeremiah 13.18 and 29.2. However, a comparison of Jeremiah 29.2 with 2 Kings 24.8–17 suggests a reference to the mother of the king. So also the age of Jehoiachin—and the observation that it is the mother of the king that is mentioned so consistently in 2 Kings alongside the reigning kings (8.26; 12.1; 14.2; 15.2, 33; 18.2; 21.1, 19; 22.1; 23.31, 36; 24.8, 12, 15, 18), and who evidently exercised a great deal of influence upon the government.

Humble yourselves. Or perhaps better with the margin, *Sit ye down low*—"i.e. descend from the throne; … as the reason that follows shows, because the kingdom is passing from you" (Keil).

For your headtires are come down. As they lost their kingdom. The *crown* is the symbol of rule.

13.19 The cities of the South. The Negeb, the dry district in the south of Judah.

Are shut up. Perhaps to be explained with Bright: "... are blockaded; None can break through"; and with NEB: "... are besieged, and no one can relieve them." Others compare Isaiah 24.10 and think of cities *shut up* by ruins blocking the entrances and with *none to open them* because all Judah has been *carried away captive.*

13.20 The personified Jerusalem is addressed all the way through verse 27. On *the flock* cf. verse 17.

13.21 When he shall set over thee as head. The Hebrew verb does have the meaning of *visit* or *punish* (as KJV). But that meaning does not result in a suitable sense here. "The phrase means also: to appoint or set over anybody; cf. e.g. 15.3. The subject can only be Jahveh" (Keil). For other places where *paqad* is rendered *appoint* or *set* see Numbers 3.10 4.27; Jeremiah 49.19; 50.44; 51.27 (appoint); Numbers 27.16; Joshua 10.18; Psalm 109.6; Isaiah 62.6; Jeremiah 1.10; 40.11. For the word *head* see Jeremiah 1.5 (KJV, *chief*).

Those whom thou hast thyself taught to be friends to thee. KJV has *captains* for *friends.* "This word is indeed the technical term for the old Edomitish chieftains of clans, Genesis 36.15ff., and is applied as an archaic term by Zechariah 9.7 to the tribal princes of Judah; but it does not, as a general rule, mean prince, but familiar, friend, Psalm 55.14, Proverbs 16.28, Micah 7.5; cf. Jeremiah 11.19" (Keil). Hebrew is *alluph*, the word rendered *gentle* in ASV at 11.19 and discussed in a note there. The reference here is to the heathen nations courted by Judah (cf. 2.14–19, 36), which would eventually be her head—first Egypt (2 Kings 23.31–35), then Babylon.

13.21a in NASB: "What will you say when He appoints over you—and you yourself had taught them—former companions (margin, chieftains) to be head over you?" This is probably as close as one can come to a literal translation. See Bright, p. 95.

13.22 And if thou say. Cf. verse 21: "What wilt thou say, etc.?"

Thy skirts uncovered. The description here and at verse 26 is likely from the public humiliation administered to prostitutes. Cf. Isaiah 47.3; Hosea 2.10; Nahum 3.5.

And thy heels suffer violence. Keil thinks of one being driven into exile barefoot; Henderson, of the sandals being torn off violently, injuring the heels. Harrison considers *heels* a "euphemism" and thinks the phrase refers to the ravishing of the body—this view following Bright who renders "your body ravished." Apparently RSV has the same view: "and you suffer violence." Others as NASB: "your heels have been exposed."

13.23 Judah has so learned (Hebrew for *accustomed* is literally *taught*, margin) the ways of evil that it has become "second nature." It cannot change. So the people will not escape this disgraceful treatment.

13.24–27 "There being no hope of improvement, nothing remained for the Jews but punishment" (Henderson).

13.25 Trusted in falsehood. Both delusive promises (7.4, 8; 6.14; 8.11) and non-existent gods (16.19–20).

13.26 Cf. Nahum 3.5. "For her lewd idolatry Jerusalem shall be carried off like a harlot amid mockery and disgrace" (Keil).

13.27 Thy neighing. As "every one neighed after his neighbor's wife" (5.8), so Jerusalem chased after idols (cf. 2.23–24).

How long shall it yet be? Not contradictory of verse 23. The unchangeable commitment of the present generation to evil does not exclude the possibility of future reform and cleansing from idolatry.

PART FIVE

Revelation on the Occasion of Drought

Jeremiah 14–17

Introduction

The heading is drawn from the occasion rather than the subject matter of these prophecies. Drought, one of the covenant curses brought upon Judah by Jehovah (cf. Deut 28.23–24), has left the land desolate and people and animals suffering. Jeremiah appeals to Jehovah on behalf of the people. But Jehovah will not hear. Judgment has been decreed and intercession cannot avail to turn it away.

I. The Uselessness of Intercession for the People (14.1–15.9)

A. Heading (14.1)

14.1 Drought. Hebrew is plural, pointing to repeated droughts or a long series of droughts (Keil), or perhaps indicating intensity or long continuance (Cheyne, Henderson).

B. The Desolute Condition of Judah Resulting From the Drought (14.2–6)

14.2 The gates. The places where the people gather (cf. Ruth 4.1–2, 11) stand for the people gathered there. Cf. Isaiah 3.26.

They sit in black upon the ground. Dressed in mourning garb. *Upon the ground* as in Job 2.13 and Lamentations 2.10. They have been brought low.

14.3 Their little ones. Not children but "inferiors" (margin) or "servants" (RSV, NASB, NBV).

And cover their heads. In humiliation and sorrow (as 2 Sam 15.30). So also verse 4.

14.4 The ground which is cracked. Literally as margin, *dismayed.* Poetic, applying such a term to the inanimate. Even the land seems to be in mourning.

14.5 The hind. The female of some animal, probably the deer (NBD). NASB, "doe." Noted for tender care of her young.

14.6 Their eyes fail. From looking for food. Cf. Job 11.20; Psalm 69.3; Lamentations 4.17.

C. Jeremiah's Intercession for the People (14.7–9). These verses are a prayer of Jeremiah on behalf of the people (v 11).

14.7 For thy name's sake. A plea similar to Numbers 14.13–19, Deuteronomy 9.25–29, Joshua 7.9 and Psalm 79.9–10; cf. Isaiah 48.9–11. Israel was called by Jehovah's name (v 9). Jehovah's reputation was bound up with the fortunes of Israel. He was the "hope of Israel, the Saviour thereof in the time of trouble" (v 8), but now seemed either not to care about Israel (v 8) or not to be able to deliver (v 9). Jeremiah therefore pleads that Jehovah bring deliverance to Judah for the sake of his own name, since he cannot plead deserving on the part of the people. See also verse 21.

14.8 A sojourner in the land. Who has no real interest in its welfare.

D. Jehovah's Reply (14.10–12). Do not pray for this people. Drought is only the beginning. Worse judgment is ahead—sword, famine and pestilence. The people are impenitent. The cup of iniquity is full (cf. Gen 15.16). They cannot be pardoned.

14.10 Unto this people. Better, *with respect to this people*, "concerning" (RSV, NBV, cf. NEB).

Now will he remember their iniquity. In fact the interests of Jehovah's name (v 7) at this point demanded their punishment. Study Ezekiel 20, noting especially verses 9, 14, 22, 39, 41–44, and Ezekiel 38.16, 23; 39.7, 13, 21–29. The entire history of Israel is explained by Jehovah's regard for his name.

14.12 The people would cry unto God "because of their trouble" (11.14), but without real faith or repentance; with idolatry still in their hearts (cf. 3.10).

E. Additional Plea (14.13) – Growing out of what Jehovah has just said: The people do not heed such threats (or such harbingers of judgment as a drought) because the (false) prophets are promising them peace, telling them they need not fear sword or famine.

F. Jehovah's Answer (14.14–18)

1. These prophets are lying and shall themselves be consumed by sword and famine (14.14–15).

2. The people shall suffer the same judgment for their wickedness (14.16–18). The false prophets are not an excuse for their continuance in apostasy and evil.

14.17 Jeremiah is led to tell the people of his great pain of heart due to the coming destruction. And note! Jehovah wants him to tell the people of his grief. Perhaps this verse explains Jehovah's choice of Jeremiah, with his deep feelings, as the spokesman for these dark days. If nothing else, perhaps this grief of Jeremiah's would touch the hearts of the people.

14.18 Vision of the overthrow of Judah. "Jeremiah, vividly realizing the future, imagines himself to be witnessing the approaching invasion, siege, and exile" (Driver).

G. Jeremiah Renews His Appeal (14.19–22). Perhaps, as Keil thinks, the command to reveal his sorrow to the people emboldens Jeremiah to renew his intercession (in spite of v 11). It is clear that Jeremiah is again addressing Jehovah. He speaks in the character of a priest (cf. 1.1), representing the people, speaking for them, giving voice to their plea.

14.19 We looked for peace. See verse 13 for why.

14.20 Sounds like a genuine confession and expression of repentance (contrast 2.23, 35 and cf. 3.13, 22b–25). But it is not treated as such in 15.1–9 and evidently is to be understood in the light of 3.10. See also 3.3–5 where it is pointed out that drought had not brought Judah to repentance.

14.21 The throne of thy glory. Referring to the temple where Jehovah was enthroned (cf. Exod 25.22; 1 Kings 8.6–11). It would be left in ruins at the destruction of Jerusalem. Put also with this plea the false confidence of 7.4, 8–11.

14.22 I.e., you alone can save; you are our only hope. A pitiful plea for Jehovah to spare the nation, the terms of which show it to arise from the conditions described in verses 2–6.

H. Jehovah's Answer: Judgment is Determined and Not to be Turned Aside by Intercession (18.1–9)

15.1 Moses and Samuel. Two men held in such favor by Jehovah that they were repeatedly able to rescue the people from ruin by their intercessions. See Exodus 32.11–12; Numbers 14.13–19; Deuteronomy 9.25–29; 1 Samuel 7.9–10; 12.17–18; Psalm 99.6.

15.2 Such as are for death. I.e., each to the destiny appointed for him. *Death* as distinguished from *sword* must mean death by disease. In 14.12 and Ezekiel 14.21 and 33.27 *pestilence* is put in place of *death.*

15.3 Four kinds. RSV, "four kinds of destroyers." NEB, "four kinds of doom." Hebrew *families.*

15.4 I will cause them to be tossed to and fro. RSV, "I will make them a horror"; NBV, "a terror"; NASB, "an object of horror." See discussion in Driver, who has "a consternation."

Because of Manasseh. In spite of Manasseh's repentance (2 Chron 33.12–17) and Josiah's reforms. The people had clung to the sins of Manasseh and had not turned to God with their hearts. Cf. 2 Kings 21.10–15; 23.26; 24.3–4.

15.7 And I have winnowed them with a fan. Not a description of the past, but referring to the divine purpose. RSV and NASB, "winnowing fork" for *fan.* Reference is to a tool used in the winnowing process by which the chaff was separated and blown away by the wind.

15.8 Against the mother. According to one alternative in KJV margin, reference is to Jerusalem as the mother city. But that would represent a change from verses 7, 8a. Perhaps the description of the fate of the mothers of young men is by the end of the passage taken as representing the fate of the mother city.

II. The Embattled Prophet Encouraged to Continue His Work (15.10–21)

Introduction

The dialogue between the prophet and Jehovah continues, but now with emphasis upon the prophet's situation rather than that of the people.

A. Jeremiah's Outcry of Complaint (15.10)

15.10 I have not lent. Such transactions are often the cause of hostility. But he had not engaged in any such activity which could account for the enemy against him. It was solely due to his preaching.

B. Jehovah's Answer: A Word of Encouragement (15.11–14)

15.11 I will strengthen thee for good. ASV margin gives another reading, *I will release thee for good*, which is accepted by NASB and by Henderson, who explains in the light of 39.11–14; 40.1–6. Jeremiah's persecutors would go into captivity, while he would be set free. Thus he would be released from persecution.

I will cause the enemy to make supplication unto thee. As in 21.1–2; 37.3; 38.14–28; 42.1–6; representing the triumph of Jeremiah's cause. Others, however, translate with the margin, *I will intercede for thee with the enemy*, and explain in the light of 39.11–14 and 40.1–6, in which case the enemy would be the Babylonians rather than Jeremiah's persecutors. Which view is favored by the context?

15.12 Can one break iron? Verses 12–14 describe the circumstances which would bring about the result of verse 11. Jeremiah's prophecies would be fulfilled. Judah would not be able to resist the powerful enemy from the north (cf. 1.13–15; 4.6; 6.1, 22; etc.). Brought to their knees by Babylon, they would come to Jeremiah in the manner described (v 11).

15.13–14 The contents of these verses show that the people are now addressed. In verse 14 where ASV supplies *them* (*I will make them to pass etc.*), KJV supplies *thee* to agree with verse 13, and NASB supplies *it*, referring to their possessions (v 13).

C. Jeremiah's Further Petition on his own Behalf (15.15–18). Jeremiah's mind remains unsatisfied. The triumph of his cause seems so far in the future. Perhaps he will not be able to survive this divine "longsuffering" in dealing with his enemies. He prays for vengeance on his enemies and that he may not perish.

15.15 Thou knowest. I.e., what he has been going through (cf. v 10).

Take me not away in thy longsuffering. I.e., in the longsuffering being shown toward Jeremiah's enemies (cf. 12.1–6 and the whole chapter with notes). A plea that his enemies may not take his life while God exercises longsuffering to them.

15.16 Jeremiah pleads that he had received the words of God with delight.

I did eat them. Cf. Ezekiel 2.8–3.3; Rev 10.9–10; also our English usage: "In our own language, if asked whether we have read such or such a book, our reply is: Read it? we quite devoured it!" (Henderson). Jeremiah had received God's words, consumed them, in a manner of speaking; the message had become a part of him.

For I am called by thy name. The reason for Jeremiah's delight in God's words. He was identified with Jehovah as Jehovah's spokesman. Cf. 7.10.

15.17 He had devoted his whole life to his message, a message of doom causing him to avoid merrymakers and worldly festivities and to seek solitude. Evidence of Jeremiah's isolation and loneliness.

Because of thy hand. Referring to the divine power which was upon the prophets (cf. Isa 8.11; Ezek 1.3; 3.14, 22; etc.).

For thou hast filled me with indignation. The divine wrath and indignation against the sin and corruption of the nation (cf. 6.11).

15.18 As a deceitful brook, as waters that fail. KJV more literally, *as a liar. Waters that fail* is literally *that are not sure,* i.e. "unreliable" (NASB). Reference to a stream that dries up in the season of drought and disappoints the one seeking water (cf. Job 6.15, in the context of verses 14–23). Contrast 2.13, "the fountain of living waters."

Jeremiah's faith is on trial. God had promised to be his protector (1.8, 17–19), and Jeremiah had started his work. But now that Jeremiah has begun to experience the opposition to his work, of which he had been given advance warning, his faith wavers. It seems that God would turn out to be a dry creekbed where no help could be found. But note! Jeremiah brings his complaint to God; he clings to God; he will not give up his faith. And mercifully, God reinforces his promises in what follows.

D. Jehovah's Encouraging Reply (15.19–21)

15.19 If thou return. I.e., perhaps, to God, turning away from the doubt and despair reflected in verse 18b; or to the work, which Jeremiah was often tempted to forsake. Cf. 9.2; 20.7–18.

That thou mayest stand before me. As a servant, waiting upon his Lord. Cf. Numbers 16.9; Deuteronomy 1.38; 17.12; 1 Kings 1.2; 10.8; 12.8; 17.1; 18.15; 2 Kings 3.14; 5.16.

If thou take forth the precious from the vile. Put *worthless* (RSV, NASB, NBV) or *base* (NEB) for *vile*. The English word *vile* is used in the old sense of *common, looked down upon* (Driver). In the manner of a refiner Jeremiah must remove the precious metal from that which is base and worthless (cf. the figure in 6.27–30). The application here is that the distrust in God reflected in verse 18b will have to be separated out in order for Jeremiah to be useful to God.

Thou shalt be as my mouth. My spokesman or prophet. Cf. Exodus 4.16 with 7.1.

They shall return unto thee. "Then shall his labours be crowned with success. They (the adversaries) will turn themselves to thee, in the manner shown in verse 11, but thou shalt not turn thyself to them, i.e. not yield to their wishes or permit thyself to be moved by them from the right way" (Keil).

15.20–21 A repetition of the promises at 1.8, 17–19. Just what Jeremiah needed at this point—a strong reminder of the commitment Jehovah had made to him. Think, for example, of the patient going into serious surgery: "Tell me one more time, Doctor. Tell me everything will be all right. Tell me good and strong. Make me believe it."[8]

It is also what we often need. When faith is on trial we need to go back to the Word and let Jehovah tell us one more time; and let his Word give us the strength we need to endure.

III. The Prophet in Relation to the Coming Judgment (Chs 16–17)

A. The Course to be Followed by the Prophet in View of the Coming Judgment (16.1–9). Jeremiah's lifestyle is to harmonize with his

[8]This good illustration was suggested by H. R. Crocker of Harpersville, Alabama in a class on Jeremiah. I had been making the point that Jeremiah needed the encouragement of Chapter 1 again. What a great illustration!

message; it is to indicate what is to come, thus to reinforce the message proclaimed.

1. Abstinence From Ordinary Family Life (16.1–4)

16.2 Cf. 1 Corinthians 7.26.

16.3–4 The reason Jeremiah is to live single. If this is to be the fate of sons and daughters and mothers and fathers, then one certainly would not want to face such conditions with a family. Jeremiah's manner of life must reflect his belief re. what is to come. His life will thus reinforce the message proclaimed.

Grievous deaths. Hebrew *deaths of sicknesses* (margin). RSV and NASB: "shall die of deadly diseases."

They shall not be lamented ... buried. Too many dead for the ordinary usages!

2. Jeremiah Not to Mourn for the Dead (16.5–7). The reason for the command (v 5a) is given in what follows (vv 5b–7). Jeremiah's avoidance of the house of mourning will foreshadow a time when there will be so many dead that the ordinary mourning rituals and customs will be out of the question. Thus Jeremiah's life is to reflect God's attitude (v 5b) and what is to come (vv 6–7).

16.6 Nor cut themselves. Heathen expressions of mourning for the dead, forbidden to Israel, but often practiced. See Lev 19.28; Deuteronomy 14.1; Isaiah 22.12; Jeremiah 41.5; 47.5; Amos 8.10; Micah 1.16.

16.7 On comfort ministered by means of the offer of food and drink see 2 Samuel 3.35; 12.17; Ezekiel 24.17; Hosea 9.4 (cf. Deut 26.14).

3. Jeremiah Not to Engage in Merrymaking (16.8–9). Again, a forecast of what was to come.

B. The Message to be Given Regarding the Meaning of the Coming Judgment (16.10–17.4)

1. The Reason for the Judgment (16.10–13)

2. The Great Regathering (16.14–15). A ray of light gleaming through the clouds, sustaining the faith and hope of the godly, keeping them from despair.

16.14 Therefore. I.e., on account of the casting forth of the people (v 13).

It shall no more be said. The coming deliverance would be so great that the former (from Egypt) would be forgotten.

3. Further Description of the Punishment (16.16–18). Before the regathering (vv 14–15), *first* (v 18) the punishment.

16.16 Fishers ... hunters. To catch them or hunt them down and kill or capture them. Other figures for the enemy: lion (4.7); serpents (8.17).

16.17 Escape will be impossible.

16.18 Carcasses. "Dead bodies" (NBV following Driver). Cf. Lev 26.30.

Their detestable things. I.e., "their detestable idols" (RSV, NBV, NASB).

4. Jehovah to Reveal Himself in the Events of History (16.19–21)

16.19 The prophet anticipates the time when the nations will realize the powerlessness and vanity of the idols.

16.20 Confirmation of the words of the nations (v 19): Making a god is totally unreasonable and foolish.

16.21 It is for this very reason, in order to bring about this result, that Jehovah must reveal himself in the events of history. His power will be put on display in the coming events and men will come to recognize his power. Cf. Isaiah's last 27 chapters, esp. chapter 44, where Jehovah reveals himself as the God of history. He reveals his purposes; history is the execution of these purposes; and prophecy the relating of his intention in advance. Thus God shows himself to be God by predicting the future and fulfilling his Word, bringing it to pass. See also Ezekiel 39.21–29 as the conclusion of Ezekiel 38 and 39. Another parallel to the concept of God revealing himself in the events of history.

5. The Necessity for Such Action: Judah's Sin is So Deeply Engraved on Its Heart (17.1–4)

17.1 Written with a pen of iron (NASB). "an iron stylus"— used for engraving upon a hard surface such as stone (cf. Job 19.24). It would write deeply and firmly. The sin of Judah was so deeply engraved upon their heart that it could not be erased.

Upon the horns of their altars. Margin according to the LXX. Sacrificial blood was smeared on the horns of the altars (Exod 29.12; Lev 4.7, 18, 25;

16.18). Reference here must be to idolatrous sacrifices. The horns of the altars, so constantly smeared with the blood of these victims, was evidence of the deep commitment of Judah to apostasy.

17.2 Whilst their children remember their altars. NASB follows Keil in its tr.: "As they remember their children, so they remember their altars etc." I.e., the idolatry is as dear to them as their children—v 2 being "a fuller and clearer disclosure of the sins written on the tables of Judah's heart" (Keil).

But Driver challenges this explanation on the ground that it "requires more to be supplied than is legitimate." Perhaps the statement is intended to show the hopelessness of the situation. The sin is deeply engraved upon the heart of the nation, and with the children already polluted by it, what hope of a reversal remains?

Asherim. In place of KJV's "groves." *Asherim* is the plural of *Asherah*. NASB margin explains it as "wooden symbols of female deities"—wooden, for they could be cut down (Exod 34.13) and burned (Deut 12.3), and in Deuteronomy 16.21 Israel was forbidden to plant "an Asherah of any kind of tree beside the altar of Jehovah." ASV margin at Exodus 34.13 says: "Probably the wooden symbols of a goddess Asherah." Asherah is mentioned in 1 Kings 18.19 and 2 Kings 23.4 as a goddess along with Baal, and 1 Kings 15.13 and 2 Chronicles 15.16 refer to images erected to her. NBD, 95, calls Asherah "a Canaanite mother-goddess mentioned in the Ras Shamra texts as a goddess of the sea and the consort of El, but associated in the Old Testament with Baal (e.g. Jdg 3.7)." G. Ernest Wright has a long discussion of "The Gods of Canaan" in *Biblical Archaeology*, pp. 107ff, which includes the following about Asherah: "While she was originally the mother-goddess (mother of various gods and goddesses, lam), in practical worship her functions in the world are frequently mixed with those of the goddesses of fertility. … The symbol of her presence at a place of worship was apparently a sacred tree or pole standing near the altar." There seems to be some confusion in Canaanite mythology whether Asherah was the wife of El and mother of Baal, or the wife of Baal. Some would likely hold one view and some another. The O. T. sometimes pairs Baal and Ashtoreth (Jdg 2.13; 10.6; etc.), sometimes Baal and Asherah (1 Kings 18.19). See further in Wright.

17.3 My mountain in the field. Jerusalem, according to Henderson, so called "on account of its elevated position." But Keil thinks of "Mount

Zion as the site of the temple." *Field* refers to the open country round about and possibly includes all of Judah.

C. General Reflections on the Sources of Ruin and of Wellbeing (17.5–18). Though expressed in a general manner, these reflections show what is back of Judah's ruin.

1. The Curse of Trusting in Man Contrasted With the Blessedness of Trusting in Jehovah (17.5–8). Stated in terms of general principles, but striking at the basic fault of Judah with its political maneuvering.

17.6 The heath in the desert. Some sort of scrubby, stunted tree, deprived of nourishment in the desert.

Shall not see when good cometh. *See* in the sense of experience; he "shall not see any good come" (RSV);—i.e., will not experience "prosperity" (NASB).

17.8 Shall not fear. Or with margin and KJV, *see—be careful.* The river does not dry up and the drought does not affect the tree.

2. The Deceptive Nature of the Human Heart (17.9–11)

17.9 The heart is deceitful. *Deceitful* is from the same Hebrew root as *supplant* in 9.4, which see for note. The primary emphasis of the present verse seems to be on the inability to know another's heart rather than on one's liability to be deceived by his own heart. The sin of Judah was deeply written on their heart (v 1). Their heart "departeth from Jehovah" (v 5). Yet they professed otherwise (cf. 3.10; 12.2). Further illustration is found in 9.8 ("one speaketh peaceably to his neighbor with his mouth, but in his heart he layeth wait for him") and in 14.14 and 23.26 ("prophets of the deceit of their own heart"). Observe also how verse 11 of the text connects greed with this deceitfulness of the heart, and compare 6.13 and 8.10 where covetousness is assigned as the motivation for the false dealing of the prophets and priests.

Now couple this passage with the warning about trust in man (v 5). It is a trust in one of deceitful heart. Verse 9b inquires *who can know it?*—i.e., the real motives of the heart; whether men might be speaking or acting as they do out of greed or for their own advantage. Verse 10 answers that God knows the heart and can repay every man according to his ways. The covetous man will receive his dues (v 11).

Exceeding corrupt. Literally as NASB and NEB: "desperately sick."

17.10 Jehovah is not deceived by the deceitfulness of the heart. He knows the heart and is able to judge a man according to his ways.

17.11 Corroborates the truth of verse 10 by means of an illustration. Verse 11 is usually understood to be an allusion "to a popular belief (arising perhaps out of the unusually large number of eggs laid by it) that the partridge brooded on eggs which were not its own: the young birds soon forsake their false mother, and so does wealth its unjust possessor" (Driver). Others suggest a different translation: *gathereth* (or *heapeth together*) (eggs) *which she does not hatch*; alluding to a bird which lays a large number of eggs which she never hatches, the nest being robbed by men.

3. Jehovah the Only Hope of Israel (17.12–13)

17.12 A glorious throne. Cf. "the throne of thy glory" (14.21). Reference to Mount Zion as the place of Jehovah's enthronement (cf. Exod 25.22; Psa 80.1; 99.1). On *set on high* cf. Ezekiel 17.23; 20.40. On *from the beginning* cf. the prophetic reference in Exodus 15.17.

17.13 From the throne to the one enthroned upon it. The temple was no ground of security for those who forsook Jehovah (cf. 7.1–15). Yet Jehovah was really enthroned there as *the hope of Israel* for those who put real trust in him (v 7).

Written in the earth. Not engraved in rock nor even written in a book where they might be preserved (Job 19.23, 24), but in the loose soil where anything written is easily swept away by the wind or obliterated by passing traffic (cf. John 8.6, 8).

Because they have forsaken Jehovah. Cf. 2.13. Without water to sustain life one will soon be gone.

4. Jehovah the Prophet's Hope and Comfort (17.14–18). In this prayer Jeremiah shows himself to be a man who has put his trust in Jehovah. At this point he overcomes the despair reflected in 15.15–18.

17.15 Shows the occasion of Jeremiah's prayer. His enemies taunt and challenge him about his message. Re. their question cf. the mockers' question in 2 Peter 3.4. "Where is the promise of his coming?" The question involves a denial of the message.

17.16 I have not hastened from being a shepherd after thee. In his prophetic office he had served as a shepherd to the people, faithfully following Jehovah's lead.

Neither have I desired the woeful day. As his enemies might have charged—i.e., that he took delight in dwelling upon his people's coming calamity, really desiring it. But to the contrary see 18.20c and cf. chapter 14.

17.17–18 Prayer for the fulfillment and vindication of his message; that he may not be put to shame and dismayed by the failure of his predictions.

D. Appendix Re. the Sabbath (17.19–27)

The connection of this passage is difficult to understand. It certainly shows that the people still "held their destiny in their own hands" and could still bring about a revocation of "the woeful day" (v 16) through repentance (Harrison). And maybe it is connected with Jeremiah's prayer for the fulfillment of his message (vv 17–18). He must continue the effort to bring the people to repentance.

Why the sabbath is singled out for special attention is not clear. Jeremiah certainly did not teach that the correction of this one failure would save the nation. But the hallowing of the sabbath is probably to be viewed as a sample of the change needed. Where that correction was made other changes would come as natural accompaniments.

Addition (5/2/08): The reluctance to honor the sabbath is no doubt a manifestation of the failure to trust Jehovah (5–8), putting greed and love of money in its place (9–11). Perhaps that explains the connection.

17.20 Ye kings of Judah. Plural as in 19.3; contrast 22.2. Harrison says it includes "the ruler and the royal princes"—in other words, the reigning king and prospective kings.[9]

[9] *Addition (2008):* Does this address to kings of Judah pose a challenge to the view that the prophecies through Chapter 20 date from the reign of Josiah (cf. 3.6–10)? Could it date from early in Josiah's reign, before the reforms were pursued so rigorously? (cf. 2 Kings 22.3). The reinstitution of the Passover dates from Josiah's eighteenth year (2 Kings 21–23; 2 Chron 35:1–19). It may be that the sabbath had also been neglected in earlier years.

We would surely like to know more about the exact relationship between Jeremiah and Josiah. We do have Jeremiah 22.15–16 in context of verses 11–17. Remember, too, Jeremiah's mourning over Josiah's death, considered worthy of note in 2 Chronicles 35:25.

PART SIX

Jeremiah's Message in Symbols and the Results of its Proclamation

Jeremiah 18–20

Introduction

The discourses of these chapters, with the reception met by them in the nation, reveal Judah's ripeness for judgment. The case is hopeless. Destruction is imminent.

I. The Potter and the Clay: Message and Results (Ch 18)

A. The Potter and the Clay (18.1–4)

18.3 The wheels. The Hebrew is a dual—the two wheels, or literally the two stones. "The apparatus consisted of two stone wheels on a vertical axle, the lower of which was spun by the feet, while the upper carried the clay which the potter shaped as the wheel revolved; cf. Ecclesiasticus xxxviii. 29–30" (Bright). Further description with an illustration is given in NBD, 90, 1012–1013.

18.4 Stress is placed upon the power of the potter over the clay. If the vessel of clay on which he works becomes marred in his hand, he is able to do something else with it—to make *another vessel, as seemed good to the potter to make it.* Jeremiah's message has to do with the power of Jehovah over the nations.

B. Interpretation of the Symbol (18.5–12)

18.5–6 The potter and the clay are shown to be a fitting representation of the relation between Jehovah and Israel. Jehovah is the potter and Israel is as the clay in his hands. Jehovah has power over the nation to do with it as seems good to him.

18.7–10 Shows the use Jehovah makes of this power over a nation. The exercise of his power with respect to any particular nation is in accord with the conduct of that nation; it is not according to an absolute, unchangeable or unconditional and eternal decree.

18.11 Application to Judah. The Hebrew verb in *I frame evil against you* is from the same root as the word *potter*. Hence: "I am shaping evil" (RSV); "I am fashioning calamity" (NASB)—working in the manner of a potter. NEB handles it thus: "I am the potter; I am preparing evil for you …" For *device* modern versions put "plan," as also in verse 12 they have "plans" for *devices*.

18.12 Reaction of the people. The call to repentance is disdainfully rejected. They are determined to continue their evil way. It is not necessary to consider these as the exact words of the people. Not many would admit, "We are too stubborn to listen." But these words express the effect of their reaction, which makes it all too clear that the call to repentance is *in vain* or "hopeless" (NASB; cf. NEB: "Things are past hope") or "no use" (NBV, NIV). "The speakers are not despondent over their state and prospects, but they would silence the troublesome preacher. This language of the Jews marks the last stage of hardened wickedness" (NBV margin). "Time has run out for Judah (cf. 2.25). National sin is so ingrained that repentance is out of the question" (Harrison).

C. The Consequences of Israel's Unnatural Apostasy (18.13–17)

18.13 The faithlessness of Israel is unheard of among the nations. Cf. 2.10–11.

18.14 "A picture drawn from natural history, designed to fill the people with shame for their natural conduct" (Keil). Some parts of Lebanon, especially Mount Hermon, are so high that they are covered with snow all year round. The melting of the snow supplies many streams which are, therefore, never dried up. Cf. Song of Solomon 4.15. This faithfulness and constancy which is found even in nature is set in contrast with the unnatural faithlessness of Israel. (*The rock of the field* is likely a reference to Lebanon itself, *the field* being the surrounding country.)

That seems to be the general sense of this verse, although exactly how it is to be translated is uncertain. Observe the KJV's additions. NIV margin explains, "The meaning of the Hebrew for this sentence is uncertain." Many emendations have been suggested. See RSV for three of these.

18.15 Vanity, KJV. Or worthlessness (cf. on 2.5), referring, of course, to "worthless gods" (NASB), "worthless idols" (NIV), "false gods" (ASV, RSV).

The ancient paths. Cf. 6.16.

To walk in bypaths. They have wandered off the main road.

In a way not cast up. Or "roads not built up" (NIV), "not the highway" (RSV), "not on a highway" (NASB), "unmade roads" (NEB).

18.16 Their own actions leave their land desolate, an object of horror to all who pass by.

An astonishment. KJV, "Desolate." Driver translates "an appalment," and the verb in 16b "appalled," but adds a note: "The same Hebrew word means also desolation; and this sense is probably also in the prophet's mind. Cf. 19.8; 25.9, 11, 18, 38, and elsewhere." NASB and NBV: "desolation." RSV: "a horror."

A perpetual hissing. RSV, "a thing to be hissed at for ever"—the word referring to "the sound midway between hissing and whistling which escapes one when one looks on something appalling" (Keil).

And shake his head. The gesture probably combining amazement with mockery (cf. Psa 22.7; 44.14; 109.25).

18.17 I will show them the back. Jehovah will turn his back on them, as they did him (2.27).

D. Reaction of the People to Jeremiah's Message—Their Enmity Against Him (18.18)

18.18 Let us devise devices. More understandable, "devise plans" (NASB) or "make plots" (RSV). Cf. 11.19.

For the law shall not perish from the priest. As Jeremiah predicted it would (4.9; cf. Ezek 7.26). They reason that they can do away with Jeremiah, for they have no need of him, since they have and will continue to have sources of information which speak far different from Jeremiah, not continually calling them to repentance. Contrast Jehovah's promise to Jeremiah in 15.11 that he would cause Jeremiah's enemy to make supplication to him in the time of trouble.

Let us smite him with the tongue. I.e., with slander and malicious charges, such as the later charges of treason, designed to destroy him. Cf. 9.3, 8; 20.10. NEB: "let us invent some charges against him."

E. Jeremiah's Prayer for Protection From His Enemies and For Their Destruction (18.19–23). This prayer is not a call for personal vengeance. Jeremiah had made every effort to bring the people to repentance. He had warned and threatened about the doom they faced if they did not repent. He had expressed agreement with the curse pronounced upon those unfaithful to the covenant (11.1–5). But he had pleaded with Jehovah not to bring destruction upon the people (14.1–15.9). Jehovah had refused his intercession, telling him that the nation was too far gone; it could not be saved. When Jeremiah sees that the people, so far from listening to him, instead were determined to get rid of him (18.18), he sees that Jehovah is correct. He therefore calls for the fulfillment of the destruction which he had threatened but which he also had labored so hard to turn aside. It is not personal vengeance that he asks, but the fulfillment of the divine judgment, the necessity of which was made so obvious by the vicious opposition to the messenger of Jehovah. Cf. also 6.11 where the wrath of Jehovah is viewed as something pent up in the prophet, which Jehovah at length tells him must be poured out upon the people. Jeremiah now heeds that order to "pour it out." But it is the wrath of Jehovah which he pours out, not his personal anger at personal offences.

18.19 Give heed to me. Contrast the end of verse 18.

18.20 A pit for my soul. Such as one might set to entrap some animal; a trap into which he is to fall (v 22b).

Remember. Cf. 14.1–15.9.

18.21 Death. Must mean "death by pestilence" (RSV, NBV), since it is distinguished from *the sword*. See on 15.2.

18.22 Describes the outcry when the "marauder" (RSV), "raiders" (NASB, NEB), "hostile troops" (Keil), or "invaders" (NIV) burst into the houses to plunder and massacre.

II. The Broken Bottle (Ch 19)

Introduction

Again symbolism is used, Jeremiah being called upon to perform a symbolic action—this time to impress upon the people the threat of impending judgment.

Harrison has the following comment re. the symbolism used: "Whereas a spoiled vessel on the potter's wheel could be reshaped, once it had hardened it was beyond reconstruction, and only fit for breaking. The earthenware container symbolized the final form of Judah's spiritual obduracy (cf. Rev 22.11), and the act of shattering it in the presence of senior citizens and priests indicated the coming doom."

A. Message at the Valley of Ben-Hinnom (19.1–9)

19.2 The valley of the son of Hinnom. "A valley to the south of Jerusalem" (NBD).

The gate Harsith. KJV (*the east gate*) derives the Hebrew from a word meaning *the sun*; but modern scholarship seems united in deriving it from a word for *potsherds* or *pottery*. Hence: "the Potsherd Gate" (RSV, NASB, etc.)—probably so called as being "the place where broken pottery was deposited" (Harrison).

19.4 Have estranged this place. Hebrew means *to make foreign* or *to treat as foreign*—hence NASB: "have made this an alien place"; "with allusion to the foreign gods (5.19, 8.19), and foreign modes of worship, introduced into it" (Driver). So what follows. NIV: "made this a place of foreign gods."

The blood of innocents. To be explained with Keil, in accord with 2.34, 7.6, and 22.3, 17, "of judicial murder or of bloody persecution of the godly." Observe especially 2 Kings 21.16 and 24.4 re. Manasseh who "filled Jerusalem with innocent blood."

Addition (5/5/08): Again, like 17.19–27, difficult to reconcile with the reign of Josiah.

19.4–5 Observe the climax: *First*, the estrangement of Jehovah's abode from him, turning it into a sanctuary for idols. *Second*, the perversion of justice in the persecution of any who opposed the apostasy. *Third*, the worst of all abominations—building altars to sacrifice their own children to idols.

19.6 Topheth. A place in the valley of Ben-Hinnom (2 Kings 23.10).

19.7 Make void. Hebrew *empty out* (margin)—a play on the word *bottle* (v 1); here used figuratively (as in Isa 19.3).

19.8 An astonishment, and a hissing. RSV, "a horror, a thing to be hissed at," as in 18.16, which see for note.

Plagues. Better, "strokes" (Driver) or "wounds" (NIV, NEB). "Lit., *blows*" (NASB margin). The word is rendered *wound* in 10.19, 14.17, 15.18, 30.14, 17, 1 Kings 22.35 and 2 Kings 8.29. See esp. the last two. "*Plague* … must be understood in its etymological sense of a severe *stroke*, or *blow* (*plege*)" (Driver).

19.9, Cf. Lev 26.29; Deuteronomy 28.53–57; Lamentations 4.10.

B. Breaking of the Bottle and Its Significance (19.10–13)

19.11 Till there be no place to bury. But perhaps better as the margin has it: "because there shall be no place else to bury." So RSV, NASB, NEB, NBV. The slaughter is so great that even this unclean place must be used for burial.

19.12 Even making this city as Topheth. Josiah had defiled this place sacred to Molech, turning it into an unclean place (2 Kings 23.10). So Jerusalem would be.

19.13 Which are defiled, shall be as the place of Topheth. Evidently the sense is as the KJV has it: "shall be defiled as the place of Topheth." See note above. So RSV, NASB, NBV, NIV.

All the host of heaven. NIV explains: "all the starry hosts."

C. Further Word of Judgment Spoken at the Temple (19.14–15). Jeremiah has now carried out the orders of verses 1–13. He returns to Jerusalem where he pronounces judgment upon Jerusalem and Judah before the people in the temple court.

III. Results of the Last Speech, Persecution and Complaint (Ch 20)

Introduction

The outcome of the last speech is the beating and imprisonment of Jeremiah, whose enemies had plotted against him before, but had not done him bodily harm.

A. Persecutions and the Message Against the Persecutor (20.1–6)

20.1 Chief officer. Hebrew *overseer* or *inspector*; evidently an official whose job was to maintain order in the area of the temple. Cf. 29.24–28.

20.2 Smote. "Beat" (RSV, NBV), "had Jeremiah the prophet beaten" (NASB, NIV), "had him flogged" (NEB).

Stocks. Hebrew root means *to twist* or *distort*; reference is to "an instrument of torture by which the body was forced into a distorted, unnatural posture" (Keil).

20.3 Magor-missabib. Meaning "terror on every side" (ASV margin); "fear round about" (KJV margin). The name expresses what the man is to be, an object of terror to himself and all those around him (v 4). The expression also occurs in verse 10, 6.25, 46.5, 49.29, and Lamentations 2.22. Pashhur was a false prophet (v 6), likely one of those who would advise alliance with Egypt and rebellion against Babylon (cf. 27.14–15). That policy would prove to be a disaster to the nation. Such a prophet would bring terror to all around him.

B. Jeremiah's Bitter Complaint, Followed by an Expression of Confidence in Jehovah (20.7–13)

Introduction

Jeremiah's enemies had plotted to take his life on earlier occasions, but they had not gone so far as actually to do him bodily harm until now. The actual beating and imprisonment is more than Jeremiah can take. He bursts forth in one of his most bitter complaints.

20.7 Thou hast persuaded me. But KJV, RSV, NASB and NIV have *deceived*, and the word does seem to have that element in practically every passage. But Proverbs 25.15 seems to be an exception. Jeremiah refers to 1.4–19. He had not wanted to be a prophet. But Jehovah had enticed him, overcoming his objections, overpowering him, and persuading him to enter the work.

I am become a laughing-stock. The consequence of his labor. His constant message was judgment to come (v 8). The people did not take him seriously. As a "prophet of doom" he came to be dismissed as one might dismiss the robed and bearded subject of many cartoons, who carries the sign announcing the end of the world. Perhaps also he was ridiculed because his message "remained unfulfilled for so long" (Harrison).

20.8 Is made a reproach unto me. Literally as RSV and NBV, "has become," with the meaning brought out in NIV, "has brought me insult and reproach all day long." The proclamation of the word has brought contempt to Jeremiah and made him an object of ridicule.

20.9 And if I say. The thought that arises in Jeremiah due to the bitter experiences resulting from his proclamation of the word. The thought occurs to him that he will just quit preaching.

A burning fire shut up in my bones. The sensation felt in his *heart*[10] was like having the marrow of his bones on fire.

I am weary with forbearing. Or *holding it in.* Perhaps NIV handles it best: "I am weary of holding it in; indeed, I cannot."

Someone has said that there are three kinds of preachers. The first has to say something. He is a paid talker who has to fill a certain amount of time each week. The second has something to say, and that is a whole lot better. But best of all is the third, the man who has something to say *and has to say it.* That is the kind of preacher Jeremiah was.

20.10 The reason Jeremiah considers such a resolution as expressed in verse 9.

For I have heard the defaming. The "talk" (Keil), "whispering" (RSV, NASB, NEB, NIV), slander, evil report. The parallel in Psalm 31.13 clarifies. Jeremiah refers to the plotting to do away with him.

Terror on every side. Some versions, like Keil, consider this an inserted description of Jeremiah's dangerous situation as his enemies plotted against him (RSV, NBV). Others take it as a quotation, part of the words of the enemies (NASB, NIV). It would then be explained as what they *in effect* are saying by their continual plotting; or could even be their *exact words* as they deliberately plot to cause him "terror on every side," perhaps with allusion to Jeremiah's prophecy (vv 3–4).

Denounce. Or "Report," meaning "to the authorities as a dangerous man" (Keil), a traitor. Compare the charges later brought against Jeremiah (26.8–9; 37.11–15; 38.4).

All my familiar friends. Lit., *every man of my peace*, i.e. all those (supposedly) on peaceable or friendly terms with him.

They that watch for my fall. Looking for some slip-up; something they could use against him; "waiting for me to slip" (NIV).

Peradventure he will be persuaded. I.e. "to say something on which a capital charge may be founded" (Graf in Keil).

[10] We would likely say mind. Cf. 23.17, 20 for example.

20.7–10 Taking Courage From Jeremiah. Do you ever become discouraged and depressed? Do you ever stagger under the burden? Do you ever wish you could get away from it all? Are you ever tempted to quit? Jeremiah is the book we need to read to overcome these feelings.

I think we are not apt to get much encouragement from someone who appears to be "untouchable," someone who can face the fiery coals without wavering or shrinking. Jeremiah was a man who carried a much greater burden than we have to bear, suffered far more than we do ... but a man who felt all that we feel in terms of discouragement, depression, and the desire to escape it all.[11] He felt all that we feel, but he went ahead and did his duty anyway. And that is to say that we can do the same. Let us, then, turn back to Jeremiah in such times of trial, and draw courage from him. Whatever encouraged and helped him can help us. So let us go to him, find out what it was that helped him to survive, and get it for ourselves.

20.11 Jeremiah overcomes the fear. Lament changes into an expression of firm confidence in Jehovah based upon the promises given him at the beginning (1.8, 17–19).

A mighty one and a terrible. Other versions: "a dread warrior" (RSV), "a dread champion" (NASB), "a mighty warrior" (NIV), "a fear-inspiring warrior" (NBV). Thus Jeremiah recalled the promise of Jehovah and realized that he was not alone; that a mighty champion, a dreaded warrior, stood beside him.

20.11b, The confidence that Jehovah was with him gave Jeremiah an assurance of ultimate victory over all his enemies.

20.12 The assurance that his persecutors would be brought down was based upon Jeremiah's knowledge of Jehovah. Jeremiah had turned his cause over to one who knows the human heart and would know where the right lies and surely take the part of the righteous.

20.13 In anticipation of ultimate victory "Jeremiah's soul rises to a firm hope of deliverance, so that in ver. 13 he can call on himself and all the godly to praise God, the Saviour of the poor" (Keil).

C. Complaint Renewed (20.14–18)

Introduction

Frankly, I wish the chapter had ended on the mountain peak to which

[11]With the present passage compare especially 9.2 and 15:9–21.

Jeremiah was exalted in verse 13. But as Jeremiah had his mountains, so he had his valleys. He would remember the promises of God and know that victory would ultimately be his. But whenever his mind then dwelt upon the visible realities of the present he would be thrown back down.

The present passage will be more understandable if we can assume the passing of some time between the feelings of verses 11–13 and those of verses 14–18. Jeremiah is again in a great spiritual struggle. He reverts to the feeling of depression. Cf. Job 3 on the whole passage.

20.16 The cities which Jehovah overthrew. Probably referring to Sodom and Gomorrah (Gen 19.25).

And let him hear a cry. I.e., let him be as one invaded by enemies, hearing the wailing of the besieged and the war cry of the invader.

Note of Time. 21.1 is the first note of time since 3.6. It seems logical to assume that all the prophecies up through Chapter 20 fall into the reign of Josiah. That is my present opinion, especially since the later prophecies reveal that Jeremiah's habit was to date his prophecies, and no other date is given for those up to this point other than the reign of Josiah (3.6). Is there anything in the first twenty chapters which cannot fit Josiah's time? What do these chapters tell us about conditions during Josiah's reign? What do they add to the picture in Kings and Chronicles? Pay special attention to the note of time given in Jeremiah 25.3–7.

PART SEVEN

Jeremiah's Message Concerning the Kings and Leaders of Judah After Josiah

Jeremiah 21–24

Introduction

Chapter 21, verse 1 provides the first definite date since the one given at 3.6. The prophecies up to this point have been from the reign of Josiah. From here on we deal with later times.

The prophecies are not arranged in chronological order. (We must pay attention to headings such as 21.1–2.) In the present section Jeremiah is more interested in theme than chronology. He begins by putting before us prophecies which date from the end of the reign of Zedekiah when Jerusalem was under siege by the Babylonians (Ch 21). Chapter 21 serves as an introduction to prophecies concerning various kings and leaders of Judah which had brought Judah to that state of affairs. Thus the causes of the destruction of Judah are set forth. Chapters 22–23 seem to be the focal point of the section. Here Jeremiah shows how Judah has been brought to ruin by corrupt leaders, kings and prophets. The consequence is judgment and the scattering of the people. But this judgment and scattering is to have a purging effect. Jehovah will find a remnant among the survivors whom he will regather and restore under the Messiah (23.1–8). Finally Chapter 24, which dates from the period following Jehoiachin's captivity, is added as a supplement to Chapters 22–23 and a confirmation of the truth set forth in 23.1–8 concerning the restoration of the remnant.

This entire analysis leans heavily upon Keil.

I. Prophecy During the Siege of Jerusalem (Ch 21)

A. Heading Stating the Occasion for the Following Prediction (21.1–2). Jerusalem was under siege (v 4). Cf. 2 Kings 25 for the occasion.

21.1 Pashhur the son of Malchijah. Mentioned in 38.1 (cf. v 4) as an official in Zedekiah's government. Not the same man as Pashhur the son of Immer (20.1).

21.2 Inquire, I pray thee. The fulfillment of 15.11.

Nebuchadrezzar. The most accurate transliteration of the Babylonian name. The other spelling, *Nebuchadnezzar* (which occurs in many passages), "may be derived from an Aramaic form of the name" (Wiseman in NBD, 873).

According to all his wondrous works. Cf. 2 Kings 19.35.

That he may go up from us. I.e., lift the siege; withdraw from the city (cf. 37.5).

B. Response to the King's Hope That Jehovah Would Deliver (21.3–7). Far from it! In fact Jehovah would use his mighty power against Jerusalem (v 5).

21.4 Keil explains thus: At this point Jewish defenders had engaged the enemy outside the walls of Jerusalem in an effort to prevent them from taking up a stronger position and blockading the city. Jehovah says he will drive these defenders back into the city.

21.5 I myself will fight against you. Not merely the Babylonians. Jehovah would strike man and beast with disease (v 6).

21.7 With the edge of the sword. "Heb. *according to the mouth of the sword* (i.e. as the sword devoureth, relentlessly)" (Driver), the sword being portrayed as an animal that bites and devours.

C. Counsel to the People as to How They May Escape Ruin and Death (21.8–10). On this often repeated advice and the charge against Jeremiah see 38.1–4, 17–19; 39.9; 52.15; and cf. the earlier counsel to submit to Babylon (Ch 27). Notwithstanding the danger, "Jeremiah, holding his duty higher than his life, remained in the city, and gave as his opinion, under conviction attained to only by divine revelation, that all resistance is useless, since God has irrevocably decreed the destruction of Jerusalem as a punishment for their sins" (Keil).

21.9 Passeth over to. "Surrenders to" (RSV, NBV, NEB, NIV).

His life shall be unto him for a prey. The same expression is used in 38.2, 39.18 and 45.5; meaning: "shall have his life as a prize of war" (RSV); "he will have his own life as booty" (NASB); "he will escape with his life" (NIV); "*lit.* his life shall be his booty" (NEB margin).

D. Exhortation to the Royal Family Re. How Destruction Can Yet Be Averted (21.11–12)

21.11 The house of the king. As NASB: "the household etc."; the royal family, including the king's court, advisers, and officials.

21.12 Execute justice. Perhaps it was such preaching which caused the temporary freeing of the slaves as a token obedience (34.8–11). But when the siege was lifted (34.21–22; 37.5) the slaves were taken back.

Observe that this failure to act in the way a king ought to act is the indictment that is now brought against the kings of chapter 22, but especially Jehoiakim. This failure of the leadership of Judah is what brought the nation to its end. (See esp. 22.3–5 and 13–19.) In this way Chapter 21 may be seen as an introduction to the section.

In the morning. Perhaps distributively as Amos 4.4, "every morning" (NASB, NIV), referring to the time when court was held. But Henderson takes Hebrew *boqer* "as an adverbial idiom" (as in Psa 46.5; 90.14; 101.8) with the meaning *early* or *speedily*. So NEB, "betimes."

Lest my wrath go forth like fire. At an even later time Jeremiah was still insisting that the city could yet be saved (38.17–23).

E. The Decree Against Jerusalem (21.13–14)

21.13 Inhabitant. Literally, *inhabitress*—feminine, referring to the daughter of Zion, the personified community of Jerusalem.

Inhabitress of the valley. NASB, "valley dweller"—so called possibly as having valleys on three sides (Harrison), *or* as being "encircled by mountains of greater height" (Keil, referring to Psa 125.2).

The rock of the plain. Cf. "mountain in the field" (17.3). "In the 'rock' we think specially of Mount Zion, and in the 'valley' of the so-called lower city. The two designations are chosen to indicate the strong situation of Jerusalem" (Keil).

Who shall come down against us? Expressing pride in their strong situation and confidence in the stronghold of Zion, *the rock of the plain*. Cf. 2 Samuel 5.6–7; Lamentations 4.12; Obadiah 3–4.

21.14 The strength of the city will not protect the people from the punishment inflicted by Jehovah.

A fire in her forest. To be explained in the light of the figure used in 22.6–7. So much timber had been used in the houses of Jerusalem that the city was like a forest. In 22.23 the personified community is called the "inhabitress of Lebanon."

II. Prophecies Regarding Various Kings and Leaders of Judah (Chs 22–23)

The various speeches delivered during the times of Jehoiakim and Jehoiachin are here in the written form joined together into a continuous whole (Keil).

A. Prophecies Re. Various Kings (Ch 22)

1. Threat of Destruction if Justice is Not Practiced (22.1–9)

22.6 Thou art Gilead ... Lebanon. These places are mentioned because of the great forests for which they were known. The royal palace is called *Gilead* and *the head* (better with various versions: *summit*) *of Lebanon* as being built of an immense amount of fine timber. It was like a great forest. Cf. verses 13–15a, 23.

I will make thee a wilderness. From a great forest to a barren wilderness.

22.7 They shall cut down thy choice cedars. Of which the palace was built. NIV, "they will cut up your fine cedar beams."

22.8–9 Not just the palace but in fact the whole city would be left in ruins. Then would be fulfilled the prediction of Moses in Deuteronomy 29.22–28. The ruined city would be a monument to Jehovah's wrath against the transgressors of his covenant (Keil).

2. Message Concerning Jehoahaz (22.10–12)

22.10 Weep ye not for the dead. Referring to Josiah, who had been killed at Megiddo (2 Kings 23.29; 2 Chron 35.24). See 2 Chronicles 35.24–25 for the long continued lamentations over Josiah.

Him that goeth away. Referring to Jehoahaz (called *Shallum* in v 11) who succeeded Josiah, but reigned only three months and was then taken away by the Egyptians as a captive (2 Kings 23.31–34).

23.11 Shallum. The name also appears among the sons of Josiah in 1 Chronicles 3.15. (Jehoahaz is omitted.) What is said about him shows that the reference is to Jehoahaz (cf 2 Kings 23.30–34). Jehoahaz might be a name taken by Shallum when he came to the throne. Cf. 2 Kings 23.34; 24.17.

3. Condemnation of Jehoiakim (22.13–19)

22.13 A woe upon Jehoiakim for building his magnificent palace through injustice—the use of forced and unpaid labor.

Chambers. Usually rendered "upper rooms" (RSV, NASB, NIV) or "roof chambers" (NASB margin, NBV, Driver); explained by Driver as "a chamber erected on the flat roof of an eastern house, with latticed windows, giving free circulation to the air, secluded and cool (Jdg 3.20, 1 Kings 17.19, 2 Kings 1.2, Dan 6.10)."

22.14 Ceiled. Better, *paneled*, according to a former meaning of the word *ceiled.*

Painted with vermillion. A red color. NASB, "bright red."

22.15 "Do you become a king because you are competing in cedar?" (NASB). He was trying to outdo everyone else in the use of this fine lumber. Is that what makes one a king?

22.15b–16 Did not thy father eat and drink? Reference to Josiah (v 18) who is set forth as a model of what a king ought to be. "Kingship and kingcraft do not consist in the erection of splendid palaces (or in the luxurious, 'playboy' life, lam), but in the administration of right and justice" (Keil). *Eat and drink*, i.e., enjoy life (Ecc 2.24–25; 3.13; 5.18; 8.15). Josiah ate and drank, but at the same time administered justice and righteousness, as David had done (2 Sam 8.15).

22.18–19 Jehoiakim will therefore meet with a horrible end. He will not be mourned either by relatives (*Ah my brother!*, *Ah sister!*) or subjects (*Ah lord!*, *Ah his glory!*). So far from receiving a royal burial, he will be dragged off like a dead donkey, thrown down somewhere outside the walls of Jerusalem and left to rot.

4. Address to Jerusalem (22.20–33). All the pronouns are feminine in Hebrew. The daughter of Zion, the personified community, is addressed.

22.20 She is called upon to go to the highest mountains to bewail her fate—*Lebanon* to the north; *Bashan* to the northeast; and *Abarim* to the southeast, the range of mountains from one of which Moses viewed Canaan (Num 27.12; Deut 32.49). Her cry is to be heard far and wide.

Thy lovers. The allies whose favor she had courted (cf. 4.30)—Egypt (2.36) and the little neighboring states (27.3).

22.22 The wind shall feed all thy shepherds. Referring to her rulers (as 2.8; 23.1–2). Neither rulers nor allies will be able to help. The verb is better translated with RSV and Driver: "shall shepherd." "The wind shall shepherd all your shepherds." The wind will be the shepherd that tends your shepherds; it will sweep them away (NASB) or scatter them (Driver). These shepherds have destroyed and scattered the sheep entrusted to their care (23.1–2). Now they are to be tended by just the sort of shepherd they deserve.

22.23 Inhabitant of Lebanon. Literally *inhabitress*, referring to the personified population of Jerusalem which is so called because of the lavish houses of the nobles and the wealthy built of cedars from Lebanon (cf. v 6).

How greatly to be pitied shalt thou be. Practically all modern versions follow the LXX: "how you will groan" (RSV, NASB, NBV, NEB, NIV).

5. Prediction Concerning Jehoiachin (22.24–30)

22.24 Coniah. This name also appears at 37.1. This man is also called *Jeconiah* (24.1; 27.20; etc.; cf. 1 Chron 3.16) and *Jehoiachin* (2 Kings 24.6, 8, 12, etc.). *Coniah* is short for *Jeconiah* which was probably the original name, since it is the name given in the family register at 1 Chronicles 3.16. Keil thinks Jeconiah changed his name to *Jehoiachin* upon coming to the throne in order to make it more like the name of his father. The reign of Jehoiachin lasted for only three months before he was taken into captivity (2 Kings 24.8–17).

The signet. RSV, "the signet ring." Very precious to ancient people (cf. Hag 2.23). *Though Coniah … were the signet* means "although he were as precious a jewel in the Lord's eyes as a signet ring" (Keil). The signet ring would be engraved with the king's official seal and would be used to impress his seal on official documents. See Exodus 28.11, 21, 36; 39.6, 14, 30 ("the engravings of a signet"); Job 38.14 ("changed as clay under the seal"; same Hebrew); Esther 3.12; 8.8, 10; Daniel 6.17 (sealed with the king's ring or signet).

Though Coniah ... were the signet upon my right hand. "It was the Divine determination, that with this prince the succession of the Davidic line in the descendants of Jehoiakim should cease—so aggravated had the wickedness of that monarch been. Supposing even that Jehoiachin had personally been held in the highest estimation by Jehovah, such was his displeasure against the father, that for his sake his son should suffer in his public and regal capacity" (Henderson). Cf. the earlier prophecy in 36.30–31.

22.25 Them of whom thou art afraid. With good reason because of the revolt of his father (2 Kings 24.1–7).

22.26 Thee ... and thy mother. See 2 Kings 24.15.

22.28 A despised broken vessel. Jeconiah's destiny was determined even though he may have been the signet on Jehovah's right hand (v 24). But when one anticipates the actual treatment Jeconiah was to receive, instead of the precious signet ring he thinks of an old broken pot that no one cares about and is fit only to be thrown into the garbage dump.

22.29 Earth. Better with margin, *land*. "The land is to take the king's fate sore to heart" (Keil). Is it because the threat of verse 30 specially concerns the land? See below.

22.30 Write ye this man childless. I.e., have him entered in the register of citizens as childless—the last of his family. Not that Jeconiah had no children, for see 1 Chronicles 3.17; but as explained in what follows: He would have no descendant on the throne. He was succeeded by Zedekiah, his uncle and a son of Josiah (2 Kings 24.17; 1 Chron 3.15). After Zedekiah no one succeeded to the throne of David in Judah.

What then is to be made of Matthew 1.11 where the legal lineage of Joseph, the adoptive father of Jesus, is traced through *Jechoniah?* One of the purposes of this genealogy is to establish the legal claim of Jesus as heir to the throne of David (Luke 1.31–33). And Matthew establishes his relation to David through *Jechoniah*. Yet Jeremiah predicts that *no more shall a man of his seed prosper, sitting upon the throne of David, and ruling in Judah.*

Henderson follows Michaelis in solving the problem by means of the observation that the descent of Jesus through Jeconiah "was only through Joseph, the husband of Mary, who though his legal, was not his real father." But the fact is, Jeremiah 22.30 is not concerned with *physical* descent (for Jeconiah was not physically *childless*) but with heirship to the throne. And Matthew has the same concern. According to Matthew, Jesus was legally and adoptively Joseph's son, hence the seed of Jeconiah, and on that basis had a claim to the throne of David. If that is not the point, then why is the genealogy of Joseph of any importance? Why publish it?

It would seem the solution must be sought along other lines. Perhaps the emphasis should be placed on *in Judah*. The passage would then mark the end of an earthly throne and faintly anticipate the heavenly rule of the Messiah which is so certainly taught in other passages (cf. Zech 6.12–13 with Heb 8.1, 4; John 18.36; Acts 2.29–36; Rev 3.21). That would make the apostrophe addressed to the *land* in verse 29 have even stronger force in the context. Observe the strong emphasis on the land at several points in this chapter (vv 10–12, 26–29; cf. vv 4–5, 22).

B. Regathering of the Flock Scattered by Bad Shepherds and Raising Up of the Messiah (23.1–8)

Introduction

The prophecy concerning the kings of Judah concludes with a brief promise showing "that, in spite of the judgment to fall on Judah and Jerusalem, the Lord will yet not wholly cast off His people, but will at a future time admit them to favour again" (Keil).

23.1–2 The future hope is introduced by means of a final summation of the condemnation against the bad rulers of Judah.

Have not visited them. Sums up the complete neglect of the sheep entrusted to their care.

I will visit upon you. Observe the word play. RSV brings it out thus: "you have not attended to them" (2b) and "I will attend to you" (2c).

23.4 Shepherds over them. Henderson thinks of the better class of leaders (Zerubbabel, Ezra, Nehemiah, etc.) in the period after the exile. Keil thinks this promise is further explained in verse 5 with the good shepherds being finally summed up in the person of the Messiah in whom they would have all the shepherds needed. He calls attention to 33.15 where the contrast of a plurality of good shepherds with evil shepherds is omitted and only the one sprout of David is mentioned, and to Ezekiel 34 where only the one good shepherd (v 23) is put in contrast with the evil shepherds (vv 1–10). Driver thinks of subordinate rulers under the Messiah. That is a possibility. Cf. 22.2 ("thou, and thy servants") and 22.22 ("all thy shepherds"). I would think of the apostles, for example.

Lacking. Or missing.

23.5–6 This passage reveals Jeremiah's concept of the Messiah—an ideal king of the future in contrast to the bad kings at the end of the kingdom of Judah. Cf. what had been said about Josiah (22.15–16). More on the Messiah and his reign in chapters 30–33.

A righteous branch. Hebrew *tsemach* is better translated *sprout* (NASB margin)—"a general term for what sprouts or shoots from the ground" (Driver). Thus in Genesis 19.25 of "*that which grew* upon the ground"; in Psalm 65.10 of the *springing* or *growth* of the earth. The messianic references to the "Branch" or "Sprout" are Isaiah 4.2; 11.1 (where a different word is used); Jeremiah 23.5; 33.15; Zechariah 3.8; 6.12.

Deal wisely. "The Heb. word means to deal with wisdom such as to command success" (Driver). So ASV margin.

Jehovah our righteousness. Hebrew *Jehovah-tsidkenu* (KJV margin) as ASV margin: *Jehovah is our righteousness.* The same name is assigned to the city of Jerusalem (33.16). It is by means of the righteous rule of the Messiah that Jehovah provides righteousness for his people. Thus the name he bears expresses the source of the righteousness provided through him.

23.7–8 Repeated almost word for word from 16.14–15. See the appendix to chapters 30–33 for discussion of such references to the land and their connection with the messianic kingdom.

C. Message Concerning the Prophets (23.9–40). After the kings the prophets were chiefly responsible for the fall of the kingdom.

1. Jeremiah's Horror at the Judgment Upon the Prophets Revealed by Jehovah (23.9–12)

23.9 ***Concerning the prophets.*** Evidently to be taken in this way as the heading of the section verses 9–40. So ASV, RSV, NASB, NBV, NIV, NEB. Cf. the similar headings at 46.2; 48.1; 49.1, 7, 23, 28.

23.9bc Jeremiah's distress and agitation of spirit over the revelation he has received.

23.10 For the land is full of adulterers. Cf. verse 14b; 9.2.

Swearing. Hebrew *alah*, usually understood as ASV margin *the curse* (RSV, NASB, NBV, NIV), according to the usage in Deuteronomy 29.19, 20, 21. (The same word is rendered *oath* in Deut 29.12, 14.)

23.11 Profane. Having no regard for what is holy, even desecrating the house of God (11b).

Their wickedness. Probably idolatry (cf. 32.34).

23.12 Punishment of their wickedness.

2. The False and Sinful Ways of the Prophets (23.13–15)

23.13 Folly. Hebrew *tiphlah*, only elsewhere at Job 1.22 and 24.12, means *tasteless* or *unsavory* (KJV margin). The cognate adjective is used in Job 6.6 of *that which hath no savor.* Bright translates "an offensive thing," with the remark: "The prophets of northern Israel ... are mentioned only to point up the enormity of the conduct of Jerusalem's prophets, who (vs. 14) are said to be even worse."

23.14 RSV brings out the contrast in accord with Bright's comment above: "But in the prophets of Jerusalem I have seen a horrible thing." Not merely insipid, but "shocking" (Bright), causing horror.

They strengthen the hands of evil-doers. Their example would have this effect, but Jeremiah may be thinking even more of their false predictions (v 17; cf. Ezek 13.22). See verse 22 for what they should have been doing.

23.15 Wormwood ... the water of gall. See at 8.14 and 9.15.

3. Warning Against Listening to the False Prophets (23.16–22)

23.16 They teach you vanity. RSV, "filling you with vain hopes." So also NBV, NIV, NEB. "They are leading you into futility" (NASB). "They make you vain" (KJV)—the most literal translation. Cf. 2.5 with note; and the end of 23.32—"neither do they profit this people at all."

23.17 Them that despise me. The LXX reads: "them that despise the word of Jehovah"—a reading accepted by RSV and NEB.

23.18 After quoting the words of the false prophets (v 17), Jeremiah offers confirmation of his charge that their message comes from *their own heart and not out of the mouth of Jehovah* (v 16). These men had not *stood in the council of Jehovah.* Jehovah did reveal his council to the true prophets (cf.

Amos 3.7), but not to these men. If they had stood in Jehovah's council their message would have been quite different (v 22). Cf. 1 Kings 22.19 for a dramatization of the idea of *the council of Jehovah.* The question is, who has had access to the council chamber of Jehovah? Who has heard his deliberations about the future of Judah?

Marked my word. I.e., paid attention, "given heed" (RSV, NASB), to it.

23.19–20 The real message of Jehovah—what these men would have heard had they stood in the council of Jehovah. The real purpose of Jehovah as contrasted with the misrepresentation of the false prophets (v 17).

In the latter days. They may doubt or deny the purpose of Jehovah now. But the time of fulfillment would leave no room for misunderstanding.

23.21–22 The final proof that the prophets of peace were not sent by Jehovah. If they had really known the purpose of Jehovah they would have warned the people and so *turned them from their evil way* (v 22) instead of encouraging them to continue in their wickedness (vv 14, 17).

4. The False Prophets Shall Not Escape the Omnipresent and Omniscient Jehovah (23.23–32).

23.23–24 The omnipresence and omniscience of Jehovah. He is everywhere; he sees all and knows all. He sees and hears what the false prophets do and say (vv 25–28), and has placed himself in opposition to them (vv 29–32).

23.25 I have dreamed. The claim of divine revelation in their dreams.

23.27 By their dreams. Not the supernatural dreams by which Jehovah sometimes revealed truth, but an ordinary dream— "the deceit of their own heart" (v 26).

23.28 The thought seems to be: Let the man who has a dream tell his dream if he must. But he must not confuse his dream with revelation from Jehovah. He must tell the people what it is—not the word of Jehovah, but only a dream; and therefore worthless—as chaff to wheat when compared with the word of Jehovah.

23.29 The power of the true word of Jehovah (such as Jehovah speaks) which will be directed against the false prophets according to the threats following in verses 30–32.

23.30 That steal my words every one from his neighbor. Practically all the commentators seem to explain in the manner of Keil: "Not inspired of God themselves, they tried to appropriate words of God from other prophets in order to give their own utterances the character of divine oracles." I suppose Keil means, for example, that they use the formula, "He saith" (v 31), i.e. Jehovah saith, in order to pass off "the deceit of their own heart" (v 26) as divine revelation. But I wonder whether the thought might not rather be that they take from the people the true words of Jehovah spoken by Jeremiah by substituting their lies (cf. Luke 8.12). They thus rob the people, replacing the wheat with chaff (v 28c).

23.32 Vain boasting. Replacing KJV's "lightness." RSV, "recklessness"; NASB and NBV, "reckless boasting." NEB similarly. Hebrew *pachazuth* (only here in OT) is derived by von Orelli from a verb meaning "to be overboiled, overweening, rash; here the presumption of false prophets." Bright says it "has the force of 'loose talk,' 'exaggerated, boastful tales,' or the like." Keil says it refers to "their boasting of revelations from God." Cf. the claim involved in "I have dreamed, I have dreamed" (v 25).

5. Ridicule of the Word of Jehovah to be Punished (23.33–40)

23.33 What is the burden of Jehovah? Hebrew *massa* is derived from a root meaning *to lift up*; hence the noun refers to something *lifted* or *taken up, a burden*. It is often used of a burden in the most literal sense (Exod 23.5; Num 4.15, 19, 24, 27, 31, 32, 47, 49; 2 Kings 5.17; 8.9; Jer 17.21, 22, 24, 27). It is sometimes applied in a figurative sense to people as a burden to be carried (Num 11.11, 17; 2 Sam 15.33; 19.35). That imagery is carried out at considerable length in Numbers 11.11–14. But that does not make the word mean *people*. It still means burden, but is used with a figurative application. Nor, I think, does the word come to mean prophecy, utterance or oracle because it is applied to certain prophecies. It is another figurative application of the word burden. When, for example, the word is used in the heading of various prophecies—"The burden of Babylon" (Isa 13.1); "The burden of Moab" (15.1); "The burden of Damascus" (17.1); "The burden of Egypt" (19.1); and often—it refers to a weighty message of judgment. But it is open to question whether *massa* ever means oracle or utterance (something taken up upon the lips, as it is usually explained).[12]

In my judgment NASB and NIV have caused the sense to be lost by

[12]See discussion on Zechariah 9.1 in E. W. Hengstenberg, *Christology of the Old Testament*, II, 1017–1020 (MacDonald Publishing Company reprint).

substituting the word "oracle" for *burden* throughout the present passage. Jeremiah's message was always a weighty burden—a message of judgment to come. Meantime the false prophets were assuring the people, "Ye shall have peace. … No evil shall come upon you" (v 17; cf. 14.13). Earlier Jeremiah had complained, "I am become a laughing-stock all the day, every one mocketh me" (20.7). The question *What is the burden of Jehovah?* is not a serious inquiry, as the following context will show. The question is asked sneeringly, with ridicule: "What new burden do you have for us today, Jeremiah?" The meaning of the whole passage turns on the word *burden* and is lost when that translation is eliminated. Observe the play on this word that runs through the passage.

What burden! Many, perhaps correctly, following the reading of LXX and Vulgate: "You are the burden." Thus RSV, NBV, NEB.

I will cast you off. Play on the word *burden*—i.e., I will disburden myself of you (Keil).

23.34–40 Because of the misuse of the word burden, they are not permitted to use the word anymore. Verses 35–37 describe how they are to speak of prophecy as the alternative to the use of the word burden.

23.36 For every man's own word shall be his burden. When someone sneers at or ridicules the word of Jehovah, as these were doing by using the word burden, his own word shall be a crushing burden which he must bear.

For ye have perverted the words of the living God. By making Jehovah's words the butt of their jokes they perverted it. What a burden to bear! That they have perverted not just the words of the human messenger but *the words of the living God, of Jehovah of hosts our God*!

23.39 I will utterly forget you. Some Hebrew manuscripts, along with the LXX, Syriac and Vulgate versions, read, "I will surely take you up." (The two words have almost no difference in Hebrew.) The Hebrew verb is derived from the same root as *massa*. The play on the word runs thus: I will take you up as a burden and throw you down.

III. The Vision of Two Baskets of Figs: Emblem of the Future of Judah's People (Ch 24)

A. The Vision: Two Baskets of Figs (24.1–3)

24.1 *Historical Setting:* After a reign of only three months, *Jeconiah* (Jehoiachin in 2 Kings; see on Jer 22.24), along with many thousands of his subjects, was carried into exile (2 Kings 24.8–17). From that time (597 BC) until the destruction of Jerusalem (586 BC) two sizable groups of Jews existed separately— one in Judah under King Zedekiah; the other in Babylonian captivity. Jeremiah remained in Judah; his younger contemporary Ezekiel had been carried away with Jeconiah and, from the fifth year of the captivity of Jeconiah (Jehoiachin in Ezek 1.1–3), did the work of a prophet among the captives.

Two baskets of figs set before the temple of Jehovah. I.e., at the meeting place of Jehovah with his people (Exod 29.42–43). Cf. the offering of the first-fruits which were to be set down before Jehovah (Deut 26.1–11). The two baskets of figs represent the two groups of people.

Smiths. NIV, "artisans"; alternative in NEB margin, "the harem." Hebrew is of uncertain meaning.

24.2 They were so bad. NASB, "due to rottenness." Or possibly bitterness. But the contrast with *figs that are first-ripe* might suggest rottenness.

B. The Good Figs Explained as Representing the Captives (24.4–7)

24.5 Keil and others connect *for good* at the end of the verse with *regard*: "I will regard the captives … for good." But in that case verse 6a would seem to be repetitious—not adding any new thought. KJV seems to be correct in connecting *for good* with *sent*: "… whom I have sent out of this place … for good." Then verse 6 elaborates the good Jehovah has in mind for them. RSV: "I will regard as good the exiles from Judah." So also NASB, NEB and NIV. Evidently wrongly. *Good* in the light of verse 6 refers to the good things Jehovah intended to do for the captives.

24.7 The building and planting (v 6) involves not only the restoration of the state but also the spiritual restoration of the people.

C. The Bad Figs Explained as Representing the People Left in the Land (24.8–10)

24.8 As the bad figs. Rotten, fit only to be thrown away. So Jehovah treats those who remain.

Them that dwell in the land of Egypt. This likely refers to people who fled to Egypt in order to escape the Babylonians (cf. chs 42–44).

The Message of Chapter 24

According to Ezekiel 11.15 the remaining inhabitants of Jerusalem considered the exiles as removed "far from Jehovah" and themselves as the heirs of the land. So it must have appeared. It must have seemed that if the nation was to have any future at all, it would lie with those who remained in Jerusalem. The present prophecy speaks to that situation. It is interesting to observe that Ezekiel, like Jeremiah, predicts that the future of Jehovah's people lies with the exiles rather than the people remaining in Jerusalem (Ezek 11.14–21).

PART EIGHT

Jeremiah's Prophecy of the Seventy Year Empire of Babylon

Jeremiah 25–29

Introduction

The events and prophecies of these chapters fall into the period from early in the reign of Jehoiakim up into the fourth year of Zedekiah. It was clear to Jeremiah that events of Jehoiakim's fourth year marked the beginning of a seventy year domination of the near eastern countries by Babylon. But Jerusalem was not destroyed when Babylon made its first appearance in Judah in 605. The chapters before us reveal the efforts of Jeremiah at this period so near the end of the kingdom of Judah to prevent the destruction of Jerusalem and the kingdom[13] and the opposition to his efforts from false prophets (chs 27–29). It becomes increasingly clear that Jeremiah's call to repentance and his counsel to submit to the yoke of Babylon will go unheeded, and that Judah will therefore be compelled to drink the cup of Jehovah's wrath right down to the dregs.

I. Jeremiah's First Announcement of Seventy Years of Babylonian Domination—given in the year that domination began (Ch 25)

A. Prediction of Babylon's Seventy Year Domination of Judah and the Surrounding Nations (25.1–11)

[13]Note especially 26.1–6, 12–13; Chapter 27.

25.1 The fourth year of Jehoiakim. This prophecy is the earliest to be given so definite a date. Earlier prophecies are dated in a more general and indefinite manner (cf. 3.6; 26.1). The preciseness here is due to the importance of the fourth year of Jehoiakim. That year marked a notable turning point for Judah. It was the year Nebuchadnezzar defeated Egypt at Carchemish in a decisive battle which determined the destiny of the near eastern world for the next seventy years (Jer 46.2). That battle ended Egypt's hopes of empire (cf. 2 Kings 23.29–24.7) and established Babylon as the master of the ancient world. In the aftermath, the Babylonians swept South and came down upon Judah for the first time, taking Daniel and some others to Babylon as hostages (Dan 1.1–7).[14] The year was 605 BC, the beginning of Babylon's seventy year empire (v 11).

25.3–7 For twenty-three years Jeremiah has warned Judah. Other prophets also have warned. But Judah would not listen.

25.8–11 Therefore, the time has come for the threats to be fulfilled.

25.11 Seventy years. Cf. 2 Chronicles 36.20–23, Ezra 1.1 and Daniel 9.1–2 on the application of this number.

B. Prediction of the Fall of Babylon (25.12–14). After seventy years of empire, Babylon will be punished.

25.12 I will punish the king of Babylon. Nebuchadnezzar was God's servant, used by him to punish Judah (v 9). But the purpose of the Babylonians' mind was not serving Jehovah. They were ambitious for empire and were out to satisfy selfish passion. They therefore incurred guilt which Jehovah would punish.

25.13 Even all that is written in this book. These words are not likely to have been part of Jeremiah's message orally delivered to Judah. But the prophecies against Israel, Judah and the nations were first written in a book in the same year (36.1–2). When the prophecies were written down this clause was probably added at that time as explanatory of *all my words which I have pronounced against it.*

25.14 Babylon to be enslaved just as they have enslaved others.

[14]Daniel 1.1 dates it in the *third* year of Jehoiakim according to the Babylonian method of dating, in which the accession year of a king was counted separately rather than being considered the first year of the reign.

C. The Cup of God's Wrath (25.15–26). To be drunk by Judah and the other nations of earth, ending with Babylon itself.

25.15 This cup of the wine of wrath. For this symbol cf. Psalm 60.3; Isaiah 51.17, 22–23; Jeremiah 13.12–14; 48.26; 49.12; 51.7; Lamentations 4.21; Ezekiel 23.31ff; Obadiah 15–16; Habakkuk 2.15–16; Zechariah 12.2; Rev 14.10; 16.19; 18.6. The nations are compelled to drink the wine of God's wrath and are left reeling and staggering like a drunk man—drunk on the wrath of God.

How was this order executed? Might there have been some real symbolic action somewhat on the order of 27.1–11, with Jeremiah offering a cup to representatives of the various nations gathered in Jerusalem? More likely the action was carried out in a vision— mentally, rather than in the outward world. The cup to be taken and offered to the nations contained wrath, rather than wine or any essence that could be literally drunk. The offering of the cup to the nations, which is done in the vision, translates into reality in terms of the actual work of Jeremiah in prophecying the doom of the nations (cf. v 13 with chs 46–51).

25.16 Because of the sword. Here figure is exchanged for reality. It is not a literal drink, but war which leaves the nations reeling to and fro like a drunk man.

25.20 All the mingled people. "I.e., probably, the mixed foreign population, settled in Egypt for trade or other purposes" (Driver). Cf. verse 24 (*the mingled people that dwell in the wilderness*), Exodus 12.38 (*the mixed multitude* that left Egypt with Israel), Nehemiah 13.3 (foreigners mixed with the people upon return from captivity; see context), Jeremiah 50.37 (foreigners in Babylon), Ezekiel 30.5 (in Egypt, as here).

The remnant of Ashdod. Probably survivors of the long siege of Ashdod (= Azotus) by Egypt under Psalletichus (663–610, Schwantes). Herodotus (ii. 159; Pelican edition, p. 165) says it lasted 29 years and calls it "the longest siege of any in history."

25.22 The kings of the isle which is beyond the sea. Or *coastland* for *isle* (margin). "I.e. Phoenician colonies on the coasts of the Mediterranean Sea" (Driver).

25.23 All that have the corners of their hair cut off. So KJV margin also. See at 9.26.

25.26 Sheshach. A name for Babylon, as is clear from 51.41. NBD, p. 1176, calls Sheshach "an artificial word, formed by the device known as Ath-bash" or Atbash—a cabalistic formula according to which the first letter of the Hebrew alphabet would stand for the last letter; the second letter would stand for the next to last; etc. *Sheshach* is the result of applying this formula to the Hebrew letters for *Babel.* See also on *Leb-kamai* at 51.1. Most scholars, liberal and conservative, seem to adopt this explanation. RSV margin calls Sheshach "a cipher for Babylon"—the word *cipher* being defined as "a method of secret writing that substitutes other characters for the letters intended, or transposes the letters after arranging them in blocks; also, a substitution alphabet so used" (WNCD).

After the other nations, Babylon also will drink the cup of God's wrath. So also verses 12–14.

D. The Message to Accompany the Cup (25.27–29)

25.29 If Jehovah punishes *the city upon which* (his) *name is called* (literally, as in 7.10), i.e., the city which belongs to him, certainly the others will not escape.

E. Jehovah's Controversy With the Nations (25.30–31)

25.30 Prophesy thou against them. Translates the offering of the cup to the nations (in vision) into the literal and external action actually taken by Jeremiah.

Jehovah will roar from on high. Like a lion roaring out of his lair, preparing to attack his prey. Cf. Amos 1.2.

He will give a shout. Hebrew "signifies the loud cry with which those that tread grapes keep time to the alternate raising and thrusting of the feet" (Keil). Cf. Isaiah 16.9–10.

As they that tread the grapes. Cf. Isaiah 63.3; Rev 14.17–20 on the treading of grapes in the winepress as a figure for divine judgment.

25.31 A noise shall come. The noise of war.

A controversy. A law-suit; a cause at law. Cf. Deuteronomy 17.8; 19.17; 21.5; 25.1; 2 Samuel 15.2; 2 Chronicles 19.8; Isaiah 34.8; Ezekiel 44.24; Hosea 4.1; 12.2; Micah 6.2.

F. Description of the World Judgment (25.32–38). Explaining the cup.

25.32 As a storm starts on the horizon and spreads, so calamity will burst forth and overtake one nation after another.

25.33 The slain of Jehovah. Those he has slain by the sword in war (vv 16, 27; cf. Isa 66.16).

25.34 Ye shepherds. Rulers of the nations.

Wallow in ashes. As in 6.26.

Ye principal of the flock. RSV, "lords," and NEB and NASB, "masters," for *principal.* Reference to the nobles—the rich and powerful among the nations ruled by the shepherds.

Ye shall fall like a goodly vessel. A fine vase, for example, shattered to pieces in the fall.

25.38 Rounds out the description begun in verse 30.

For their land. Keil takes this clause as offering the evidence that the lion has *left his covert.*

The oppressing sword. *Sword* is italicized, but appears in some manuscripts (NEB margin) and in the LXX. Cf. 46.16; 50.16.

II. Message of Jeremiah and Response of People and Leaders Early in the Reign of Jehoiakim (Ch 26)

A. Jeremiah's Address in the Court of the Temple (26.1–6). (Cf. 7. 1–15, though that is an earlier address.) It is an effort even at this late date to stop the plunge toward ruin. The prophet speaks briefly and sharply, in the hope that even at so late a date the people might yet listen, turn, and avert the impending doom.

26.1 In the beginning of the reign of Jehoiakim. Not necessarily earlier than the previous message in Jehoiakim's fourth year (25.1). In 28.1 the middle of Zedekiah's fourth year is said to fall in the beginning of his reign. It is likely that this message shortly followed that of chapter 25 and the first Babylonian invasion of Judah. After that event Jeremiah would be able to face the nation with some hope that now they would listen.

26.2 Diminish not a word. "Do not hold back a word" (RSV). "Do not omit a word!" (NASB). Jeremiah is not permitted to soften the threat by the omission of even a single word; he must "proclaim the word of the Lord in its full unconditional severity" (Keil).

B. Reaction of Priests, Prophets and People (26.7–9). Observe what groups lead in the opposition—priests and prophets as distinguished from princes (cf. vv 10–11).

26.8 Thou shalt surely die. The penalty prescribed in the law for a prophet who speaks what Jehovah has not commanded him to speak (Deut 18.20). Contrast Jeremiah's reply (v 15).

C. Jeremiah on Trial (26.10–24)

1. Court Convened (26.10). NEB is probably right to put "officers" for *princes*. Reference is to officials of the government. NASB has "officials" in verses 11–12.

2. The Charge Against Jeremiah (26.11). Cf. verse 9 and the charge against Stephen in Acts 6.11–14.

3. Jeremiah's Defence (26.12–15)

4. Two Cases Put Forth as Precedents Showing What Ought to be Done to Jeremiah (26.16–23). This section is probably to be interpreted as follows: Verse 16 gives the final outcome arrived at due especially to the influence of Ahikam (v 24). Verses 17–23 show the arguments that took place in the assembly before that verdict was reached. These arguments were put forth by *certain of the elders of the land* (v 17). But some of them argued one thing and some another, as explained below.

(a) The Case of Micah (26.17–19). Put forth by one group, who urged on the basis of this precedent that Jeremiah not be executed. They combined Micah 3.12 with the facts of 2 Kings 18–19 in their argument. (The scriptures do not say, however, that Hezekiah made his plea on account of Micah's prophecy.)

29.19 Thus should we commit great evil against our own souls. "But we are about to bring great evil upon ourselves" (RSV). "But we are committing a great evil against ourselves" (NASB). I.e., by making themselves responsible for innocent blood (v 15).

(b) The Case of Uriah (26.20–23). Best explained as a continuation of what was said by "certain of the elders" (v 17) rather than a historical appendix attached to the account of Jeremiah's trial. The verses continue the account of the trial. Some elders offered Micah as one precedent for urging the course they advocated; now others put forth a second precedent, nearer in time and showing the attitude of the present king, in opposition to the first view (Henderson). The expressions "this city" and "this land" (v 20) sound more like what might have been said by a speaker who had the subject immediately before him (vv 6, 9, 11, 12, 15, 18) than the words of a historian who likely would have identified the city and land more particularly. Cf. the comment on *the words of this covenant* in 11.2. (*Against* my argument, however, put verse 21, considering that Jehoiakim's princes were present at this trial. But this manner of referring to them can possibly be accounted for by the fact that the passage is a written summary of the trial which might not give the exact words of the speaker in this instance.)

26.22–23 Jehoiakim was a vassal of Pharaoh-necoh in his early years. Harrison points out that "international treaties often contained extradition clauses, and this was doubtless part of the vassalage terms imposed by Egypt."

5. Final Outcome (26.24). If I have been correct in the preceding, one or more speakers have used Uriah as a precedent to urge that Jeremiah be put to death. Now we see that Jeremiah only escapes that end through the support of an influential man. *Ahikam the son of Shaphan* had been an official in Josiah's government; he was among those sent to Huldah (2 Kings 22.12–14); he was also the father of the future governor Gedaliah, who was also friendly to Jeremiah (Jer 39.14; 40.5). Likely he remained in an influential position as a holdover from the government of the good king Josiah. *Observe two points:*

1. One of the ways used by Jehovah to fulfill his promises and to preserve the life of Jeremiah.

2. The attitude of the *princes* of Judah at this time as opposed to that of the priests and prophets. These princes were carried away with Jehoiachin's captivity in 597 BC (2 Kings 24.14). The princes under Zedekiah are different men and take a different attitude toward Jeremiah (37.14–15; 38.4–6, 24–28). These last princes are "bad figs" (Ch 24), completely aligned with the views of the false prophets and priests.

III. Controversy Over and Vindication of Jeremiah's Prophecy of the Seventy Years During the Reign of Zedekiah (Chs 27–29)

Introduction

The historical setting is early in the reign of Zedekiah. Read 2 Kings 24.10–17 in order to understand the allusions to Jehoachin's captivity, which began in 597 BC, at which time also Zedekiah's reign began.

This section deals with Jeremiah's controversy with false prophets over the prediction of a seventy year domination of the world by Babylon. This prediction was challenged by false prophets who assured the people that the captivity would not last long and encouraged revolt against Babylon. In this section Jeremiah confirms and vindicates his prediction of the long duration of Babylonian supremacy and warns kings and people to bear the yoke placed upon them.

A. Message to Foreign Nations and to Judah Urging Submission to the Yoke of Babylon (Ch 27)

1. Message to Foreign Kings Through Their Ambassadors Gathered in Jerusalem (27.1–11)

27.1 Jehoiakim. So KJV and ASV text (but not the margin). Evidently an error which has crept into the Hebrew text at the hand of some copyist who must have been recalling 26.1. It should read *Zedekiah*, as proved by verses 3, 12, 20; 28.1. Most later translations simply put Zedekiah in the text, following the reading of the Syriac translation. See RSV, NASB, NEB, NBV.

27.2 Bonds and bars. Reference to an ox's yoke which "consisted of a wooden bar, or bars, held about the animal's neck, or lashed to the horns, by cords or leather thongs" (Bright). Cf. "the bars of your yoke" in Lev 26.13. Put "thongs" (RSV) or "cords" (NEB) for *bonds*. Jeremiah was to wear the yoke as a symbol of the Babylonian yoke to which the nations must submit. The wearing of the yoke would dramatize his message and impress it upon his audience.

27.3 And send them. Older commentaries usually explain that Jeremiah was to make several yokes and send one to each king. But *them* is in Hebrew a suffix consisting of only one letter, and one manuscript of the

LXX omits *them*, reading simply *send to etc.* This reading is followed by most modern scholars. Thus: "send to" (NEB), "send word to" (RSV, NASB), "send a message to" (NBV). Bright thinks *them* was carried over from verse 2 by some copyist.

The messengers that come to Jerusalem. The purpose of their coming is not expressly stated. But judging from Jeremiah's message to them, they likely came together for the purpose of forming a coalition to resist and overthrow Babylon.

27.4 Their masters. The kings who had sent them.

27.6 And the beasts of the field. Indicating "the unlimited extent of Nebuchadnezzar's empire" (Henderson), the completeness of his dominion over the territory.

27.9–10 The false prophets encouraged revolt, the effect of which would be captivity and destruction.

27.11 Babylon was content to bring the nations into subjection and under tribute, except in cases of stubborn resistance and revolt, as might be learned by comparing 2 Kings 24.1 with verses 10ff and 25.1ff.

2. The Same Message to Zedekiah (27.12–15)

3. Message to Priests and People of Judah (27.16–22)

27.16 The vessels of Jehovah's house. Which were taken away at the time of Jehoiachin's (= Jeconiah's, v 20) captivity (2 Kings 24.13).

Shall now shortly be brought again. Cf. 28.3.

27.17 Wherefore should this city become a desolation? As it surely would if they revolted (vv 8–11). By promising that Babylon was soon to fall (v 10; cf. 28.1–11) the false prophets encouraged revolt. But their promises were false; and, if acted upon, would bring Babylon back down upon Jerusalem to its utter destruction.

27.18 What true prophets, with real insight into the council of Jehovah (cf. 23.16–22), would be doing instead of encouraging revolt.

27.19 For *pillars*, *sea*, and *bases* see 1 Kings 7.13–47.

27.20 Jeconiah. Jehoiachin in 2 Kings 24.8–17.

27.22 They shall be carried to Babylon. Fulfilled 52.17–19 and 2 Kings 25.13–17.

Then will I bring them up. As in Ezra 1.7–11.

B. The Controversy With the False Prophet Hananiah (Ch 28)

1. Hananiah's Prophecy (28.1–4). We hear what the false prophets were saying, right out of the mouth of one of them, directly contradicting Jeremiah in 27.16–22.

2. Jeremiah's Answer and Hananiah's Response (28.5–11)

28.6 Amen. Jeremiah's agreement is explained and limited by what follows.

Jehovah do so. RSV: "May the Lord do so; may the Lord make the words which you have prophesied come true," etc. NBV, NEB and NASB similarly. Jeremiah desires that also. Nothing would please him more.

28.7–8 But one must remember that the earlier prophets predicted war and calamity, not peace. Therefore only a *threatening* prophecy can carry the presumption of being true, since only these would agree with earlier predictions.

28.9 When a prophet predicts peace, contrary to all these earlier witnesses of God, only the fulfillment can show him to be a true prophet. Cf. Deuteronomy 18.21–22.

28.10–11 Instead of being content to await the issue of the conflict, Hananiah takes the yoke off Jeremiah's neck (cf. 27.2) and breaks it, in that dramatic fashion seeking to reinforce and give strength to his prophecy, as if such theatrics could really prove anything.

And the prophet Jeremiah went his way. With no bombastic and dramatic outburst to try to top that of Hananiah. The calmness of Jeremiah is noticeable. He would not speak or act without revelation from Jehovah. He simply waits upon Jehovah. Later, revelation does come, and then Jeremiah speaks (vv 12–16).

3. The Prophecy Against Hananiah (28.12–16)

28.13 But thou hast made. The LXX has "I" for "thou." Some prefer that reading. But the fact is, Hananiah's false prophecy and the dramatic breaking of the wooden yoke encouraged revolt against Babylon, which brought Babylon down upon the nations with even greater force. The prophet had only replaced a wooden yoke with one not so easily broken. "Thou" fits the case quite as well as "I."

28.16b Cf. Deuteronomy 13.5.

4. Death of Hananiah (28.17). Jeremiah had said that the event would determine whether Hananiah had spoken the truth (v 9). Hananiah, however, did not live two years to see the outcome. His death occurred just two months after his prophecy (cf. v 1). One would think such a dramatic fulfillment of Jeremiah's prediction would strengthen his authority as a spokesman of God. But the truth is, it was not a lack of evidence that kept the people from listening to Jeremiah. They were stubbornly committed to apostasy; they did not want to believe; and no amount of evidence would convince them. Cf. Luke 16.31. Seed must be planted in the right soil to germinate and bear fruit.

C. Letters to the Captives in Babylon (Ch 29)

Introduction

As in Jerusalem, so in Babylon, false prophets kept alive the hope of a speedy end to Babylonian domination and the captivity. Jeremiah therefore sends letters to Babylon to counter that false hope which kept the chastisement of the captivity from having its full moral effect on the hearts of the people. The date is not precisely given, but likely is early in the reign of Zedekiah (v 2). Ezekiel would begin his preaching among the captives in the fifth year of the captivity (= Zedekiah's fifth year) (Ezek 1.1–3).

1. The First Letter (29.1–23)

(a) Introduction to Jeremiah's Letter (29.1–3)

29.1 The residue of the elders. Those that have survived and remain alive among the captives (cf. 39.9).

29.2 See 2 Kings 24.10–17.

29.3 The mission of these men is unknown. Jeremiah takes advantage of their being sent to Babylon to send a message to the captives.

(b) The Captives Counseled to Prepare for a Long Stay in Babylon and to Seek the Peace of Babylon (29.4–7). Their welfare lies not in the overthrow of Babylonia but in its peace.

(c) Warning Against Putting Trust in the False Prophets (29.8–9). The message of these prophets can be gathered from the contrasting message of Jeremiah and by comparing the message of Hananiah and the false prophets of Judah (Ch 28).

(d) Justification of the Preceding Counsel (29.10–14). Jehovah has good planned for the people, but it will be carried into effect only after the seventy years of Babylonian rule.

29.10 After seventy years are accomplished for Babylon. Pointing back to 25.11–12 and to be computed from the date of that prophecy.

29.12–14 This hopeful future was dependent upon their turning to God from the heart, which they would not do as long as they entertained the false hopes encouraged by the false prophets.

(e) The Final Doom Upon Jerusalem and Its Remaining Inhabitants (29.15–20)

Verse 15 clarifies the reason and occasion for such an announcement to the captives of Babylon, and shows that Jeremiah's prediction was in direct opposition to the views set forth by the false prophets in Babylon. *The people said*, Jehovah has raised up prophets in Babylon. What these prophets said is clear from Jeremiah's reply. Jeremiah's answer to this saying of the people (v 15) is given in verse 16: *Thus saith Jehovah* (as over against *what ye have said*, v 15). Evidently the prophets were supporting their prediction of a short captivity by appealing to the continued existence of the kingdom in Judah. A king remained on the throne of David; the city had survived; the temple remained. The partial captivity could easily be restored and the temple treasures returned to Jerusalem. Jeremiah takes the ground from beneath them by predicting the complete destruction of the kingdom and the scattering of the remaining people.

The destruction of Jerusalem and the temple was a critical turning point. As long as Jerusalem stood, the false prophets had a thread from which to suspend the hopes offered to the people and could succeed in their opposition to Jeremiah in Judah and Ezekiel in Babylonia. But the complete ruin of city and kingdom dealt a shattering blow to those false hopes and left the captives severely shaken. When word reached Babylonia that Jerusalem had fallen Ezekiel's "mouth was opened" in a way that it had not been open before (Ezek 33.21–22). He could begin to gather a more receptive audience; the people would be more ready to listen; and the remnant that would eventually return from captivity would begin to appear. From our vantage point we are able to perceive that the calamitous events which seemed like such a great disaster to the nation were in reality necessary to its survival and to the fulfillment of the divine purposes for that nation.

(f) Punishment of the False Prophets in Babylon (29.21–23)

29.22 Shall be taken up a curse. The time would come when as bad an end as one could wish for an enemy would be that he may end up like these prophets.

Roasted in the fire. Explained by Daniel 3.6, and evidently referring to a Babylonian mode of execution.

2. A Second Letter in Response to the Letter of the False Prophet Shemaiah (29.24–32). Some time passes between the letter of verses 1–23 and this prophecy. *Shemaiah*, one of the false prophets in Babylon, incensed over Jeremiah's letter to the captives, sent a letter back to Jerusalem to the people and especially the priest Zephaniah, calling for Jeremiah's punishment. This section describes Jeremiah's response as ordered by Jehovah.

29.29, Zephaniah's motivation is not revealed. He was probably just letting Jeremiah know what was going on in Babylon. He does not appear to be unfriendly to Jeremiah (cf. 37.3).

PART NINE

Jehovah's "Good Word" Concerning the Future of His People

Jeremiah 30–33

Introduction

This section sums up Jeremiah's hope for the future—Jehovah's "good word" toward Israel (cf. 29.10). To this point references to a future hope have been woven into a message whose dominant theme was judgment to come because of national apostasy and covenant disloyalty (cf. 3.11–4.2; 16.14–15; 23.5–8; 24.4–7; 29.10–14, 32). But the note of hope is the dominant note of this section. Jeremiah gathers up the briefer promises given heretofore in order to present a comprehensive statement of the hope for the future held out to the people of God. Judgment must come. But God was not through with Israel. Brighter days are ahead. The section is often called "The Book of Consolation" because of the hope for the future embodied therein. These chapters would provide the godly remnant with "a strong anchor of hope" to sustain them through the difficult and trying times through which they must pass.

The necessity for such assurances as are provided in these chapters will be realized if we will imagine ourselves to be Jews living at the time of Jeremiah. The nation faced what appeared to be total destruction. Jerusalem was to be left in ruins, the temple and the city burned, the king removed from his throne, and the people carried into exile. It looked like the end for the Jews. Was Jehovah through with the Jews? What had become of the covenant with Abraham? What about Jehovah's commitment to David? (2 Sam 7.11–16).

This section answers these questions and provides the reassurances that were absolutely needed to sustain the faith of the godly in the trying times that were ahead. The promises of these chapters would be the barrier against despair that was demanded by the times.

Introduction and Statement of the Subject (30.1–3)

30.2 Write thee all the words. The reason is explained in verse 3. The words relate to the future—beyond the time of captivity. Thus the reason assigned also gives the subject of the following prophecy. That reason, as also verse 4, seems to suggest that reference is only to the words of hope contained in this section (chs 30–31 or 30–34) rather than including all the prophecies of Jeremiah. Likely these words were not read or proclaimed publicly, but written in a book for the consolation of the godly—Jeremiah himself and others like him.

I. Jehovah's Words Concerning Israel and Judah: Words Concerning Future Good (30.4–31.40)

A. Heading (apparently of Chs 30–31) (30.4)

B. Deliverance of Israel Through Judgment Upon the Nations (30.5–24)

1. A Great World Judgment, Out of Which Israel Will be Delivered (30.5–11). *Note:* Jeremiah's horizon would seem to be defined by the prophecies of judgment in Chapters 46–51, which suggests the application of this passage. Cf. also chapter 25.

(a) Description of a Terrible Judgment (30.5–7). A time of great suffering, but "Jacob" will be "saved out of it."

(b) The Time of Israel's Deliverance and Restoration (30.8–9)

30.9 David their king. Cf. 23.5; Ezekiel 34.23–24; Hosea 3.5. Reference to the Messiah—a second David; a sprout raised up unto David. So 23.5 and 33.14–26 explain. Driver explains: "the ideal king of the future, as David was of the past." This passage must be explained in the same way as the "Elijah" prophecy is explained in the New Testament (Mal 4.5, with Matt 11.14; 17.10–13; Luke 1.17; John 1.21).

(c) On the Ground of This Prediction Israel is Encouraged to Take Heart (30.10–11).

30.11 In measure. Literally, *in judgment* (margin), which Driver explains: "i.e. in a judicial spirit, not in anger (Psa 6.1, 38.1)."

Note on Jeremiah's Standpoint: Observe how he is placed right in the middle of the catastrophe, though it is actually future.

2. The Severe Affliction and Chastisement of Israel to be Followed by Healing (30.12–17). A further development of the thought in verse 11. Israel is to be severely chastised for its sins. But Jehovah will not make a full end of them. He will punish Israel's enemies and bring salvation to Israel.

(a) The Wound (30.12–15)

30.13 None to plead thy cause. I.e., to take up your case and execute justice (cf. 5.28; 22.16); "thy claims against thy heathen oppressors" (Hitzig, in Keil). "The words (of this verse) are partly borrowed from a court of justice, and partly from medical practice" (Henderson).

30.14 All thy lovers. Allies; nations allied with Israel. Cf. 2.18, 33, 36; 22.20, 22.

(b) Healing (30.16–17). Jehovah takes up their case, executes justice, administers healing.

(c) The Restoration of Israel (30.18–22)

30.19 Glorify. "Honor" (NASB), "bring them to honor" (Keil), "make them honored" (RSV).

They shall not be small. "Insignificant" (NASB), "lightly esteemed" (Keil).

30.21 And their prince shall be of themselves. Not a foreign ruler. Cf. Deuteronomy 17.15.

And I will cause him to draw near. The prerogative of special chosen ones, priests (Exod 19.22, 24; 20.21; 24.2; Num 16.5).

For who is he? RSV: "for who would dare of himself to approach me?" NASB: "For who would dare to risk his life to approach me?" Who would lay his life on the line in approaching me? See Exodus 19.21; 33.20; 34.3; Numbers 8.19. The ruler is given a special privilege reserved only for a few—Moses, priests. God brings him near (v 21b). Only so would one dare approach God.

On the whole verse compare the "priest-king" prophecies: Psalm 110.4;

Zechariah 6.12–13. The latter is also a "Branch" prophecy, which further ties it in with Jeremiah. See on verse 9 above.

30.22 Describes the covenant relation. Cf. the covenant renewal words of Deuteronomy 26.16–19; 27.9; 29.1, 10–13.

4. The Storm to Break Upon the Wicked (30.23–24). A resumption of the thought of verses 5–11. The judgment upon the wicked is necessary to the saving of the nation; it is the prelude to restoration. The judgment is upon the wicked of all nations, including Israel, which had to be purged of evil. The covenant relation described in verse 22 cannot be fulfilled otherwise. The verses, therefore, prepare us for Chapter 31. Cf. 23.19–20—almost identical.

30.24 In the latter days. God's purposes would not be thoroughly understood until the fulfillment came. We are put on notice that we cannot expect to understand this section apart from the fulfillment. So with many prophecies. The failure to appreciate this point and to understand Old Testament prophecy in the light of New Testament application leads to endless speculation and frustration.

C. Deliverance for All Israel (Ch 31)

1. Announcement of the Renewal of the Covenant Relationship With All the Families of Israel (31.1). See note and passages referred to at 30.22. Observe how the general announcement is broken down in what follows, so as to make clear that both northern and southern kingdoms are included. *At that time* refers to "the latter days" (30.24).

2. Deliverance for the Northern Kingdom (31.2–22)

31.2 The people that were left of the sword. "Survived" (RSV, NASB). Reference to the captives of the Northern Kingdom.

31.3 Jehovah appeared of old unto me. Jeremiah speaks as representative of the people of Israel in captivity. *Of old* should probably be "from afar." Thus margin, KJV margin, RSV and NASB. Reference to Zion. People are in exile.

31.4 O virgin of Israel. Yet see Jeremiah 3.6. She had played the harlot. But here is a few beginning and complete forgiveness (cf. 50.20). Note similarity to Hosea 2.19–20: Not "take back," but "*betroth.*" A completely new relationship. A new people, born again. Reference to the spiritual people of the new covenant. So Hosea. So here (vv 31–34).

31.5 And shall enjoy. Hebrew as margin: *profane*, or *make common*. The firstfruits were not for common use (cf. Lev 19.23–25). To *make common* = to enjoy for oneself. See this same usage in Deuteronomy 20.6; 28.30. The curse of Deuteronomy 28.30, 39 is lifted.

31.6 Let us go up to Zion. The old schism being ended; the breach healed.

31.8 With them the blind and the lame. Includes even the weak and frail, who might not be expected to be able to make a long journey. All of God's people are included.

A great company. Hardly true of the return after captivity (cf. Ezra 2.64–65 with 2 Sam 24.9). Reference is to the regathering under the new covenant (vv 31–34).

31.9 Weeping. Tears of joy.

31.10 The word to be heard by the "nations" (= Gentiles) and proclaimed by them that Jehovah is ready to gather his scattered people.

31.12 Shall flow. Cf. Isaiah 2.2, "and all nations shall flow unto Zion." They come to learn of the ways of Jehovah (v 3). Does this help explain "the goodness of Jehovah" in a manner true also to the present context?

Unto the goodness of Jehovah. The good things provided by Jehovah, according to the following apposition. Cf. also verse 14: "my people shall be satisfied with my goodness."

31.14 With fatness. The fat pieces of the sacrifices intended for the priests. Many sacrifices would be offered.

31.15 A voice is heard in Ramah. Some mention that the captives of Judah were brought to Ramah (40.1), but the context here deals with the northern kingdom. More likely the reference is to Ramah as being near Rachel's tomb. At least that is a fair assumption. Ramah was in Benjamin (Josh 18.25). Rachel's tomb was "in the border of Benjamin" (1 Sam 10.2). Josephus (*Antiquities*, Book VIII, Chapter xii, Paragraph 3) says Ramah "was forty furlongs distant from Jerusalem." "It is probably to be identified with Er-Ram, 5 miles north of Jerusalem, near the traditional tomb of Rachel" (NBD, 1076).

Rachel, the wife of Jacob who so desperately desired children (Gen 30.1), became the mother of Joseph (Gen 30.22–24), hence the ancestress of Ephraim (Gen 41.52; Jer 31.18, 20). She is poetically depicted as *weeping for her children ... because they are not*—i.e., either dead (cf. Gen 42.36) or carried away into captivity.

Quotation in Matthew 2.17–18. A secondary and parallel fulfillment. The death of the boy babies was the same situation all over again. Note "Then was fulfilled" (Matt 2.17) in contrast with "that it might be fulfilled" (vv 15, 23).

31.16 Thy work shall be rewarded. Some think of the work of bearing and bringing up children; others of the lamentation, which would not be fruitless.

31.18–19 Basis of the hope (v 17), Ephraim's change of heart. Ephraim comes to recognize that his suffering was chastisement for his sins and greatly desired; he desires correction, is penitent, sorrowful over his shameful past.

31.20 Jehovah still has mercy for Ephraim when he changes. If Jehovah, though he must speak against and punish him, still remembers him, Ephraim must surely be regarded as a dear son—though undeservedly. Compare the father of the prodigal son (Luke 15).

31.21–22 Encouragement to return, without hesitation or delay. For *O virgin of Israel* see note on verse 4. Observe she is also called *O backsliding daughter* (v 22).

A woman shall encompass a man. A difficult statement. Two points to be noted: **1.** It refers to "a new arrangement of the relations of life." **2.** It "is mentioned as a motive which should rouse Ephraim (= Israel) to return without delay to the Lord and to his cities."

Nobody knows for certain what the statement means. *Views*: **1.** It describes the new relation between Jehovah (= man, husband) and the virgin of Israel (= woman). The rule is that the man seeks and embraces the woman. But the "new thing in the earth" is the new relation under the new covenant (vv 31–34). No longer does Jehovah's wife forsake him or even hold herself aloof from him, waiting to be sought by her husband. Instead she will lovingly embrace and cling to her husband. *So* Keil, Driver, et al.

2. The female as the weaker sex is wonderfully strengthened by God so that she need fear no enemy. She is able to be the protector of the man. See Deuteronomy 32.10 and Psalm 32.10 for this use of the language. So Gesenius and Henderson. The view seems to be adopted by RSV: "a woman protects a man."

3. NEB adopts the view of Ewald, et al, which requires a slight change in the text: "a woman turned into a man"—the view thus explained in Driver: "... there will be no more need for the 'virgin' of Israel to be timid or hesitate: frail woman that she is, she will be wonderfully endowed by Yahweh with the strength and courage of a man."

4. "Quite possibly we have here a proverbial saying indicating something that is surprising and difficult to believe, the force of which escapes us" (Bright, 282).

Special Note on Restoration of Northern Kingdom: Hosea deals with the same subject in passages (1.10–2.1, 23) the application of which is fixed by New Testament quotations (Rom 9.25–26; 1 Pet 2.9–10). When God rejected Israel (Hos 1.9) they were no more than Gentiles. But in the church Israelites and Gentiles alike become the people of God.

3. Deliverance and Blessing of Judah (31.23–26)

31.23 O habitation of righteousness. Cf. 2 Peter 3.13.

31.26 Jeremiah received this revelation in his sleep. Cf. Daniel 2.1ff, 19; 7.1. His sleep was *sweet*, for finally the revelation received was a message of comfort and hope rather than "violence and destruction" (20.8).

4. The Nature of the Deliverance Promised to Israel and Judah (31.27–34)

(a) Building and Planting of the Combined Israel and Judah on an Individual Basis (31.27–30)

31.27 Cf. Hosea 2.21–23.

31.28 The second part of Jeremiah's commission (1.10). God to be as watchful over his word of hope as he was over his word of destruction (cf. 1.12).

31.29–30 Compare also the treatment of this proverb in Ezekiel 18.1–4. The point is elaborated more fully all through Ezekiel 18. Observe also the connection with the apparently messianic passage just preceding in Ezekiel 17.22–24, just as the parallel here precedes the "new covenant" passage. This connection is extremely important. God's covenant had been with a physical nation. When the nation apostatized it was destroyed and many innocent individuals suffered the consequences. But Jeremiah and Ezekiel predict the time when God would enter into covenant with men on an individual basis. It would be a covenant with spiritual men. The concept of God's dealing with people on an individual rather than a national basis is a prerequisite to understanding the new covenant and to the idea of a spiritual kingdom. No doubt the innocent often still suffer temporarily for the sins of others. But the new covenant has to do with something else—a person's spiritual relationship with God.

Perhaps Jeremiah 3.14 should be related to this passage also.

(b) God's New Covenant With Israel and Judah (31.31–34). The concept of individual responsibility set forth in verses 29–30 and the parallel in Ezekiel (see note above) is a key to understanding this passage. The former covenant was made with a physical nation, including believers and unbelievers. True, God desired the law to be on the hearts of the people (Deut 6.4–9). And it was written on some hearts (Psa 1.2; 119.10–16, 47, 97, etc.). But many were unbelieving idol worshippers. Judges 17.6 and 21.25 do not mean a person could not have done right if he wanted to without a king to enforce the law. The fact is, most did not want to. But a strong king would often whip the people into an outward conformity to the law. Such a man was Josiah. In his days there was an outward return to God, but idolatry was in the heart. See Jeremiah 3.6–10. But the new covenant is not a covenant with a physical nation, but with individuals who submit themselves to God's law—the converted, the true believers. That distinction is the key to understanding this passage.

31.33 I will put my law in their inward parts. Not in an immediate sense. Not that he would force or compel them. Men are moral beings, creatures of choice, not robots. God would teach them (John 6.44). Those who receive this teaching and voluntarily submit to God's law are the parties to this new covenant. Hence it is entirely a spiritual relation rather than national.

And I will be their God. Fulfillment of the covenant relation. See at 30.22.

31.34 And they shall teach no more … saying, Know Jehovah. Jeremiah had to teach Judah to know Jehovah (cf. 9.23–24). They were in the covenant, but did not know Jehovah. None such would be in the new covenant. No one can enter this relation without knowing Jehovah (John 6.44; Heb 11.6). Incidentally, what of infant membership in the light of this description of the nature of the new covenant?

5. Permanence of Jehovah's Relationship With Israel (31.35–37)

31.35–36 Since time began sun and moon have traveled their daily courses. The waves have never ceased their ebb and flow. As constant as these, so God's faithfulness in Israel. God will always have his Israel.

Ordinances. "Fixed order" (RSV, NASB).

31.37 If … beneath. Impossible! Just as impossible that God will cast off all Israel—though the unbelieving will not be spared. Cf. Romans 11.1–5.

6. The Holiness of the New Jerusalem (31.38–40). Even areas formerly unclean would be "holy unto Jehovah."

II. Jeremiah's Purchase of Hanamel's Field The Symbol of Restoration to the Land After Exile (Ch 32)

Introduction: Harrison calls the chapter "a practical demonstration of faith in the future of the nation." "This chapter is important because it provides a tangible demonstration of Jeremiah's faith and hope for the future restoration of his people."

A. Historical Introduction: Time and Circumstances (32.1–5). This sketch of the time and circumstances under which Jeremiah was to buy a field show how little hope the present offered as to Judah's future. Jerusalem was under siege, soon to fall and to go into exile. Jeremiah was confined, not knowing what would become of him.

32.1 Tenth year of Zedekiah. During the siege of Jerusalem (v 2), which began in Zedekiah's ninth year (39.1).

32.2 Shut up in the court of the guard. NEB has "the court of the guard-house attached to the royal palace." Driver explains: "A part of the court surrounding the Palace railed off to guard prisoners in, whom it was not desired to throw into the common dungeon: their friends had free access to them, but they might not pass beyond the area in which they were confined." The ASV translation "suggests a court in which a body of men, called the 'guard,' were stationed." But the Hebrew word "is quite different from the word rendered 'guard' (of a body of men)"; it "means either *the court of keeping* or *guarding*, or *the court of the guard-place* (the court in which the place of guarding was)" (Driver). Harrison says it was "apparently a stockade within the palace grounds."

See 32.6–15 for the access to these prisoners; 37.15, 16, 20–21 for distinction from "the prison in the house of Jonathan" and "the dungeon-house" and "the cells"; 38.1–3 for Jeremiah's access to the people; 38.6, "the dungeon (or pit) of Malchijah … that was in the court of the guard."

Chapters 37–38 give details of the circumstances under which Jeremiah was imprisoned.

32.3–5 Explains how Jeremiah came to be imprisoned. Verses 2–5 are parenthetical, explaining the circumstances. Verse 6 then connects with verse 1; it is not an answer to Zedekiah's question. The message of Jeremiah referred to by Zedekiah was evidently often repeated from the time the siege began. See chatper 21; 34.1–5; 37.16–17; 38.17–23.

B. Purchase of the Field and Significance of the Transaction (32.6–15)

32.7 The right of redemption. See Lev 25.13–17, 23–34, for laws governing the sale of property, and esp. verse 25 for *the right of redemption*. God did not want land which he had given to the tribes and families of Israel for a hereditary possession to fall permanently into the hands of strangers.

32.9 Seventeen shekels of silver. Not much money. But see Lev 25.13–17 for the basis of determining price. See also Keil's discussion.

32.10 I subscribed the deed. Literally as KJV margin: "wrote in the book" or scroll. Keil translates "in the letter" and explains this as "the usual letter of purchase."

And sealed it. In the sense "to make sure by sealing" (Keil), as Isaiah 29.11. Two copies were made—one sealed, one opened (vv 11–12). The open one gave easy access to the deed; the sealed copy assured that if the other were damaged, defaced, or tampered with, a perfect copy would yet remain.

32.12 The witnesses that subscribed the deed of the purchase. I.e., who wrote in the scroll as witnesses to attest the transaction.

32.14 That they may continue. I.e., protected from damp, decay and destruction.

32.15 Brings out the significance of the symbolic transaction.

C. Jeremiah's Prayer for Additional Revelation (32.16–25). The action Jeremiah was to take and its meaning had been made clear. But the actual state of things so greatly contrasted with the promised future that it posed a great strain upon human faith. Under these conditions Jeremiah pleads for additional revelation about Judah's future—revelation which would give support to faith under trial.

32.24–25 closes the prayer by presenting the great contrast between the promise and the present situation. The prophet lays the problem before the Lord; as it were, pleading for more food for faith. Jeremiah has expressed confidence in the infinite might of Jehovah. He desired only some further word as a support for faith in these circumstances.

D. Jehovah's Answer (32.26–44)

1. Introductory: Nothing is too hard for Jehovah (32.26–27). Confirms Jeremiah's words (v 17): "Yes, it is really so" ... reinforcing faith.

2. The city will assuredly be taken and destroyed because of the sins of the people (32.28–35).

3. But just as certainly the people will be restored (32.36–44).

32.39 One heart and one way. They had gone astray, turned every one to his own way (Isa 53.6).

32.40 I will not turn away from following them. NASB as KJV simply, "I will not turn away from them, to do them good"—literally as KJV margin: "from after them."

And I will put my fear in their hearts. The uninterrupted bestowal of the blessings implies faithfulness on the part of the people, which God secures by putting his fear in their hearts. Cf. note on 31.33b.

III. More Restoration Promises (Ch 33)

A. Introductory: The Invitation to Call Upon Jehovah for Revelation (33.1–3)

33.2 That doeth it. I.e., the things about to be revealed and of which Jehovah had already spoken.

That formeth it to establish it. Reference to the purpose of God, which is formed in order to be carried into effect. Jehovah does not form purposes only to let them come to nothing, but he forms them to establish them.

33.3 Great things. The things revealed in the following verses.

B. "Repair of the Injuries and Renewal of the Prosperity of Jerusalem and Judah" (Keil) (33.4–13)

33.10–11 Return of joy and gladness—a joyous life. Reversal of 7.34, 16.9 and 25.10.

The voice of them that say, Give thanks. I.e., Praising God for such blessings.

33.12–13 Shepherds and their flocks again in the land.

That numbereth them. Counting them as they pass out of the fold in the morning and into it at night.

C. Restoration of the Davidic Monarchy (33.14–26)

1. Promise of the Branch of David: Kings and Priests (33.14–18). Cf. 23.5–6.

33.17 David shall never want a man. Reference to 2 Samuel 7.12–16 according to the form of 1 Kings 2.4; 18.25; 9.5; 2 Chronicles 6.16; 7.18.

33.18 The priests the Levites … to offer burnt-offerings. The time would come, however, when the sacrifices would have served their purpose (Heb 10.18); when only spiritual sacrifices would be offered (Rom 12.1–2; 1 Pet 2.5; Heb 13.15–16). Then all Christians would be priests—stones (Matt 3.9) turned into living stones (1 Pet 2.5).

Understand this verse, with verse 22b, in the light of Isaiah 66.21. It must be explained in the spiritual terms of the gospel. All men, whether Jews or Gentiles, may be the seed of Abraham through faith (Gal 3.7, 26–29). So also, Levites are taken from among the Gentiles (Isa 66.21), and all Christians are priests (1 Pet 2.5, 9; Rev 1.6; 5.10.

2. The Certainty and Immutability of the Covenant With David and With the Levites (33.19–22). Such assurances were necessary to sustain the faith of the godly; to keep them from giving up amidst the trials of the exile.

33.20 My covenant of the day. Cf. Genesis 9.8–17 with 8.22.

3. Preservation of the Seed of Jacob and of David (33.23–26). Cf. 31.35–37.

33.26 To be rulers. Jesus is the last of the Davidic rulers (Luke 1.32–33). His kingdom will have no end, and he will never need a successor.

Addendum to Chapters 30–33: *The Jews and the Land*

A. The conditional element in Prophecy: Jeremiah 18; cf. Jonah 3.4.

B. Conditions upon return from captivity: Lack of prosperity and the reason: Haggai 1.7–11; Zechariah 1.1–6; chs. 7–8; Mal 1.2–5; 3.7.

C. Rejection of Christ: Matthew. 21.43; 23.37–39; Chapter 24.

Note: Zion to be the place of refuge (Obad 17); but not the literal fortress (Matt 24.16).

D. Neither Jew nor Greek in Christ: Galatians 3.26–29.

E. God's purpose fulfilled in the church: Not in the Jewish nation: Book of Ephesians contrasted with Acts 15.1, 5.

F. What about the land? Jesus predicted destruction and scattering. But what is the New Testament expectation for the future? A regathering to Palestine? If that is still the hope of the Jews we would expect some reference to it in the New Testament, just as the Old Testament prophets before the exile had predicted scattering to be followed by regathering and return. But what is found in the New Testament? See John 4.20–24; Romans 4.13; Galatians 3.16 (Note reference to "land" passages!); 4.25–26; Philippians 3.20; Hebrews 10.34; 11.13–16; 12.22 (in context); 13.14; Rev 21–22. Observe especially the passages written "to the Hebrews." Likely this book was written in the shadow of the Roman destruction of Jerusalem. But that would be no great disaster to Christian Jews. Their hopes were not tied to that city.

G. Future of the Jews: Romans 9–11:[15] In Chapter 11 Paul raises the same issue that is discussed in Jeremiah 31.35–37 and 33.23–26. (This section of

[15]See my *Thinking Through Romans* for full discussion of these chapters.

Jeremiah can help us to understand the problem of Romans 9–11.) Paul's thesis is: God has not cast off his people. He makes three points: **1.** The rejection is not complete—a remnant is saved (vv 1–10). **2.** The rejection is not final—others can still be saved (vv 11–24). **3.** As God works in history his purpose is "mercy upon all" (vv 25–32).

All Israel in verse 26 refers to physical Israel (contrasted with Gentiles and so all through chs 9–11), but to that Israel which is worthy of the name—the real Israel; the believing Israel (cf. 9.6). Paul did not expect a turning to God on the part of all (physical) Israel. Read 9.6–13, 27–29; 11.5–8, 14 ("some"), 23 ("if"—conditional).

And so in verse 26 means *in this manner*, which is defined by verse 25 to mean *under these circumstances*—i.e., with "a hardening in part" persisting in Israel all through the ages until the end of time when the last Gentile has been converted. Under these conditions all the real Israel will be saved.

And so is not *and then.* Paul is not referring to a salvation of Israel at the end of time, but to a process that was going on in his day and that proceeds all through the age. Compare verses 30–32 with verses 11–14.

PART TEN

The Conquest and Destruction of the Kingdom of Judah

Prophecies and Events to the Fall of Jerusalem

Jeremiah 34–39

Introduction

Keil supplies an appropriate heading for Chapters 34–45: "The Labor and Suffering of Jeremiah Before and After the Conquest and Destruction of Jerusalem." The section can be subdivided thus:

1. Prophecies and Events to the Fall of Jerusalem (chs 34–39).

2. Words and Experiences of Jeremiah After the Fall of Jerusalem (chs 40–44).

3. A Message for Baruch (ch 45).

I. Attitudes During the Reigns of Jehoiakim and Zedekiah (Chs 34–36)

A. Two Prophecies Re. the Siege and Destruction of Jerusalem (Ch 34)

1. A Word for Zedekiah Re. the Outcome of the Siege and His Own Fate (34.1–7). The prophecy announces the hopelessness of Zedekiah's position. Likely coming early in the siege when Zedekiah might have had hope of defeating and driving off the Babylonians through the help of Egypt, it lets him know the outcome of the siege in advance. If he had received the word with a believing heart he would have been able to plan his conduct accordingly.

34.5 The burnings. RSV translates verse 5b, "And as spices were burned for your fathers, … so men shall burn spices for you etc." NASB similarly. Cf. 2 Chronicles 16.14; 21.19. Spices were burned in honor of the dead. Cf. our custom re. flowers at funerals. The verse means that Zedekiah would have an honorable burial as befits a king.

They shall lament thee. Contrast 22.18–19.

2. Prophecy Re. the Liberation of Slaves (34.8–22)

(a) Occasion of the Prophecy (34.8–11). Verses 21–22, with chapter 37, make the situation clear. Zedekiah evidently hoped, by freeing the slaves, to impress God and thus bring the lifting of the siege (cf. Jeremiah's message to Zedekiah in 21.11–12). But when the siege was lifted the slaves were brought back under bondage.

(b) The Breach of Faith Set Before the People (34.12–16)

34.13 Out of the house of bondage. Given in Deuteronomy 15.15 as the motive for obeying this law.

34.14 Cf. Exodus 21.2; Deuteronomy 15.12.

(c) The Curse to Come Upon the People for this Violation of Their Sworn Covenant (34.17–22)

34.17 I proclaim unto you a liberty. They were God's servants, brought under his protection (Lev 25.55). Now he sets them free from this relation and turns them over to the sword, etc.

34.18 And I will give. Hebrew is literally, *And I will give the men … the calf which they cut etc.* (margin). RSV adds the word "like" in the following, but probably has the thought correct: "And the men … I will make like the calf etc." NEB and NAB similarly. The view is also defended in Keil, 86–87. See further below.

The covenant which they made before me. See verses 8–10, 15. But the first reference ("my covenant") probably refers to the covenant of verses 13–14.

34.19 That passed between the parts of the calf. Cf. Genesis 15.10, 17. Reference is to the ceremony by which they entered into the covenant. The symbolism seems to be as explained in the New Berkeley Version note: May I be as this calf if I violate the covenant.

34.21 That are gone away from you. Chapter 37 explains this temporary withdrawal of the Babylonians.

B. Israel's Faithlessness Condemned by the Example of the Rechabites (Ch 35)

Introduction

(1) *Times and Situation.* The necessary background may be gleaned from verse 11 compared with 2 Kings 24.1–2. The presence of invaders in Judah had driven the nomadic, tent-dwelling Rechabites to take refuge in Jerusalem. Jehovah takes advantage of their presence and puts them before Judah as a condemning object-lesson.

(2) *The Rechabites* were a branch of the Kenites (1 Chron 2.55), descendants of Moses' father-in-law (Jdg 1.16). They had entered Canaan with Israel and maintained a nomadic life in southern Judah (Jdg 1.16; 1 Sam 15.6; 27.10; 30.29).[16]

1. Loyalty of the Rechabites to the Principles of Their Father (35.1–11)

35.6–7 See 2 Kings 10.15, 23 for another reference to Jonadab the son of Rechab. This man wanted his people to maintain the simple nomadic life; to stay clear of the corrupting influences of the more settled life.

35.11 The only reason they are in Jerusalem now.

2. The Application—Contrast Between the Faithfulness of the Rechabites to Their Father and the Disloyalty of Judah to Jehovah (35.12–15)

35.13 Will ye not receive instruction? I.e., take a lesson in loyalty from this example.

3. The Punishment to Come Upon Judah (35.16–17). This model of loyalty condemns Judah for unfaithfulness.

4. The Blessing Pronounced Upon the Rechabites (35.18–19). A predic-

[16]Heber the Kenite, however, had separated from the main body of Kenites and lived in northern Palestine. See Judges 4:11, 17; 5.24.

tion of their survival as a distinct people to serve Jehovah. See *Smith's Bible Dictionary*, III, 2681 for the traces of evidence of their continued existence. But two points must be made: **1.** We must keep in mind the conditional element in prophecy (Jer 18). **2.** Whether any such people will be saved is, of course, dependent upon their acceptance of the Christ (John 14.6; Acts 4.12).

C. Attitudes Toward the Word of God During the Reign of Jehoiakim (Ch 36). This chapter is also of special importance as showing how the prophecies of Jeremiah came to be put in written form.

1. The Prophecies of Jeremiah Written on a Scroll (36.1–8)

36.1 The fourth year of Jehoiakim. Judging from verse 9, late in the year. The public reading ordered does not seem to have been done until the ninth month of the fifth year. The announcement of the seventy year dominion of Babylon came in the fourth year of Jehoiakim (ch 25). That year was extremely significant—it was the year of Nebuchadnezzar's decisive defeat of Egypt at Carchemish (46.2) and marked the beginning of the seventy year Babylonian domination of the eastern world. It was the beginning of the fulfillment of the threats Jeremiah had issued over the preceding 23 years (25.3). Perhaps now at last, now that the fulfillment had begun, hearts would be softened and the people would be ready to listen (36.3).

36.5 I am shut up. Margin, *restrained.* The language is not further defined. It could refer to imprisonment (as in 33.1 and 39.15), but evidently does not in this case. Verse 19 shows that Jeremiah could hide himself from the authorities. Driver translates "detained," comparing 1 Samuel 21.7, and thinks "probably by some ceremonial uncleanness." But this is unlikely since it persisted over several months. Chapter 26 suggests a more likely explanation. (The message referred to there may not be of much earlier date than chapter 36. Cf. 26.1 with 28.1.) Jeremiah may have been prohibited from coming to the temple—possibly, as chapter 26 makes likely, under threat of death. RSV translates, "I am debarred from going to the house of the Lord." So also NBV, which translates "restrained" and adds in a marginal note: "Under a temple interdict." The Hebrew word does not in itself mean "imprisoned." Compare the usage in Deuteronomy 11.17, 2 Chronicles 7.13, Isaiah 66.9 and Jeremiah 20.9.

36.8 A "headline" summary of what is given in detail in verses 9–10.

2. Reading of the Book to the People in the Temple (36.9–10)

36.9 Proclaimed a fast. "It would appear that fasts were being proclaimed in times of national crisis" (Harrison). The time appeared ripe for the message of Jeremiah. Cf. Joel 1.13–14; 2.12–17 for how such fasts are to be understood.

3. Reading of the Book to the Princes at the Palace (36.11–19)

36.12 *On the Officials Named:* The name of *Elishama the scribe* is found also at 41.1 and 2 Kings 25.25. "Scribe" is usually explained in such contexts as secretary or Secretary of State—an important official in the government. *Elnathan the son of Achbor* is mentioned also in 26.22. *Shaphan* had been the scribe (or secretary) in Josiah's government (2 Kings 22.3, 8), and is called "Shaphan the scribe" in verse 10. His son *Gemariah* is likely a brother to Ahikam, Jeremiah's protector (26.24). The others are otherwise unknown.

36.17–18 Baruch's attestation to the genuineness of the document. Cf. Jeremiah's insistence on the authority of his message (26.12–15).

4. Reading of the Book to Jehoiakim (36.20–26)

36.23 Jehoiakim's action is best brought out by the following translations: "As Jehudi read three or four columns, the king would cut them off with a penknife etc." (RSV). "As Jehudi read three or four columns, the king would snip them off etc." (NBV). The basis of this translation is that the tense of the Hebrew verb for *cut* implies *repeated* action (Driver; NBV margin). Thus Harrison explains: "As Yehudi read the scroll a few columns at a time, the king would cut off that section and burn it, until the entire scroll had been used up." Take note of the cold-blooded nature of the action; it was not a matter of flying off in an angry rage.

The penknife. Hebrew refers to *a scribe's knife* which was used for trimming the reed pens and "for trimming or cutting the papyrus rolls" (Harrison).

36.24 Contrast 2 Kings 22.11 (cf. 1 Kings 21.27).

5. The Punishment to Come Upon Jehoiakim (36.27–32)

36.30 Cf. 22.18–19. Jehoiachin, Jehoiakim's son, reigned only three months and was replaced by Zedekiah, a brother of Jehoiakim (2 Kings 24.6, 8, 17).

II. The Experiences and Words of Jeremiah During the Siege and Capture of Jerusalem (Chs 37–39)

A. Attitude Toward the Word of God During the Time of Zedekiah (37.1–2)

B. Zedekiah's Appeal to Jeremiah During the Temporary Lifting of the Siege (37.3–5). Verses 4–5 explain the state of affairs: (1) Jeremiah was free to come and go; hence two of Zedekiah's officers are sent to him. (2) The approach of the Egyptian army and the raising of the siege seemed to give hope that the city would be saved.

37.3 Pray now ... for us. In the light of verse 7 ("to inquire of me") compared with verse 17 ("Is there any word from Jehovah?") Zedekiah seems to be merely seeking revelation concerning the final outcome of the present state of affairs.

C. Jeremiah's Reply to Zedekiah (37.6–10). Jeremiah cuts off every hope. There is no hope for the city even if nothing were left of the Chaldean army but mortally wounded men.

D. Arrest and Imprisonment of Jeremiah (37.11–15)

37.12 To receive his portion there. No reference to the purchase in chapter 32. That transaction did not take place until Jeremiah "was shut up in the court of the guard" (32.2). Bright translates, "to attend to a division of property among his people there"—"literally 'to divide there among the people.'" Henderson thinks Jeremiah's object was to "avail himself of the produce of the property which he possessed there, and which he might require during the further siege of the city." But the meaning is really uncertain.

37.13 Thou art falling away. I.e., deserting. A plausible accusation in the light of Jeremiah's message to the people that the only way to save one's life was to pass over to the Chaldeans (21.9).

37.15 Indicates a change of attitude in the princes since the days of Jehoiakim (26.16, 24; 36.11–19, 25). The princes are different men. Some of those during Jehoiakim's reign had been carried over from Josiah's government (cf. note on 36.12). But the better class of princes had been carried into captivity with Jehoiachin (2 Kings 24.10–17).

E. Secret Interview With Zedekiah and Result: Jeremiah Moved to the Court of the Guard (37.16–21). Verses 19 and 21 would seem to show that the Chaldeans had returned.

37.19 Where now are your prophets? The false prophets had been bold before. And Zedekiah had relied upon their advice. But now they are nowhere to be found, and Zedekiah is left to sneak in and inquire of Jeremiah. The prophets have been put to shame by the failure of their prophecies.

The king of Babylon shall not come against you. Cf. 28.1–4 for a sample of the message of these false prophets.

Introductory Note: The Situation in Chapter 38

The number of fighting men is evidently greatly reduced (v 4); famine has set in (v 9); the number of deserters has become large (v 19)—hence it is the last period of the siege.

F. Jeremiah's Message Heard by the Princes (38.1–3). Though confined in the court of the guard Jeremiah was in position to speak to those who came there, and repeated his prediction that all resistance was fruitless. Cf. 21.8–10.

38.1 Jucal. Spelled Jehucal in 37.3.

G. The Accusation of Treason, Resulting in Jeremiah's Imprisonment in the Pit (38.4–6)

38.4 He weakeneth the hands. I.e., undermining the morale. The charge was doubtless true. Jeremiah's message would make men unwilling to sacrifice their lives in defence of the city, it being a hopeless cause. However, Jeremiah was not expressing a personal opinion, but declaring the word of God—and that out of love for his people, it being his conviction that the nation could only be saved through submission. The courage Jeremiah sought to weaken was not a heroic courage based on trust in God, but a fleshly and foolish obstinacy which could only bring ruin. Hence the injustice of the charge.

38.5 Observe this display of weakness in Zedekiah.

38.6 Dungeon. Better, *pit* or *cistern*. "An underground pit, such as most houses had, for the storage of water" (Driver). "... a cistern which had been emptied of its water during the siege, and in which nothing remained but the slime at the bottom" (Henderson). Cf. 2 Kings 18.31 and Proverbs 5.15 for such private cisterns.

H. Jeremiah Rescued by Ebed-melech, But Kept in the Court of the Guard (38.7–13)

38.10 Thirty men. Why so many? Keil says, to effect the rescue against any attempt of the princes to prevent it. But Zedekiah seems afraid of them (vv 5, 24–26). Driver and Harrison suggest that the original text may have been *three* (*slsh*) instead of *thirty* (*slsm*).

38.11 Under the treasury. Where there seems to have been some kind of storeroom.

I. The Last Interview Between Jeremiah and Zedekiah (38.14–28)

1. Zedekiah's Inquiry (38.14–16)

2. Jeremiah's Counsel: Surrender to the Babylonians and Preserve the City (38.17–23)

38.17 If thou wilt go forth. I.e., surrender to them—the same message Jeremiah had repeatedly announced. But how contrary to all human expectations!

38.21–22 Consequences if he does not surrender.

Hath showed me. In vision.

Thy familiar friends. Intimate and trusted advisers. They had "led him into a hopeless struggle with the Chaldaeans, and then, when he was in difficulties, turned back and deserted him" (Driver).

3. Zedekiah's Order to Jeremiah: Keep the Subject of the Interview Secret From the Princes (38.24–28). Such weakness of character is a guarantee that this interview also is doomed to be fruitless.

38.26 I presented my supplication. Which doubtless would be true. He would simply leave untold the main burden of the interview, which information the princes had no right to anyhow.

J. The Capture of Jerusalem (39.1–3). Situation: The Babylonian officers enter and take up a position in the lower city. Cf. 52.4–7 and 2 Kings 25.1–4 on verses 1–2.

K. The Fate of Zedekiah and of the People of Jerusalem (39.4–10)

39.9 The account is much condensed. This actually took place one month after the fall of the city (52.12; 2 Kings 25.8ff).

L. Provision for Jeremiah (39.11–14)

39.12 Do unto him even as he shall say unto thee. Cf. 40.4.

39.14 Out of the court of the guard. This is an extremely condensed account of what happened. See 40.1ff.

Gedaliah. Who was made governor (40.5). His father *Ahikam* had earlier given protection to Jeremiah (26.24).

That he should carry him home. I.e., apparently to Gedaliah's residence as governor (40.5–6). The comparison with verse 12 and chapter 40 shows that the whole account is condensed.

M. Consolatory Message to Ebed-melech (39.15–18). This message dates from prior to the fall of Jerusalem; it is a supplement to chapter 38. Cf. 38.7–13 on *Ebed-melech* and why he is granted this promise.

39.18 Thy life shall be for a prey unto thee. Cf. 21.9; 38.2.

PART ELEVEN

The Conquest and Destruction of the Kingdom of Judah

Words and Experiences of Jeremiah after the Fall of Jerusalem

---

Jeremiah 40–45

I. The Governorship and Assassination of Gedaliah (Chs 40–41)

A. Jeremiah's Fate at the Fall of Jerusalem (40.1–6). Cf. the condensed version at 39.11–14. This fuller account shows that Jeremiah was not freed immediately from the court of the guard (39.14).

40.1 Ramah. Five miles north of Jerusalem according to the probable identification.

40.2–3 The mode of expression is Jeremiah's, but Nebuzaradan may have expressed the thought that Jeremiah's predictions had now been fulfilled.

40.4 Nebuzaradan is carrying out an order of Nebuchadnezzar (39.11–14).

40.5 Now while he was not yet gone back. Jeremiah appears to hesitate for a moment. Nebuzaradan ends the indecision in this manner.

B. Return of the Scattered Peoples[17] and Their Peaceable Settlement Under Gedaliah (40.7–12).

---

[17]Some having sought refuge in the fields, some in surrounding countries.

40.7 All the captains … in the fields. At the conquest these had evidently found places of refuge.

40.9 These men must have been concerned for their safety since they had borne arms against the Chaldeans. Gedaliah assures them of safety and protection, provided they accept Chaldean authority and peaceably cultivate the soil.

40.10 To stand before the Chaldeans. I.e., as their servant (cf. 1 Kings 10.8), in which position he would be able to represent the Jews and maintain their interests.

40.11–12 Some Jews had taken refuge in Moab and other countries.

C. Gedaliah Forewarned of the Assassination Plot (40.13–16)

D. The Murder of Gedaliah and of Certain Others at Mizpah, Including Jews and Chaldeans (41.1–3)

41.1 The seventh month. Just two months after the destruction of Jerusalem and the appointment of Gedaliah (52.12)? It is not altogether certain that it was the same year. Chapter 40.12 seems to indicate that enough time has elapsed to gather a harvest.

And there they did eat bread together. Ishmael and his men were received hospitably and acted most treacherously.

E. Pilgrims From the North Murdered and the People Remaining at Mizpah Carried Away Captive (41.4–10)

41.5 Men from Shechem. Although Harrison thinks these pilgrims may have been Judeans who had moved north after the fall of Samaria, it is possible that they were pious descendants of Israelites who were living among the heathen colonists (2 Kings 17.24–26). Since Hezekiah (2 Chron 30.11) or Josiah (2 Chron 34.9) such people had attended feasts in Jerusalem; now come to the site of the recently destroyed city.

Having their beards shaven. All signs of mourning. They were evidently in mourning on account of the destruction of Jerusalem.

Having cut themselves. A heathen mourning custom (16.6), forbidden to Israel (Deut 14.1).

To the house of Jehovah. I.e., to the site where it had been.

41.6 Weeping all along. Pretending sympathy with them. Another indication of the treacherous character of Ishmael.

41.8 We have stores hidden. Cisterns or underground storehouses were often used to keep grain. Such a supply of goods would be important to Ishmael in the times.

41.9 Which Asa the king had made. Not specially mentioned in the history of Asa's reign, but see 1 Kings 15.16–22 and 2 Chronicles 16.1–6 for Asa's fortifications. This pit was probably a cistern for water supply.

41.10 Jeremiah was evidently among these captives (42.1ff).

F. Defeat of Ishmael by Johanan, Liberation of the Captives, and the Plan to Flee into Egypt (41.11–18)

II. The Word of Jehovah Concerning the Flight to Egypt (Ch 42)

A. The Request for Guidance From Jehovah (42.1–6). The people really do not intend the absolute commitment to obedience which their words express. Their minds are already set on going to Egypt. They had no idea Jehovah would tell them to remain in the land under the present circumstances. They only wanted to know how best to carry out their settled purpose. They wanted guidance only within this limitation.

B. Revelation From Jehovah in Response to the People's Request: The Future of the People (42.7–22)

1. The Counsel to Remain in the Land Without Fear—the Way to Recovery (42.7–12)

2. Warning—the Disaster Certain to Follow Flight into Egypt (42.13–17)

3. Jehovah's Testimony Against a People Bent on Going to Egypt (42.18–22). Cf. verse 5: "Jehovah be a true and faithful witness amongst us." This section assumes that the people will go into Egypt. In fact that point had already been decided when the people came to Jeremiah.

III. Jeremiah's Prediction of Nebuchadnezzar's Invasion of Egypt (Ch 43)

A. Reaction to Jeremiah's Speech—the Flight to Egypt (43.1–7)

43.2 Thou speakest falsely. But cf. their commitment (42.1–3, 5–6). They evade the obligation to which they have committed themselves by this charge against Jeremiah. And this in spite of all the recent confirmation of Jeremiah's message! Cf. note on 28.17.

43.7 Tahpanhes. A town "on the N. E. frontier of Egypt" (Driver).

B. Revelation at Tahpanhes Regarding the Invasion of Egypt (43.8–13)

43.9 Hide them in mortar in the brickwork. RSV: "hide them in the mortar in the pavement. The Hebrew words are of uncertain meaning. Hebrew for *mortar* occurs only here. Hebrew for *brickwork* "elsewhere (2 Sam 12.31; Nah 3.14) denotes a "brick-mold' or 'brick-kiln,' but here perhaps a 'terrace of brickwork' (cf. KB)" (Bright). But surely it is easier to think of Jeremiah as slipping some stones into the brickkiln than laying them in the pavement himself. *Great stones* cannot, of course, be thought of as anything like a boulder, but only great in comparison with very small stones. The *brickkiln* is not to be thought of as something *always* present "at the entry of Pharaoh's house." It was likely there for the purpose of laying some pavement. Jehovah predicts that Nebuchadnezzar's throne would be set upon the stones hidden in the brickkiln and thus becoming a part of the pavement. The purpose of this action is not explained but it would certainly add dramatic force to Jeremiah's prediction of the coming of Nebuchadnezzar and likely would be remembered by the Jews when the fulfillment came.

43.10 His royal pavilion. The Hebrew is of uncertain application. Keil thinks of "the gorgeous tapestry with which the seat of the throne was covered." But others think the reference is either to the carpet on which the throne stood or to the canopy above it.

43.11 Death. As distinguished from *the sword*, obviously refers to death by some other means—*pestilence* (RSV), *plague* (Bright). Cf. 42.22.

43.12 As a shepherd putteth on his garment. Usually explained of the ease with which he clothes himself with Egypt. "… As easily as the shepherd in the open field wraps himself in the cool night in his mantle, will be be able to grasp Egypt with his hand and fling it round him like an easily managed garment, in order then to leave the land as an absolute conqueror, clothed in this attire of booty, in peace, without an enemy" (Ewald).

43.13 The pillars of Beth-shemesh. *Beth-shemesh* means "the house of the sun." The probable reference is to the city of *On*, called *Heliopolis* (city of the sun) by the Greeks, "about 6 miles N. E. of the modern Cairo, where there was a famous Temple dedicated to the sun, with an avenue of obelisks in front of it, built by Thothmes III, of the eighteenth dynasty (c. 1500 BC)" (Driver).

That is in the land of Egypt. Distinguishes this place from the Beth-shemesh in Canaan.

Babylonian Invasion of Egypt. A fragmentary inscription of Nebuchadnezzar mentions an invasion in his 37th year (= 568/7 BC).

IV. Message Concerning the Idolatry Practiced by the Jews in Egypt (Ch 44)

Introduction

Chapter 44 contains the last recorded message of Jeremiah. (The prophecies in chs 45–51 are of earlier date.) The continuation of pagan practices in Egypt shows that the Jews "had failed completely to grasp the significance of the catastrophe which had overtaken Jerusalem" (Harrison). Jeremiah's last word is, therefore, a message of judgment.

A. The Threat of Punishment for Idolatry (44.1–14)

1. Heading (44.1). Harrison thinks the reference is to Jewish colonies established in Egypt before the fall of Jerusalem. But what in the text leads one to such an idea? Does not the text lead us to think of the Jews who came to Egypt along with Jeremiah? But in that case we must assume the passing of some time since the message delivered at Tahpanhes (43.8–13). The Jews have now settled in various cities of Egypt.

2. Reminder of the Calamity Which Befell Judah Because of Idolatry (44.2–6)

3. Application to the Present (44.7–10)

4. Punishment Yet to Come (44.11–14). Because they remain impenitent (v 10), Jehovah will punish them severely.

44.14 Save such as shall escape. Clarifying "none ... shall escape" (v 14a). Only an inconsiderable handful of fugitives; so few as to be beneath notice. The Jews undoubtedly planned to return to Judah after the Egyptian sojourn, when the Chaldean threat was over. But the only return would be that of a few fugitives who would somehow manage to escape the coming judgment.

B. Answer of the People to Jeremiah's Threat (44.15–19)

44.15 A great assembly. The people were evidently gathered for a festival in honor of an idol.

44.17–18 Every word that is gone forth. Vows to sacrifice to the queen of heaven. Cf. verse 25.

The queen of heaven. See at 7.18.

For then had we plenty of victuals. They could probably offer a plausible argument. The troubles started with the death of Josiah—first the Egyptians, then the Babylonians were upon them. So as long as they worshipped the queen of heaven all was well. Josiah's reform was followed by the time of trouble. They would ignore the real cause of the judgment (indicated in Jeremiah's early chapters) and construe history to suit their purposes.

44.19 "At the beginning of verse 19 one LXX MS, followed by the Syriac, reads: 'And all the women answered and said', ..." (Harrison). Whether that preserves the correct text or not, the last part of the verse shows that the wives are speaking.

Cakes to worship her. Margin, *to portray her.* RSV, "cakes for her bearing her image." Evidently cakes in the shape of the moon, or possibly with its image stamped upon them.

Without our husbands. I.e., without their knowledge and approval (v 15); without which a woman's vow would not be binding (Num 30). Evidently the thought is: Why this tirade against the wives? We acted with the consent of our husbands. Are they arguing that the husbands therefore are the responsible parties?

C. Jeremiah's Reply (44.20–30)

1. Refutation of the People's Reasoning (44.20–23). The idolatry is the very cause of the disaster which has befallen them. Did they think God had forgotten the idolatry which they had not renounced from the heart? (cf. 3.10). It was because he could no longer endure such abominations that the evil came.

44.23 Therefore this evil is happened unto you. Note connection with verse 23a. The "evil" is exactly the consequence threatened in the law against such abominations.

2. Repetition of the Threat of Punishment (44.24–28)

44.25 Establish then your vows. Or as KJV: "ye will surely accomplish your vows, etc." So Keil. God appeals, exhorts, and threatens. But he does not compel. They will go on in their sin, but must suffer the consequences.

44.26 My name shall no more be named. None would be left to name it (v 27).

44.27 All the men. Modified and clarified in verse 28. Cf. note on verse 14.

44.28 Shall know whose word shall stand. I.e., be proved true. The fulfillment would determine who was correctly interpreting the history of Judah. See notes on verses 17b–18 and 20–23.

3. Sign of the Coming Punishment (44.29–30). The sign of their certain punishment would be the fall of Pharaoh Hophra into his enemies' hands.

Pharaoh Hophra is the pharaoh called Apries by the Greeks, "fourth king of the XXVIth Dynasty, who reigned for nineteen years, from 589 to 570 BC He was an impetuous king, over-ambitious to meddle in Palestinian affairs" (K.A. Kitchen, NBD, 536). James H. Breasted points out that "the date of Zedekiah's rebellion coincides with the accession of Apries" (*A History of the Ancient Egyptians*, condensed version, 408).

Hophra's Downfull. A disastrous campaign in Libya was followed by a revolt of Egyptian troops, who held Hophra "personally responsible for the defeat." Hophra sent Ahmose (Amasis in Herodotus), one of his nobles, "to try to argue the rebels into submission." But instead, the disaffected soldiers proclaimed Ahmose king in the place of Hophra. In the struggle that followed Hophra was killed. The historical source of this account can be found in the Penguin edition of Herodotus, pp. 166–169, 296, from which the quotations are taken. See also Breasted, pp. 410–412.

Pharaoh Hophra is mentioned by name in the Old Testament only at Jeremiah 44.30. He is the pharaoh referred to in several other passages, however.

V. A Message for Baruch (Ch 45)

Background and Content of Chapter 45

This message goes back to the fourth year of Jehoiakim (v 1). The chapter is an appendix to Chapter 36. The recording of Jeremiah's messages of judgment in a book leaves Jeremiah's scribe Baruch discouraged and depressed. Driver well describes the content of the chapter: "Words of mingled reassurance and reproof, addressed to Baruch, in the depression and disappointment which overcame him, after writing the roll of the fourth year of Jehoiakim."

45.3 Jehovah hath added sorrow to my pain. Like Jeremiah (15.18), Baruch had felt *pain* at the moral corruption of the nation and the attitude toward the word of God manifested therein. *Sorrow* was *added* by the threat of judgment, that feeling being freshly increased and intensified by the writing of the messages.

45.4–5 *Answer to Baruch's Complaint.* Jehovah's answer has a stern character. The judgment has been decreed. But perhaps also verse 4 calls upon Baruch to appreciate what Jehovah himself is feeling as it is necessary to tear down what he himself had built. Verse 5 adds comfort and reassurance to alleviate Baruch's pain and sorrow. When calamity is striking "the whole land," an individual must not expect great temporal prosperity for himself. It is a lot if he can escape with his life as a booty ("prey" in ASV and KJV; "prize of war" in RSV). Baruch will receive that much, though flight may be necessary (*in all places* etc.).

PART TWELVE

Jehovah's Word Concerning Foreign Nations: Egypt, Philistia, Moab, Ammon, Edom, Syria, Arabia, Elam

Jeremiah 46–49

Introduction

Chapters 46–51 contain prophecies concerning foreign nations. (A heading is supplied by Jeremiah himself at 46.1.) Similar collections may be found for comparison in Isaiah 13–27, Ezekiel 25–31, and Amos 1.1–2.3. See also Obadiah and Nahum. Jeremiah's prophecies are connected with Chapter 25, in which Jeremiah made the prediction in the first year of Babylon's dominion that all the nations, ending with Babylon itself, would drink the cup of the wine of the wrath of God. Now we see how that prediction will be carried out. As Driver puts it, "Chapter 25 may be regarded as an introduction to these prophecies: it acquaints the reader with Jeremiah's general view of the political situation, which is then illustrated, and poetically developed, with reference to particular countries, in the present prophecies." The prophecies are of earlier date than the immediately preceding section. See especially 46.2, 49.34 and 51.59–64. Some general observations concerning this section will be offered at its close.

I. Two Prophecies Concerning Egypt (Ch 46)

A. The Defeat of Egypt at Carchemish (46.2–12)

1. Heading (46.2)

Pharaoh-neco reigned in Egypt c. 610–595 BC At the fall of the Assyrian Empire, Neco participated in a brief contest with Babylon for control of the ancient near eastern world, and in fact brought Judah under Egyptian dominion for a short time (2 Kings 23.29–24.7).

Carchemish was a great commercial city and fortress located near Haran and about 260 miles N.N.E. of Damascus. It commanded the main crossing of the Euphrates. Wiseman (NBD, 200) has listed the main references to Carchemish in ancient writings. It is first mentioned in an 18th Century BC text as an independent trade center. Later it was claimed by the Egyptian Pharaoh Thuthmosis III. Still later it was a Hittite fortress, but in 1110 BC it was ruled by an independent king. It was conquered by the Assyrians (see Isa 10.9) and placed under an Assyrian governor. In 609 BC, as the Assyrian empire collapsed, Pharaoh-neco was able to regain control of the city (cf. 2 Chron 35.20) and made it an Egyptian outpost. But in 605 the Egyptians were attacked and decisively defeated by the Babylonians under Nebuchadnezzar.

The Battle of Carchemish (605 BC) was the political turning point of the age. It ended Egyptian hopes of empire and placed Babylon in control of the ancient near eastern world. The battle marked the beginning of Babylon's seventy year empire.

2. Call to the Egyptian Army to Prepare for Battle (46.3–4). Take note of Jeremiah's poetic dramatization of the situation. The commands sound like orders barked out by Egyptian officers.

3. Vision of Egypt's Defeat (46.5–6). Suddenly the prophet sees the great army meeting with disastrous defeat.

4. Egyptian Ambition Checked and Humbled at Carchemish (46.7–12)

46.7–8 A second stanza begins. Egypt sets out, ambitious for empire, like a great overflow of the Nile, determined to "cover the earth."

46.9 Cush and Put, the Ludim. Allies of Egypt.

46.10 Meaning of the battle: Jehovah's "day of vengeance."

46.11 The blow struck Egypt is one from which they shall not recover.
Gilead … balm. Cf. 8.22.
Virgin. Unforced, unviolated, undefeated.

46.12 The report of Egypt's disgrace goes out to all nations.

B. The Invasion and Conquest of Egypt by the Babylonians (46.13–26). Cf. Ezekiel 29.32

46.13 How that Nebuchadrezzar ... should come. Nebuchadnezzar was not immediately able to follow up the victory at Carchemish (605 BC) with an invasion of Egypt. But a fragmentary inscription of Nebuchadnezzar mentions an invasion in his 37th year (= 568/7 BC). Cf. the prediction of Ezekiel (29.17–20) in 570 BC

46.14 A call to arms, followed in verses 15ff with a decription of Egyptian defeat. *Migdol* and *Tahpanhes* were towns on the northern frontier of Egypt; *Memphis* (KJV, *Noph*, a transliteration of the Hebrew), the northern capital, "situated on the Nile, at about 15 miles from the apex of the Delta" (NBD).

Stand forth. NASB, "Take your stand and get yourself ready"; NIV, "Take your positions and get ready." A call to prepare for defence.

For the sword hath devoured round about thee. Referring to countries surrounding Egypt, probably especially those on the northern frontier, since the enemy comes from the north (v 20). The countries on Egypt's frontier have already fallen. She is next.

46.15 Thy strong ones. Many think of soldiers: "thy valiant men" (KJV), "your mighty ones" (NASB), "your warriors" (NIV); others, of horses (as in 8.16 and 47.3). But over 50 Hebrew manuscripts and the LXX and the Vulgate versions all read the singular *thy strong one.* In addition, the verb *swept away* (better perhaps, *become prostrate*, NASB; or *will be laid low*, NIV) is singular in Hebrew, and so are the following pronouns (Driver). RSV follows the LXX: "Why has Apis fled? Why did not your bull stand?" Similarly NEB. "Apis was the sacred bull revered as the incarnation of the god Ptah (later of Osiris)" (Bright). Cf. Psalm 22.12, literally *strong ones of Bashan* = bulls; so also Psalm 50.13 68.30; Isaiah 34.7; Jeremiah 50.11 where bulls is literally *strong ones*. Keil and others, however, think of the Pharaoh.

Drive them. Or *thrust him down* (RSV; cf. ASV margin; NASB, NIV).

46.16 Let us go again to our own people. Referring to foreigners living in Egypt. Cf. the reference to hired mercenaries in verse 21, though this verse does not necessarily refer to soldiers.

46.17 They cried there. "Some ancient versions read: Call the name of Pharaoh a big noise" (NASB margin), including the LXX. The reading involves only a different pronunciation of the same consonants.

But a noise. NASB, "but a big noise"; NIV, "only a loud noise." And following the LXX as explained above: "call the name of Pharaoh, king of Egypt, 'Noisy one who lets the hour go by'" (RSV); "Give Pharaoh of Egypt the title King Bombast" (NEB); "Big noise"—perhaps with some play on his personal name or royal titles (Bright). Harrison suggests "Loudmouth." Cf. verse 25 ("them that trust in him") with Ezekiel 29.6–7, 15–16. Pharaoh turns out to be "all talk"—tall on promise, short on performance.

The appointed time. The time of grace; the period after Carchemish when Pharaoh might have made peace with Babylon and averted invasion. Instead he continually threw himself against Babylon and invited invasion. Henderson, however, explains: The time after Carchemish when he might have prepared for defence.

46.18 Like Tabor among the mountains. Standing out above all that surrounds. So would Neb., the invader of Egypt, tower above all other kings.

46.19 Daughter that dwellest in Egypt. Personification of the population of Egypt.

Furnish thyself to go into captivity. "Literally *make thee articles for exile*" (Driver). "Prepare yourselves baggage for exile" (RSV). Similarly NASB, NEB. "Pack your belongings for exile" (NIV). The same expression in Ezekiel 12.3: "Prepare thee stuff for removing (or, exile)."

46.20 The gadfly (margin). Accepted by most in place of *destruction*, agreeing with *heifer*. NASB, "a horsefly," with margin, "Or, possibly, *mosquito*." A figure for the enemy. Cf. Isaiah 7.18.

46.21 Her hired men. Mercenary soldiers. Herodotus mentions Greek mercenaries used by Egypt (ii. 152, 154, 163; Penguin edition, pp. 163, 164, 167–168).

Like calves of the stall. Calves kept in the stall for fattening. Hence: Well fed, fat. Pharaoh depended upon them and therefore abundantly provided for them. (Keil refers to Herodotus II. 152, 163.) Well cared for and nourished, they were like fattened cattle, but of no use in war (v 21b).

46.22a The margin is clearer: *Her sound is like that of the serpent as it goeth.* Perhaps with RSV: "She makes a sound like a serpent gliding away"; or NIV: "Egypt will hiss like a fleeing serpent ..." Hebrew is not just *voice* (KJV) but a *sound* of any kind. It may be the sound of the serpent slithering away in the grass rather than its hiss. So Egypt has been brought down to the dust (cf. Isa 29.4). The multitudes of Egypt are compared to a *forest* (v 23; cf. Isa 10.15–19, 33–34). The enemy armies are like wood choppers that cut down the forest (vv 22b–23a). The fleeing Egyptians are like serpents trying to slip away through the grass.

46.23 Though it cannot be searched. As translated, this clause describes the forest. Cf. RSV: "though it is impenetrable"; NIV: "dense though it be." The margin suggests an alternative, putting *for* in place of *though*. In that case the army would be described as countless. See what follows.

46.25 Amon of No. *No* (No-Amon in Nah 3.8) is the city called *Thebes* by the Greeks—the capital of Upper (Northern) Egypt. No corresponds to Egyptian for *the city*. No-Amon would mean *the city of* (the god) *Amon* (Kitchen in NBD, 890). See also Kitchen's article on the god Amon in NBD, 31: "He was first prominent as a local god of Thebes ... became chief god. Later ... Amun became state god, 'king of the gods.'"

Her kings. The plural probably refers to the rulers of nations allied with Egypt (Henderson), (though Keil thinks "all the kings who ever ruled Egypt"). It would correspond to *them that trust in Pharaoh*.

46.26 And afterwards it shall be inhabited. Prediction of future restoration after the time of its conquest and destruction. Cf. 48.47; 49.6, 39; Ezekiel 29.13–14.

C. Epilogue: Concluding Promise to Israel (46.27–28). (These verses are repeated from 30.10–11.) Jeremiah has spoken of the punishment of *them that trust in Pharaoh* (v 25). Israel was in that class. These verses provide assurance of the future destiny which the true Israel has to hope for.

II. Prophecy Concerning the Philistines (Ch 47)

47.1 Before that Pharaoh smote Gaza. *Gaza* was one of the five Philistine cities. Pharaoh's attack on Gaza is of uncertain date. The LXX omits this clause, in fact "for the whole of verse 1 has simply, *On the Philistines*." Driver therefore thinks it is possible that the LXX preserves the correct reading, the additional clause being supplied later by someone who wrongly saw in Pharaoh's conquest of Gaza the fulfillment of the prophecy (cf. v 5a). (The enemy, however, was to come *out of the north*; undoubtedly the reference is to the Babylonians.)

47.2 For this representation of an invading enemy under the figure of waters that overflow and flood a land cf. 46.7–8; Isaiah 8.7–8.

47.3 Translates the figure into reality.

The fathers look not back to their children. They are put in such terror by the invading enemy that they can think only of getting away and do not even turn back to help their children.

47.4 To cut off from Tyre and Sidon every helper that remaineth. *Tyre and Sidon* were Phoenician cities located on the northern coast of Palestine. Philistia, on the other hand, was on the southern coast. Evidently the Philistines were allies of Tyre and Sidon, and Jehovah works to cut off all remaining allies of these Phoenician cities. NASB: "every ally that is left."

The isle of Caphtor. The margin puts *seacoast* for *isle.* RSV and NASB: "coastland." The Hebrew may mean either *island* or *coastland. Caphtor* probably refers to the island of Crete (NBD, 199), but Driver says "either Crete or Cilicia." In any case it was the land from which the Philistines originally came (Amos 9.7).

47.5 Baldness. A sign of deep, painful sorrow and mourning. Cf. 16.6; Deuteronomy 14.1; Micah 1.16.

Cut thyself. Also a sign of mourning. Cf. 16.6; 41.5; Deuteronomy 14.1; 1 Kings 18.28.

47.6 NIV supplies the words *you cry* after *Jehovah*, evidently considering verse 6 "the cry of the Philistines for mercy" (Driver). But it may be simply the outcry of the prophet himself, overcome by the vision of destruction he sees. Observe that it is the *sword of Jehovah* that has been turned loose on the Philistines.

III. Prophecy Concerning Moab (Ch 48)

Introduction

Moab was located on the fertile plateau east of the Dead Sea. The Moabites were descended from Lot, as were the Ammonites (Gen 19.37–38). For earlier prophecies against Moab see Isaiah 15–16 and Amos 2.1–3. See also the brief prophecy of Ezekiel (25.8–11). Jeremiah has drawn heavily upon Isaiah. The outline below is an effort to break the chapter up into units and provide headings which would accurately represent the content of each unit. The results of the labor of others is different at points, and I am not confident that I have completely succeeded. But I hope the outline will be an aid in reading and not a distraction.

A. Prediction of the Complete Devastation of Moab (48.1–10)

48.1 Nebo. Refers to a city rather than the mountain (Num 32.3, 38).

Misgab. Means *the high fortress* and is not used elsewhere as a proper name. RSV (the fortress), NASB (the lofty stronghold) and NIV (the stronghold) do not so take it here. Keil thinks the terms refers back to *Nebo* and *Kiriathaim*, which are treated as representative of the mountain country of Moab.

48.2 "The renown of Moab is no more" (Driver, followed by RSV, NBV and NEB). Its fame, its glory, is gone. But cf. 49.25 (Damascus called "the city of praise") and 51.41 (Babylon called "the praise of the whole earth"), which seem to give the preference to NIV: "Moab will be praised no more." Similarly NASB.

In Heshbon they have devised evil against her. Heshbon is a Moabite city, evidently to be thought of as now captured by the enemy, who now, in Heshbon, plan the complete destruction of Moab. Cf. verse 45: "a fire is gone forth out of Heshbon." "In the Hebrew there is a play on the name in 'devised'" (Driver). The wordplay cannot be reproduced in English.

Come. The evil plotted against Moab.

Thou also, O Madmen. "The name of the Moabite town Madmen sounds like the Hebrew for *be silenced*" (NIV margin), another wordplay impossible to represent in translation.

48.4 RSV, "a cry is heard as far as Zoar," follows the LXX. "The difference in the Heb. is slight" (Driver). So also NBV and NEB.

48.6 There is no safe place left in the country. The Moabites must take to the desert to save their lives. Cf. 17.6 on *like the heath in the wilderness* and the contexts of each passage.

48.7 Thou hast trusted in thy works. I.e. their own undertakings or "achievements" (NASB), probably referring especially to their "strongholds" (RSV, NBV) or "defences" (NEB). Some think the LXX, which reads *in your fortifications* in place of both terms *in thy works* and *in thy treasures*, may preserve the original reading.

Chemosh. Moabite god (1 Kings 11.7).

48.8 Destruction everywhere! Complete!

48.9a According to most of the older translations, a dramatic presentation indicating that the devastation will fall upon Moab so suddenly it will need wings to escape. But the translation is extremely uncertain. NIV has, "Put salt on Moab, for she will be laid waste." Cf. NEB margin (Text is different yet!) and NASB margin. See Bright, 320 for discussion of various attempts at translation and their basis.

48.10 The destruction is the work of Jehovah and that work must be pursued with all zeal. This curse will be upon Babylon if it does not carry out the work of Jehovah with vigor. Cf. 50.25.

B. The Power and Security of Moab to be Shattered and the Entire Country Devastated before the Enemy (48.11–25)

48.11 For a long time Moab had been settled in its land, secure against the enemy. It had not been carried into captivity, but rather had been *at ease*. It is compared to a fine wine left to settle and thus to develop taste and scent. *He hath settled on his lees* ("that which settles at the bottom, as of a cask of liquor, esp. wine; sediment; dregs," WNCD), *and hath not been emptied from vessel to vessel*. The symbolism is especially appropriate here because of the fame of Moab's vineyards (cf. vv 32–33).

Therefore his taste remaineth in him. *Taste* and *scent* are "figures expressive of Moab's national character, and its spirit of haughty independence (v 29)" (Driver).

48.12 Them that pour off. Not *wanderers* (KJV), which obscures the continued use of the figure, but *tilters* (Driver, followed by RSV, NBV and NEB). The figure refers to workers whose job is to pour off the wine or to empty it *from vessel to vessel* (v 11).

And break their bottles in pieces. They go about their work recklessly, even smashing the bottles.

48.13 Chemosh. The Moabite god in whom they had misplaced their trust.

Bethel. The site of one of the golden calves reverenced in the northern kingdom (cf. 1 Kings 12.29).

48.14 We are mighty men. "We are mighty warriors, and men valiant for battle" (NASB). No longer will Moab be able to boast of its power.

48.15 His chosen young men. "The choice of his young men" (KJV margin); "the flower of his young men" (Driver); "her finest young men" (NIV).

48.17 The strong staff ... the beautiful rod. Evidently referring to the ruler's scepter; symbol of rule or government.

48.18 Thou daughter that dwellest in Dibon. Personification of the population of Dibon.

Come down from thy glory. "Your place of honor" (NEB).

Sit in thirst. Or "on the thirsty ground" (NEB); "the parched ground" (RSV, NASB, NIV). The verse is similar to Isaiah 47.1.

48.19 Inhabitant of Aroer. Literally as margin, *inhabitress*. As frequently, the population of a city is personified and represented as a woman.

Stand by the way. The road.

Ask him that fleeth. Fugitive from the war. Aroer was located on the Arnon (Deut 2.36; 3.12; 4.48; Josh 12.2). The Moabite stone says King Mesha of Moab "built Aroer and made the road by the Arnon" (NBD, 85). Evidently fugitives would try to go past Aroer and escape over the Arnon.

What hath been done? "What has happened?" (RSV, NASB, NEB, NIV).

48.20–25 The question (v 19b) is answered. "Moab is utterly crushed and helpless; the entire country is at the invader's feet" (Driver).

Horn ... arm. Symbols of power. For *horn* cf. esp. Deuteronomy 33.17; Psalm 75.4–5, 10. The *arm* is the place where one's strength resides, that with which one does any kind of work or fights.

C. The Humbling of Moab's Pride (48.26–30)

48.26 Make ye him drunken. Explained by 25.15–29.

Magnified himself against Jehovah. Cf. verse 42. The reason for the destruction of Moab. Such pride and arrogance as emboldens him to exalt himself against Jehovah (cf. v 29). Probably done through opposition to Jehovah's people. See esp. verse 27, and cf. Isaiah 10.10–11; 36.18–20.

Wallow in his vomit. The other occurrences of the Hebrew verb are: Job 27.23; 34.37; Lamentations 2.15 (clap); Numbers 24.10; Jeremiah 31.19; Ezekiel 21.12 (smite); Job 34.26 (strike). The verb means to clap or "to strike, frequently of striking the hands together; here it signifies to fall into his vomit, i.e. to tumble into it with a splash" (Keil). *Splash* (Driver, NASB margin, NBV) seems to fit better than *wallow*.

Shall be in derision. "An object of ridicule" (NIV), "a laughingstock" (NASB).

48.27 Was he found among thieves? They wagged their heads in mockery as if Israel were a caught thief.

48.28 Over the mouth of the abyss. "At the mouth of a cave" (NIV after NEB) or in the rocky sides of deep gorges.

48.29 The synonyms are heaped up to give emphasis to Moab's pride. That was its character—"settled on his lees," safe, secure (v 11), trusting in its own accomplishments and wealth (v 7), proud, haughty, even challenging Jehovah himself (vv 26, 42). "Pride goeth before destruction, and a haughty spirit before a fall" (Prov 16.18).

D. Lamentation Over Moab (48.31–39)

48.31–32 The vision of terrible devastation causes even the prophet to feel sympathy for the wicked nation.

With more than the weeping of Jazer. Meaning, in the light of Isaiah 16.9, *more than Jazer weeps* (cf. NIV). Others: "More than the weeping for Jazer" (NASB; cf. RSV; NEB).

Thy branches passed over the sea. Reference to the Dead Sea. Song of Solomon 1.14 mentions "the vineyards of Engedi" which was across the Dead Sea from Moab. "The extensive cultivation of the grape is set forth under the figure of a vine whose tendrils stretch out on all sides," says Keil. But Driver may be more to the point: "Sibmah … must have been famous for its vines (cf. Isa 16.8, 9), and this verse must describe the area over which the vines derived from Sibmah extended."

Even to the sea of Jazer. Isaiah 16.8, from which our passage is drawn, has *even unto Jazer.* So LXX reads here. *The sea of* is possibly the error of a copyist who repeated *sea* from the previous line.

48.33 The shouting shall be no shouting. Explain in the light of 25.30 and Isaiah 16.9–10. The Hebrew *hedad* refers to "the loud cry with which those that tread grapes keep time to the alternate raising and thrusting of the feet" (Keil on 25.30). But in 51.14 *hedad* is the battle shout of an attacking enemy. In the present text Jeremiah has said that the wine will cease from the winepresses. The shout of men treading the grapes will be no more. There will be shouting indeed, but not the joyful shout of the treaders of grapes; rather, the shout of the attacking foe.

48.34 The cry is heard from place to place, all over the land.

To Eglath-shelishiyah. The parallelism seems to call for a proper name rather than a translation in the manner of KJV. But Keil, Driver and NBV translate "the third Eglath." So reads the LXX. This Eglath is thus distinguished from other towns of the same name.

The waters ... shall become desolate. I.e. "dried up" (NIV), the enemy having stopped up the springs (cf. 2 Kings 3.25).

48.36 Like pipes. Most other versions: "like a flute" (RSV; so NASB; NIV; NBV)—the instrument used in a lamentation over the dead (Matt 9.23).

The abundance that he hath gotten. On which Moab had depended (v 7).

48.37 The signs of deep mourning.

48.38 Like a vessel. Good for nothing; fit only to be smashed. Cf. 22.28.

48.39 A derision and a terror. "A laughingstock and an object of terror" (NASB).

E. The Judgment Upon Moab Which Brings It to Such a Sorrowful End (48.40–46)

48.40 He shall fly as an eagle. The enemy, swooping down upon Moab.

48.41 And the heart of the mighty men. Moab's mightiest warriors will be frightened and anxious like the heart of a woman experiencing birthpains.

48.43–44 Destruction is inescapable. "He who flees from one danger falls into the other" (Keil). Cf. Isaiah 24.17–18 for this description.

48.45–46 Derived from Numbers 21.28–29; 24.17.

48.45 Fugitives can find no refuge in Heshbon. It is from that city that the destruction of Moab was planned and the fire of war went forth. Cf. verse 2.

A flame from the midst of Sihon. The original passage has "from the city of Sihon" (Num 21.28). Sihon was the ancient Amorite king who lived in Heshbon (Num 21.34). Could Sihon be a poetic designation of Heshbon? So the parallelism suggests.

The tumultuous ones. Literally *the sons of tumult*. Referring to Moab's warriors, or perhaps to the Moabites generally (vv 26, 29, 42).

F. Closing Ray of Hope for Moab in the Latter Days (48.47). Cf. 12.15; 46.26; 49.6, 39. The prophecy closes with a note of mercy—the future would see a turn in Moab's fortunes. Moab would cease to be a people (v 42), yet would be restored. The restoration would seem to involve only individuals rather than a national recovery, and likely was to be fulfilled in Christ. The last line is a note indicating that the prophecy concerning Moab ends at this point. Cf. 51.64b.

IV. Prophecies Concerning Various Small Nations (Ch 49)

A. Ammon (49.1–6). Cf. Amos 1.13–15.

49.1 Ammon. Situated just north of Moab in the territory east of the Jordan. Descended, as were the Moabites, from Lot (Gen 19.37–38).

Why then doth Malcam possess Gad? See Judges 11.13 and Amos 1.13 for the longstanding tendency of Ammon to claim and encroach upon the territory of Israel. When the Israelite tribes east of the Jordan were carried into exile by the Assyrians, the Ammonites had evidently moved in upon the tribal territory of Gad. They acted as if Israel had no sons and no heir who would eventually return to the land.

Malcam. The word means *their king* (KJV). But the original Hebrew had no vowels, and probably the word should be pronounced *Milcom* as in modern versions (RSV, NBV, NEB, NASB margin). Milcom was "the god of the children of Ammon" (1 Kings 11.5, 33). Another name for Milcom was *Molech*, and this name is put into the text of NIV. See also on verse 3.

49.2 A desolate heap. Or "a mound of ruins" (NIV).

Her daughters. The daughters of Rabbah (also in v 3) were the surrounding small towns or villages dependent upon Rabbah, the capital. For this usage see Numbers 21.25; 32.42; and esp. Joshua 15.45 in context.

49.3 Ai. Otherwise unknown. Not the city west of the Jordan.

And run to and fro among the fences. Or "hedges" (KJV, RSV). Hebrew *gederah* refers to sheep folds in Numbers 32.16, 24, 36; Zephaniah 2.6; "hedges" in 1 Chronicles 4.23; Psalm 89.40; Jeremiah 49.3; Nahum 3.17; "wall" in Ezekiel 42.12 (cf. *geder* in v 10). Not necessarily sheep folds. It could also refer to the walls or hedges enclosing vineyards. Cf. the situation in Numbers 22.24—a path between vineyards with a wall on each side. The situation here seems to be that the cities have been laid waste and can give no protection, and the people have to scramble about across the country and try to get away the best way they can.

Malcam. See on verse 1. The parallel passage in 48.7 confirms the application to Milcom, the Ammonite god.

49.4 Thy flowing valley. Not an antithesis to the preceding as in KJV margin: *thy valley floweth away.* (So also NASB and NEB.) The description of Ammon's *confidence* continues all through verse 4, and the antithesis does not start until verse 5. Perhaps: *thy valley flows,* to be explained somewhat as NIV: "your valleys so fruitful." Cf. references to "a land flowing with milk and honey" (Exod 3.8, 17; etc.). The point of verse 4 is that Ammon's trust in her wealthy, fertile land will be of no avail.

O backsliding daughter. Cf. 31.22 (re. Israel). Perhaps applied to Ammonites as being descendants of Lot.

Who shall come unto me? Or "against me" (RSV and NASB). "Who will attack me?" (NIV).

B. Edom (49.7–22). Cf. Obadiah 1–9

1. Jehovah's Oath: Edom to be Completely Destroyed (49.7–13)

49.7 Edom. Descendants of Esau (Gen 36.1, 8–9) who lived in the territory between the Dead Sea and the Red Sea. So Edom was a brother nation to Israel, yet historically had behaved in a most unbrotherly manner. Cf. esp. Numbers 20.14–21; Amos 1.11–12; Obadiah.

Is wisdom no more in Teman? It is uncertain whether *Teman* was a town or a district of Edom. Bright thinks it is here "a poetic appellation for the entire land." Jeremiah describes a terrifying judgment facing Edom "before which his wise men shall stand not knowing what to advise, and unable to find out any means for averting the evil" (Keil).

49.8 Dwell in the depths. I.e., deep in the desert where the enemy would not be likely to pursue them.

Dedan. A city by this name located in the Arabian desert southeast of Edom is indicated on Map 7 in NBD. The Dedanites were a commercial people. The caravans (Isa 21.13) and merchants (Ezek 27.15, 20) of Dedan are mentioned. Evidently Edom was on their caravan routes and they are warned to turn back lest they be caught up in Edom's fate.

49.9–10 Grape-gatherers would not normally take every grape. They would miss some, which would be left for gleaners. But Jehovah has determined to strip Edom completely bare. Nothing and nobody (at least among the fighting men, for see v 11) will be spared.

His secret places. Or "his hiding places" (RSV, NASB, NEB, NIV).

49.11 A word of comfort while implying severity of treatment. The severity is that the men will be so completely exterminated that no one will be left to care for their widows and children. But Jehovah will have a special regard for them and they can look to him for protection.

49.12 They to whom it pertained not to drink. Translate as the margin: *they whose judgment* (or *sentence*) *was not etc.* The parallel in 25.28–29 shows the reference is to Israel. They, if anybody, would have escaped the cup of the wine of divine wrath (cf. 25.15), but did not. That being so, surely Edom cannot expect to escape. The statement does not, of course, imply injustice in the judgment on Israel. Israel's apostasy had made it like any pagan nation and they were therefore treated as such. Not even the people of Jehovah were exempt from judgment under these conditions.

2. The Proud Nation to be Brought Down (49.14–18). Cf. Obadiah on verses 14–16.

49.14 An ambassador is sent among the nations. I.e., a messenger sent from Jehovah to summon the nations to a war against Edom. The idea is that Jehovah is behind the attack on Edom.

49.16 Thy terribleness. I.e. "the terror you inspire" (NIV), "the horror you inspire" (RSV), "the dread for you" (NBV), "the terror of you" (NASB).

The pride of thy heart. To be taken in apposition with *thy terribleness*, the construction being as in KJV, NBV, et al. "The pride of Edom increased because the other nations were afraid to make war on him in his rocky dwelling, so difficult of access" (Keil).

That dwellest in the clefts of the rock. "The allusion is to the physical topography of Edom. Its capital, Petra, lay in an amphitheatre of mountains, accessible only through the narrow gorge, called the *Sik*, winding in with precipitous sides from the W.; and the mountain sides round Petra, and the ravines about it, contain innumerable rock-hewn cavities, some being tombs, but others dwellings, in which the ancient inhabitants lived" (Driver). See also the article "Sela" in NBD, 1158.

49.18 Edom to be left a desolate wasteland like Sodom and Gomorrah.

3. Jehovah's Counsel Against Edom: Edom to be Attacked by a Powerful Enemy (49.19–22)

49.19 He shall come up like a lion. Either Jehovah (RSV, NIV, NEB) or the unnamed enemy. Parallels can be found for either—Jehovah (25.30, 38, also with the wine figure, 25.27–39, as here in verse 12); a human enemy (4.7; 50.17). The nearest antecedent is "I" (= Jehovah) in verse 16. And the enemy that attacks Edom so far (vv 7–18) has been Jehovah, except in verse 14 where a *plurality* of nations is called to battle against Edom. On the other hand, the whole passage implies Jehovah's use of a human conqueror, and the verse is highly dramatic and the enemy could be mentioned suddenly without previous mention—which would not be unusual in such a passage.

From the pride of the Jordan. Referring to the jungle thicket about the Jordan, the lair of lions (RSV, NASB, et al). See on 12.5 and cf. 4.7: "A lion is gone up from his thicket, ..."

Against the strong habitation. NASB has "a perennially watered pasture," with margin: "enduring habitation." The margin seems to be from Driver who explains: "i.e. an abode of long standing, and likely to endure." The translation "pasture" fits the imagery of a lion attacking sheep.

For I will suddenly make them run away from it. The Edomite "flock" to be quickly driven from its habitation.

And whoso is chosen. Having chased the Edomites from their land, Jehovah appoints over it whatever ruler he chooses.

For who is like me? None is his equal in power. None can prevent it. Or perhaps: Who is like God able to bring one into judgment? See what follows.

And who will appoint me a time? Meaning as KJV margin: "convene me in judgment." "I.e. who will summon me to meet him in a court of law, or in a trial of strength? Exactly the same expression occurs in Job 9.19" (Driver). Who can bring God into court to account for his actions?

And who is the shepherd? The ruler (cf. 2.8; 23.1; etc.) who can "stand against" (NIV) or "stand his ground before" Jehovah. What ruler can stand before Jehovah to defend his flock?

49.20 Surely they shall drag them away. Against taking *the little ones* or *the least* as the subject of the sentence (KJV and ASV margin) see Keil. The enemy attacking Edom is compared to a lion attacking a flock. The Edomites are compared to the weakest and most helpless sheep of the flock being dragged off by a lion.

49.21 "The fall of Edom will be so fearful, that the earth will tremble, and the cry of anguish from the perishing people will be heard on the Red Sea" (Keil).

49.19–21 Repeated in the prophecy against Babylon (50.44–46).

49.22 Repeated from the prophecy against Moab (48.40–41).

C. Syria (49.23–27)

49.23 Evil tidings. Bad news of an enemy's approach.

They are melted away. Description of a loss of courage and resolve. Cf. Exodus 15.15; Joshua 2.9, 24; Psalm 75.3; and Ezekiel 7.17 ("all knees shall be weak as water"). Contrast something solid, prepared to put up stiff resistance.

There is sorrow on the sea. Better "anxiety" for *sorrow* (NASB, NEB). An implied comparison. The anxiety they feel at the approach of the enemy has them in agitation and turmoil like the tossing of the sea.

49.24 The citizens of Damascus turn to flee, but panic takes hold and they are so possessed with trembling and fright that they cannot take effective action and escape.[18]

49.25 Amazement expressed that the city has not been abandoned through the flight of its citizens. It is terrible. Panic keeps them from getting away (as v 24 explains). Verse 25 is possibly the exclamation of a citizen of Damascus. But some ancient versions have *the city of joy* rather than *the city of my joy*, which would permit the words to be explained more easily as an expression of the prophet's own feeling.

The city of praise. RSV, "the famous city"; NBV, "the renowned city."

49.26 Shall be brought to silence. NEB, "lie still in death."

49.27 Cf. Amos 1.4, 14. *Ben-hadad* is the name borne by more than one Syrian king, at least two and probably three. See Kitchen in NBD, 140–141 and Harrison in *Introduction to the Old Testament*, 187–188.

D. Arabians (49.28–33). After the heading (v 28a), this prophecy consists of two stanzas (vv 28b–30 and 31–33), each beginning with an order to the enemy to make war on the Arabians. Observe how, except for the concluding lines (vv 30, 33), each stanza covers the same ground.

---

[18] I have followed Keil in explaining verses 24–25.

49.28 Kedar. "Kedar, in its restricted sense, denotes a nomadic tribe which inhabited the Syro-Arabian desert, but the name is often used in Scripture and in rabbinical literature as a collective term for the Bedouin generally" (NBD, 688).

The kingdoms of Hazor. *Hazor* cannot here refer to any of the several cities of Palestine bearing this name. NBD, 508 calls it "an area occupied by semi-nomadic Arabs." But the probable meaning of the name is "'settlement' or 'village'" (NBD, 507), and many take it here as a collective term used to distinguish Arabians who lived in fixed settlements from the nomadic tribes who lived in tents and wandered about. *The kingdoms of Hazor* would then be "the regions of the settled tribes, ruled by their own princes or sheiks; cf. 25.24" (Keil). Isaiah 42.11 mentions "the villages that Kedar doth inhabit." Cf. Genesis 25.16.

Which Nebuchadrezzar king of Babylon smote. A hundred years ago Keil could write, "But we have no historical information as to the time when this took place." But the Babylonian Chronicle published by D. J. Wiseman in 1956 records "the actual attack by Nebuchadrezzar on Arabs south-east of Damascus in 599 BC" (NBD, 688). See Wiseman, *Chronicles of Chaldean Kings*, 32.

Arise ye. Jehovah gives the order! He uses Nebuchadrezzar for his own purposes.

The children of the east. The name commonly given to the tribes living in the desert east of Palestine (cf. Jdg 6.3; Job 2.3; Ezek 25.4).

49.29 The property and wealth of the Arabians to be carried off. For the phrase *Terror on every side* see 6.25; 20.3, 10; 46.5; cf. Lamentations 2.22.

49.30 Dwell in the depths. I.e., deep in the desert where the enemy will not pursue.

49.31 Arise, A second stanza begins. The command to Neb. is repeated. The command is to attack a nation that feels secure without city walls. Living outside the usual path of hostile armies they did not feel the need of strong fortifications. Their territory could therefore be easily conquered.

49.32 Them that have the corners of their hair cut off. Discussed at 9.26.

I will bring their calamity from every side of them. Note parallelism with "Terror on every side" in verse 29.

E. Elam (49.34–39)

49.34 Elam. An important and extremely ancient nation lying east of Babylonia in "the plain of Khuzistan, watered by the Kerkh river, which joins the Tigris just north of the Persian Gulf" (NBD, 355). They were remote from and had not come into relation with Israel.

49.35 The bow of Elam, the chief of their might. Evidently the Elamites were known for skill with the bow (cf. Isa 22.6). When Jehovah says he will break this "mainstay of their might" (RSV, NIV), which likely stands (by synecdoche) for all weapons, he means he will render them powerless before their enemies.

49.36 And upon Elam will I bring the four winds. Verse 37 translates figure into reality: "Elam is to be attacked on all sides by enemies, and be scattered in every direction" (Keil).

49.38 I will set my throne in Elam. I.e., to judge. Cf. 1.15–16; 39.5; 43.10; 52.9.

49.39 Cf. 46.26b; 48.47; 49.6.

PART THIRTEEN

Jehovah's Word Concerning Foreign Nations (2), And Historical Appendix

Jeremiah 50–52

I. Prophecy Concerning Babylon (Chs 50–51)

Introduction

1. The seed of this prophecy is found at Chapter 25. Note especially verses 11, 12 and 26. The nations will drink the wine of God's wrath during Babylon's seventy year dominion. After that Babylon shall drink of the same cup.

2. Two major themes of the prophecy: (a) The fall of Babylon. (b) The liberation of Israel from bondage.

3. These chapters are important not only in their own context but also as a part of the background of the book of Revelation. Consider especially Revelation 17–18, but also 14.8 and 16.19.

A. Heading of Chapters 50–51 (50.1)

B. Announcement of the Fall of Babylon (50.2–3). Jeremiah sees the fall of Babylon as if it were already accomplished, and commands that the news be published to the nations.

50.2 Set up a standard. Or a banner (RSV), signaling the news.

Babylon is taken. "Captured" (NASB); conquered.

Bel ... Merodach. Marduk, the supreme god of Babylon, and *Bel* a title of Marduk meaning "Lord." The Babylonian gods are exposed as weak and helpless, unable to deliver.

50.3 Out of the north ... a nation. The enemy is identified in 51.11 as the Medes; but note "the kings (plural) of the Medes." The Medes are allied with others; hence "a company of great nations" in 50.9.

C. The Liberation of Israel (50.4–10). The fall of Babylon brings the deliverance of Israel. They come out of captivity, seeking God, returning to Zion.

50.4 Weeping. With tears of penitence, say some; but perhaps also of joy.

50.5 They shall inquire. "They shall ask the way to Zion, with faces turned toward it" (RSV: similarly NASB).

Come ye. Encouraging and exhorting each other.

50.6 Israel now turns to God in the manner of verses 4–5 because of the misery into which he has fallen because of his sins, vers. 5–7" (Keil).

Their shepherds. Rulers (23.1–4 in context, and often).

They have turned them away on the mountains. Keil thinks the reference is to the "every high hill" on which idols were worshipped (cf. 2.20; 3.2; 17.2; etc.).

Their resting-place. Referring to the place where flocks of sheep lie down to rest (KJV margin; cf. 33.12; 50.19). Their *resting-place* is Jehovah, who is called *the habitation of righteousness* and *the hope of their fathers* in verse 7.

50.7 We are not guilty. Not true. Israel needed to be punished. But the enemies were evil in motive and act, and would be held accountable. See verse 14. Cf. 2.3.

50.8 Call to Abandon Babylon. See also this call in 51.6, 45, 50; cf. 50.28. Such a call presupposes a time when Israel *could* flee. In the time of Babylon's power their oppressors held them fast and refused to let them go (50.33). But in the period between the Persian occupation of Babylon and the complete destruction of the city, which came later, they could leave. Some remained in Babylon even after Cyrus' decree (Ezra 1.1–4) permitting them to return to their homeland (Zech 2.6–7; 6.9–10). But to remain there would be disastrous. They must flee to avoid being caught up in the sin and punishment of Babylon.

Be as the he-goats. Which try to push their way out of the fold first.

Israel is called to lead the way out of captivity—to have the eagerness of the he-goat.

50.9 A company of great nations. The Medes and their allies. Cf. 51.11, 27–28.

Their arrows. "Their arrows are like a skilled warrior who does not return empty-handed" (RSV; similarly NASB), but returns only after taking his prey (v 10).

50.10 The plunderers of Chaldea will be satisfied with her wealth. All will find enough.

D. Babylon's Devastation (50.11–13)

50.11 Because. RSV, NEB, et al put "though" for *because* three times in this verse.

That plunder my heritage. The people and land of Jehovah. Cf. 12.7–13.

That treadeth out the grain. Cf. Deuteronomy 25.4. But NASB margin notes: "Another reading is, *in the grass.*" RSV: "a heifer at grass." In either case reference is to a heifer grown "fat and sassy," meaning a people proud and independent.

50.12 Your mother. The nation as a whole distinguished from the individuals making it up (her children). Cf. Hosea 2.2–4; 4.5.

The hindermost of the nations. "The last of the nations" (RSV); "the least of the nations" (NASB). Imagine such a prophecy in the fourth year of Zedekiah (51.59–60).

E. The Order to Babylon's Enemies (50.14–16)

50.14 For she hath sinned against Jehovah. Cf. verses 28, 33. Such statements provide the light in which the fall of Babylon must be viewed. It is a matter of divine vengeance. See verse 15 below.

50.15 It is the vengeance of Jehovah. Observe the emphasis given to this point (cf. 50.18, 28, 29; 51.6, 11, 24, 34–36, 44, 45, 47, 49, 52, 56b).

50.16 Every one to his own people … to his own land. Referring to foreigners living in and about Babylon.

F. The Restoration of Israel and the Punishment of Its Enemies (50.17–20)

G. Jehovah's Vengeance Against Babylon Described (50.21–28)

50.21 Jehovah's order to the enemy to attack Babylonia.

Merathaim … Pekod. The latter has been shown to be an actual place in Babylonia. The name refers to the *Puqudu*, a people of East Babylonia (cf. Ezek 23.23). It is therefore likely that *Merathaim* also refers to some actual place. Bright follows Driver in suggesting the probable identification with "the district of *marratim* at the head of the Persian Gulf"—hence Southern Babylonia. NBD, however, calls this identification "questionable." In any case the names likely were used by Jeremiah for the sake of a wordplay. *Merathaim* is a dual in form and derived from a root meaning *to rebel*—hence *double rebellion* (ASV margin), suggesting the intensity of Babylon's rebellion against Jehovah (cf. v 24). *Pekod* means *visitation* or *punishment.*

50.22ff The consequence of Jehovah's order (v 21).

50.25 The attack upon Babylon is Jehovah's work (cf. 48.10). The enemies of Babylon are only weapons in his hands. Cf. "sword of Jehovah" in 47.6 (cf. Isa 34.5–6); also 49.37, "I will send the sword after them." See also especially Isaiah 10.5, 15.

50.26–27 Further address to the enemy.

Her bullocks. Likely to be explained in the light of Isaiah 34.5–7; Jeremiah 48.15; 51.40 with reference to the young warriors of Babylon, who are to be slaughtered like sacrificial animals.

50.28 The glad cry of the Jews is heard as they flee to proclaim in Zion the vengeance Jehovah has taken.

The vengeance of his temple. For its profanation and destruction.

H. The Fall of "Pride" (50.29–32)

50.29 Continues the address to the enemy interrupted by verses 27b, 28.

Recompense her. Stresses the idea of divine vengeance involved in the judgment upon Babylon. It is a due recompense for what Babylon has done. The reason assigned for judgment is that *she hath been proud against Jehovah*, referring especially to Babylon's insolence in destroying Jehovah's temple (v 28) and holding his people captive (v 33). Such presumption must be punished.

50.31 O thou proud one. Hebrew is literally "O Pride" (margin). So also in verse 32 *the proud one* is literally "Pride." It is the name by which Babylon is addressed. Babylon is the personification of pride. How else account for their storming into the temple, despoiling and wrecking as they did?

I. The Utter Destruction of Babylon (50.33–40)

50.33–34 Help define the pride and arrogance for which judgment falls upon Babylon. Verse 38b adds another reason for judgment.

Redeemer. Hebrew *goel* was used of the nearest of kin who took up the cause of another and acted on his behalf in some way—right of redemption (Lev 25.23–25; Ruth 2.20; 3.9–13, with note in margin on verse 9; 4.1–6; Jer 32.6–8); Ruth 4 referring also to the Levirate Law (Deut 25.5–10); avenger (Hebrew *goel*) of blood (Num 35; Deut 19; Josh 20). Jehovah as the strong Redeemer of Israel takes the part of Israel and frees them from oppression. Cf. also esp. Psalm 19.14; 119.15–16 in context; Job 19.25 in context; Proverbs 23.10–11.

That he may give rest to the earth. RSV: "that he may give rest to the earth, but unrest to the inhabitants of Babylon." Babylon had formerly given unrest to the earth (Isa 14.16–17). Now the tables are turned. Cf. Isaiah 14.3–7.

50.35–38 Description of the way in which Jehovah takes up the case of Israel as its Redeemer. The pleading of Israel's cause (v 34) involves more than words. The judgment falls upon all that is in Babylon—inhabitants generally, princes, advisers, prophets and diviners, warriors, horses and chariots, mercenaries, treasures, waters (vv 35–38).

Boasters. In place of KJV's "liars." Cf. Isaiah 44.25, "the signs of the liars (or boasters)," and the pairing of the word with "diviners." Reference is to such as the prophets, soothsayers and astrologers of Babylon.

All the mingled people. Foreigners; mercenaries or allies.

Drought. Hebrew has the same consonants as the word for *sword* used throughout verses 35–37. The vowels are later additions. It is uncertain whether the reading should be *sword* (which would be no more incongruous in verse 38 than in verse 37c; it would not be understood literally) or *drought.*

Mad over idols. They act like madmen (cf. 25.16) —one deprived of reason. The devotion to idolatry is an insanity.

Idols. Hebrew is literally *terrors* (margin)—referring to the idols as objects of terror.

50.39–40 The state of complete desolation in which Babylon is left by the judgment.

J. Agents of the Judgment: The Enemies Brought Against Babylon by Jehovah (50.41–46). The description is taken from two earlier passages.

50.41–43 Quotation from 6.21–23. The descriptions of the Babylonians is here adapted to their enemies who would be of the same character.

Many kings. See on verses 3, 9; cf. "the kings of the Medes" (51.11) and the "kingdoms" listed in 51.27. Reference to the Medes and their allies.

50.44–46 Quotation from 49.19–21. See notes there.

50.46 Cf. 49.21. The noise of the fall of little Edom is heard at the Red Sea; but the noise of the fall of Babylon resounds among the nations. NASB, after Keil and Driver: "At the shout, 'Babylon has been seized!' the earth is shaken, and an outcry is heard among the nations." Hebrew for *noise* means "*sound* or *voice* (viz. of the following words)" (Driver, who renders it *tidings*). Keil explains it of the effect upon the world of the news of Babylon's fall—the anxiety, fear and uncertainty.

K. The Complete Destruction of the Babylonian Army (51.1–4)

51.1 Leb-kamai. Means "the heart (or midst or center) of them that rise up against me" (KJV; ASV margin), but should be understood as a proper name—as NASB margin puts it, "a code name for Chaldea." Evidently a cabalistic formula called "Atbash" was used. The first letter of the Hebrew alphabet would stand for the last letter; the second letter would stand for the next to last; etc. According to this formula *Leb-kamai* would be Chaldea according to the Hebrew spelling. The name *Sheshach* is another example of this usage (v 41 and 25.26). This explanation seems to be adopted by most scholars, liberal and conservative alike. This "playing with words" is used apparently because of the meaning that results from the transformation of letters. The name Leb-kamai would describe Chaldea as "the center of God's enemies"—the place where all enmity against Jehovah has its heart and center (Keil). Cf. Rev 17.5 where Babylon the great is described as "the mother of the harlots and of the abominations of the earth"; also Genesis 10.8–10; 11.1–9 for the beginning of organized revolt against Jehovah, which took place in Babylon.

A destroying wind. Better with RSV, NASB, et al: "the spirit of a destroyer." Hebrew for wind and spirit is the same word. Keil points out that the verb "is nowhere used of the rousing of a wind, but everywhere means 'to rouse the spirit of any one,' to stir him up to an undertaking; cf. Haggai 1.14, 1 Chronicles 5.56, 2 Chronicles 21.16, and 36.22." Jeremiah has this usage in verse 11. Hebrew for *destroyer* would be used substantively as in 4.7. Possibly the figure of winnowing, if it is present at all in verse 2, plays upon the double meaning of the Hebrew for spirit and wind. Keil, however, mentions some passages where the Hebrew verb refers to the scattering of a nation without reference to the figure of winnowing. See Lev 26.33; Jeremiah 49.32, 36; Ezekiel 5.10; 12.15; etc.

51.3–4 "These strangers shall kill, without sparing, every warrior of Babylon, and annihilate its whole military *forces*" (Keil).

L. The Judgment Upon Babylon and the Liberation and Vindication of Israel (51.5–10)

51.5 Reasons given for this destruction of Babylon: (1) God has not forsaken Israel or Judah. He acts on their behalf. (2) The guilt of Babylon (cf. "her iniquity" in v 6).

51.6 For the reasons assigned (v 5) Babylon will be destroyed, and the Israelites in Babylon must flee in order to avoid being caught up in her sin and punishment. For the historical circumstances that clarify this call to abandon Babylon see note on 50.8.

51.7 A golden cup. Cf. 25.15ff. *Golden* indicating Babylon's wealth and splendor. Cf. verse 13.

51.8 Wail for her. An ironical address to the captive nations. They are called upon to lament the fall of Babylon and try to heal her injuries. Probably this anticipates the cry that would be raised among many captives: "Instead of abandoning Babylon we must do something to help her." But it is soon apparent that the case is hopeless and that they must abandon Babylon in order to save themselves (v 9). Any parallels in modern circumstances?

51.10 Jehovah hath brought forth our righteousness. The judgment upon Babylon is at once a condemnation of Babylon's guilt (vv 5b–6) and a vindication of the righteousness of Israel's cause. Cf. Psalm 37.6 and the whole psalm. Perhaps light is cast on Israel's "righteousness" by 50.20. (1) It is a righteousness based on forgiveness. (2) It is the righteousness of the remnant that remains.

M. The End of Babylon Decreed by Jehovah (51.11–14)

51.11–12 Who is addressed? Henderson thinks the Babylonians are being called to prepare for the defence of Babylon. But more likely Babylon's enemies are addressed and summoned to prepare for an attack on Babylon. (See notes on v 12a.) Then the second half of each of these verses explains the reason for preparation, an important point: Jehovah is back of the attack on Babylon. The Medes are only instruments used by him.

The kings of the Medes. Keil explains the plural as referring to the heads of the various provinces of the Medes; Boutflower: "the chiefs of the Median clans." But see verses 27–28. "Kings" is distinguished from "governors" and "deputies." Note "kingdoms" in verse 27. Perhaps all the kings in "the land of their dominion"—i.e. vassal kings or allies—are included. The *Septuagint* has "the king" and is followed by Driver.

Set up a standard. The signal flag indicating the direction an army was to take and the point of attack.

Make the watch strong. Explained by 2 Samuel 11.16.

Set the watchmen. Hebrew does not refer to sentinels looking out for the approach of the enemy but to "'watchers' in the sense of *guarders, blockaders*; cf. the corresponding verb in 2 Sam 11.16)"—hence "men to watch and keep the city close by blockading it" (Driver).

Prepare the ambushes. As in Joshua 8 and Judges 20.29–48. KJV margin explains *ambushes* as *liars in wait.*

51.13–14 Now Babylon is addressed. (We must appreciate the poetic and dramatic effect as now one, then the other is addressed.) Neither the strategic position of Babylon on the Euphrates nor the immense wealth which makes possible the building of strong fortifications can prevent the city's destruction.

The measure of thy covetousness. "I.e. the limit put to thine unjust gain" (Keil). But NASB margin points out that literally the words read "the cubit of your being cut off." Hence Driver: "the cubit where thou shalt be cut off," and NBV: "the thread of your life is severed." Perhaps as in Isaiah 38.12 the figure is of a piece of cloth or a thread measured out to the point where it is to be cut off."

Jehovah of hosts hath sworn by himself. God has decreed it—it is absolutely certain.

Though I have filled thee with men. Reading as the margin. See Keil for defence. Not even the tremendous population that Babylon has can prevent its ruin.

As with the cankerworm. Apparently one stage of the development of the locust.

Shall lift up a shout. Reference to "the shout of victory" (RSV) which would be "like the song of grape treaders" (NASB margin; cf. 25.30).

N. The Almighty Jehovah Contrasted With the Nothingness of Idolatry (51.15–19). The passage is repeated from 10.12–16, probably for the purpose of suggesting the certainty of Babylon's fall, once it has been decreed by Jehovah (vv 11–14). Let no one doubt that the mighty world power can be brought down. Consider who has decreed and sworn it! The destruction of Babylon is certain and the Babylonian gods will be helpless to prevent it. Keil writes: "In chap. 10 Jeremiah wished, by means of this announcement, to combat the fears of the idolatrous people for the power of the heathen gods; here he seeks by the same means to destroy the confidence of the Chaldeans in their gods, ..." But the last part is most unlikely. Rather, is not the message for Israel, one that would build confidence in Jehovah and his power to overthrow Babylon?

51.19 And Israel is the tribe. Israel omitted here in Hebrew text. Contrast 10.16. NASB, after Keil, suggests reading, "For the Maker of all is He, and of the tribe of His inheritance"—referring to Israel. The LXX reads: "For the former of all things is his inheritance" (Driver). But that is a thought completely different from 10.16.

O. The Instrument of Destruction to be Recompensed for its Evil (51.20–24). It is difficult to determine who is addressed in verses 20–23. Because of verse 24 Driver thinks the Medes are addressed. But verses 25–26 make it more likely that the address is directed toward Babylon. NASB translates the verbs in verses 20–23 as presents, which is possible (Driver); then begins verse 25 with "But." Verses 20–26, then, will fit into the context thus: Babylon is a great power—a hammer (vv 20–24), a destroying mountain (vv 25–26). But Babylon is only a tool in the hands of the almighty Jehovah (vv 15–19), who will bring judgment upon it.

51.20 My battle axe. NASB has "war-club," with explanation in the margin: "literally shatterer." "War-club" is from Driver, who explains: "The word signifies properly something that *shatters* or *dashes in pieces* (cf. Nah 2.1)"; it is cognate with the verb rendered *break in pieces* in verses 20–23. Cf. 50.23 where Babylon was already called "the hammer of the whole earth."

51.24 Israel is addressed. Jehovah uses Babylon, then destroys it.

P. The Destroying Mountain to Become a Burnt Mountain (51.25–26)

51.25 O destroying mountain. "The prophet now changes the metaphor of a war-club for that of a volcano, which, pouring forth floods of lava, spreads destruction over all the surrounding country" (Henderson).

Roll thee down from the rocks. Off its solid foundation.

A burnt mountain. "I.e. as barren and desolate as an extinct volcano" (Driver).

51.26 Babylon will be so turned to ashes that no stone of any value will be left for rebuilding. That marks the utter end of Babylon.

Q. The City of Babylon Taken by a Powerful Alliance (51.27–33)

51.27–28 The alliance against Babylon. Summons to the nations to attack Babylon.

Set ye up a standard. A banner or ensign around which the armies are to rally.

As the rough cankerworm. One stage in the development of the locust. Likely with emphasis on both number and destructiveness."

51.29a The earth quakes before the advance of this mighty force.

51.30–32 The fall of the city. Messengers come from all directions to inform the king that every quarter of the city is in enemy hands.

The passages. Literally, *crossing-places.* Babylon was built on the Euphrates.

51.33 Like a threshing-floor at the time when it is trodden. "I.e. trodden down hard, in readiness for the threshing" (Driver); meaning prepared and ready for judgment.

R. The Destruction of Babylon Explained as Jehovah's Response to Jerusalem's Complaint Against Babylon (51.34–40)

51.34–35 Dramatically Jerusalem is introduced as speaking, uttering its complaint against Babylon and calling for judgment. The judgment strikes Babylon, therefore, because of its offences against the people of God.

Like a monster. Hebrew *tannin* usually refers to a large sea- or river-monster such as the crocodile (cf. Psa 74.13; Ezek 29.3).

51.36–37 Jehovah's answer (vv 36–40). Jehovah will take up the cause of Judah and turn Babylon into a desert, heaps of ruins.

51.38–39 Babylon will be surprised by judgment day as they growl like lions over their prey and engage in revelry. Cf. Daniel 5, and the following from Herodotus i. 191 (Penguin edition, pp. 90–91). Recall that the Euphrates River flowed through the city of Babylon. After describing how Cyrus diverted the course of the Euphrates, permitting an army to ford the river and enter the city, Herodotus says "the Babylonians were taken by surprise. The Babylonians themselves say that owing to the great size of the city the outskirts were captured without the people in the centre knowing anything about it; there was a festival going on, and even while the city was falling they continued to dance and enjoy themselves, until hard facts brought them to their senses." See also Xenophon's *Cyropaedia* vii. 23.

S. The Astonishing End of Babylon (51.41–44). "The fearful destruction of Babylon will astonish the world" (Keil).

51.41 "An exclamation of astonishment regarding the conquest of the city which was praised throughout the world" (Keil).

Sheshach. Another code name for Babylon. See at 25.26 and cf. 51.1.

51.42 The sea. Explained in the light of 46.7–8; 47.2; Isaiah 8.7–8; 17.12–13. A figure for enemy troops that pour into Babylon in overwhelming numbers. Cf. verses 55–56.

51.44 Bel. See at 50.2.

That which he hath swallowed up. The treasures taken as spoil from conquered nations. Henderson refers to how such treasures would often be deposited in a temple. Cf. 1 Samuel 5.2.

T. The Repeated Warning to Abandon the Doomed City (51.45–49). Cf. 50.8; 51.6. Israel is warned to flee (v 45). Yet they need not despair when the rumors of war are heard; the end is not yet (v 46; cf. Matt 24.6; Mark 13.7; Luke 21.9). Yet these rumors are the harbingers of the judgment to come (v 47), and Israel must take warning and get out.

U. Further Assurance and Encouragement (51.50–53)

51.50 Ye that have escaped the sword. I.e. Babylon's sword (v 49). Refers to the Israelites that have survived. They are called upon to remember Jehovah and Jerusalem and hasten their return.

51.51 Though they "have escaped the sword" they have been humiliated and disgraced before their enemies.

51.52–53 Jehovah's answer is that Babylon will be repaid. Its mighty defences (v 53) shall be to no avail.

Though Babylon should mount up to heaven. Cf. Genesis 11.4; Isaiah 14.12–13.

Fortify the height of her strength. Hebrew for *fortify* is "lit. *cut off*, i.e. *make inaccessible*, the regular meaning of the Hebrew word rendered *fortify*" (Driver). *The height of her strength* is explained as "the height in which its strength consists" (Keil). Reference is to the great wall surrounding Babylon. See verse 58 below.

V. Final Word of Judgment Upon Babylon (51.54–58)

51.54 An exclamation. It is as though Jeremiah were transported into the future and saw the destruction as accomplished. He exclaims at what he sees.

51.55 Destroyeth … the great voice. Referring to the noise and bustle of the great city.

And their waves. I.e. of the enemy, which comes down upon Babylon like waves of the sea (v 42).

51.57 And I will make drunk. On the wine of his wrath (cf. 25.15).

51.58 And the peoples shall labor for vanity. Taken from Habakkuk 2.13. The tremendous exertion involved in the building of the city is all in vain. The people are only building for the fire that will reduce Babylon to ashes.

W. Epilogue: Jeremiah's Charge to Seraiah (51.59–64). The message sent to Babylon, with the accompanying symbolic action, was doubtless intended to strongly impress upon the captives the message of Jeremiah that Babylon would fall after seventy years and Israel be restored.

51.59 Seraiah the son of Neriah. Evidently a brother of Baruch. See 32.12, 16; 36.4.

Chief chamberlain. Better with margin: *quartermaster.* So RSV and

NASB. KJV's *a quiet prince* is wrong. Hebrew for *quiet* means "rest, place of rest" (*Young's Anal. Conc.*). Seraiah was the official in charge of arrangements for the resting-place when the party stopped for the night.

51.64 Thus far are the words of Jeremiah. A statement added by the collector of the prophecies, indicating that the words of Jeremiah end here and chapter 52 is a historical appendix added by someone else.

Reflections on Chapters 46–51

A. Jehovah is revealed as the God of history and the God of all the earth, not just a tribal or national deity. It is he who controls the destiny not only of the small nations but even of the great powers.

B. The great nations are only tools in his hands (50.9, 21, 25; 51.7, 20). He uses them to accomplish his purposes, then holds them accountable for their own misdeeds.

C. Judah might seem to be only a small state tossed about between great powers. But the truth is, God is in control and is working out his purposes.

D. Great nations are held accountable in history for their wrongdoing just as individuals will be held accountable at the end of time.

E. The fall of Babylon was not just a matter that a stronger nation had finally arisen, but rather a matter of divine vengeance (50.14–15, 17–18, 24, 28, 29; 51.6, 11, 24, 36, 56). So also the defeat of Egypt (46.10).

II. Historical Appendix: The Fall of Jerusalem and the Captivity (Ch 52)

Introduction

The last verse of Chapter 51 separates "the words of Jeremiah" from this chapter. Chapter 52 was not, therefore, written by Jeremiah, but attached to his prophecies by another writer or compiler. Its contents agree almost word for word with 2 Kings 24.18–25.30. Driver thinks verses 1–27 were "excerpted from 2 Kings 24.18–25.21" and verses 28–30 "taken by the compiler from some independent source." But Keil thinks, because of the differences in the two accounts, that both must have been taken from another and common source—some document giving a fuller description of the fall of Judah than we have in our Old Testament books; that

that explanation would account for the likenesses and also the differences between the two.

Why this record is added to Jeremiah's prophecies is not explained. It may have been, as Driver thinks, "for the purpose of showing how Jeremiah's principal and most constant prediction was fulfilled." See further on verses 31–34.

Cf. also Jeremiah 39.1–10.

A. Brief Account of the Character of Zedekiah's Reign (52.1–3)

52.3 Cf. the KJV with the corrected translation in ASV, NASB, and other versions. Some difficulty has been felt in the statement that Zedekiah's evil came to pass "through the anger of Jehovah." But compare the repeated "God gave them up" in Romans 3.24, 26, 28, which was a manifestation of divine wrath (v 28). Evidently evil kings like Jehoiakim and Zedekiah were a punishment of the attitudes long present in the nation, even during the reign of Josiah (3.6–10).

B. The Siege, Capture and Destruction of Jerusalem, and the Captivity of the People (52.4–30)

1. The Capture of Jerusalem and the Fate of Zedekiah (4–11)

2. The Destruction of the City and the Captivity of the People (12–16)

3. The Spoiling of the Temple (17–23)

4. Various Executions (24–27)

5. Summary—the Number of Captives Taken at Various Times (28–30)

52.28 At this point 2 Kings 25.22–26 has an account of the appointment and assassination of Gedaliah. It is omitted here. But it was given even more fully at 40.7–43.7. The passage verses 28–30 is not in 2 Kings. Nor is it in the Septuagint here.

In the seventh year. I.e. of Jehoiachin's captivity (2 Kings 24.10–17). Cf. 25.1 where "the fourth year of Jehoiakim" corresponds to "the first year of Nebuchadrezzar."

Three thousand Jews and three and twenty. Ten thousand in 2 Kings 24.14. But verse 16 points out that seven thousand were soldiers. The number here evidently excludes soldiers, and is an exact number, whereas 2 Kings 24.14 gives a round number.

52.29 Eighteenth year. Nineteenth year in verse 12, perhaps from a different source which followed a different method of dating. Cf. the note on 25.1.

52.30 The three and twentieth year. We have no other certain information about captives being taken in this year. Pfeiffer thinks "this deportation may have been brought on by the disorders which followed the murder of Gedaliah" (*Exile and Return* in O. T. History Series, p. 17). But did Gedaliah's governorship last that long?

C. The Exaltation of Jehoiachin (52.31–34). Cf. 2 Kings 25.27–30. The effect of this account both here and in 2 Kings is to close the books on a hopeful note. Jeremiah had predicted the overthrow of Judah and the destruction of Jerusalem. But he also looked beyond the dark days of judgment and foresaw a brighter future. Judah would be restored. And God had not forgotten his covenant with David (2 Sam 7.11–16; Jer 23.5; 33.14–26). Beyond the darkness of the present in which the house of David was brought so low Jeremiah could see a king of the future seated on the throne of David. The rise of Jehoiachin in the captivity may have been just the glimmer of light needed to keep alive the hope of God's remnant through this time of trial.

Archaeological References to Jehoiachin

References to King Jehoiachin have been discovered by archaeologists in both Palestine and Babylon. W. F. Albright mentions three different jar-handles each bearing the same stamp, "Belonging to Eliakim, steward of Yaukin." Yaukin has been shown to be an abbreviated form of Jehoiachin. These stamps show that while Jehoiachin was in exile "his estates in Judah continued to be managed by a steward" named Eliakim (D. J. Wiseman in NBD, 602). Eliakim was "steward of the crown property of king Joiachin while the latter was a captive in Babylonia" (Albright, *The Biblical Archaeologist Reader*, 107), or as others define his position, "administrator of the personal or crown property of Jehoiachin" (*Documents From Old Testament Times*, edited by D. Winton Thomas, p. 224).

The Babylonian discoveries were in the form of nearly 300 cuneiform tablets found in the ruins of what must have been "an important public building, probably one of the main depots for the distribution of supplies from the royal storehouses," located "near the famous Ishtar Gate" in Babylon (Albright, 107). These tablets contain records of the distribution of rations of oil and barley to "individuals who are either prisoners of war or otherwise dependent upon the royal household" (Oppenheim in *The Ancient Near East, An Anthology of Texts and Pictures*, edited by James B. Pritchard, 205). "Whether all these people were exiles, or whether some were employees of the king, it is impossible to say" (Martin in *Documents From Old Testament Times*, 86).

Among those receiving rations are listed several Judeans, but also people of other nationalities. But of special significance is "Yaukin, king of Judah," a name which appears several times in the tablets.

What of the significance of these tablets? They show (1) that "in Babylon Jehoiachin was treated as a royal hostage and received rations from the Babylonian court" (Wiseman in NBD, 602); (2) that "Jehoiachin was regarded by the Babylonians as legitimate king of Judah" (Albright, 111). (Albright might also be correct in the opinion that the Babylonians were holding Jehoiachin "in reserve for possible restoration to power if circumstances should seem to require it.") Cf. Ezekiel's method of dating prophecies from the year of Jehoiachin's captivity (1.1; cf. 8.1 20.1; 24.1; etc.).

An interesting and full discussion is provided in the Albright article referred to above. Besides the references above see G. Ernest Wright, *Biblical Archaeology*, 179–181, and other works on Biblical archaeology.

Also from DeWard Publishing

Heritage of Faith Library

The Man of Galilee
Atticus G. Haygood

Dr. Haygood's apologetic for the deity of Christ using Jesus Himself as presented by the gospel records as its chief evidence. This is a reprint of the 1963 edition. The Man of Galilee was originally published in 1889. 108 pages. $8.99.

Jesus and Jonah
J.W. McGarvey

McGarvey's defense of the historicity of the Biblical account of the book of Jonah based on Jesus' teaching about Jonah—which is the same as His teaching regarding the historicity of the rest of the Old Testament. This would indicate that Jesus either accepts all of it as historical or none of it as historical. Since the New Testament makes it plain that Jesus accepts the Old as historical, McGarvey argues that the denial of the Jonah story makes Jesus either a liar or a fool.

Original Commentary on Acts
J.W. McGarvey

McGarvey's classic commentary on Acts, attractively re-typeset and added to our Heritage of Faith collection.

A Guide to Bible Study
J.W. McGarvey

A brief handbook that gives a brief summary of facts regarding the making and the purpose of the Bible; its chief divisions; short sketches of the various books, serving as introductions to their study; and various other material of an interesting and helpful sort to the reader and student of the Bible.

Coming Soon

Natural Theology
William Paley

DeWard Original Publications

Beneath the Cross: Essays and Reflections on the Lord's Supper
Jady S. Copeland and Nathan Ward (editors)

The Lord's Supper is rich with meaning supplied by Old Testament foreshadowing and New Testament teaching. Explore the depths of symbolism and meaning found in the last hours of the Lord's life in *Beneath the Cross.* Filled with short essays by preachers, scholars, and other Christians, this book is an excellent tool for preparing meaningful Lord's Supper thoughts—or simply for personal study and meditation. 329 pages. $14.99 (PB); $23.99 (HB).

The Growth of the Seed: Notes on the Book of Genesis
Nathan Ward
A study of the book of Genesis that emphasizes two primary themes: the development of the Messianic line and the growing enmity between the righteous and the wicked. In addition, it provides detailed comments on the text and short essays on several subjects that are suggested in, yet peripheral to, Genesis. 537 pages. $19.99.

The Big Picture of the Bible
Kenneth W. Craig
In this short book, the author summarizes the central theme of the Bible in a simple, yet comprehensive approach. Evangelists across the world have used this presentation to convert countless souls to the discipleship of Jesus Christ. Bulk discounts will be available, as will special pricing for congregational orders. 48 pages, color. $4.99.

Boot Camp: Equipping Men with Integrity for Spiritual Warfare
Jason Hardin

According to Steve Arterburn, best-selling author of *Every Man's Battle,* "This is a great book to help us men live opposite of this world's model of man." *Boot Camp* is the first volume in the IMAGE series of books for men. It serves as a Basic Training manual in the spiritual war for honor, integrity and a God-glorifying life. 237 pages, $13.99 (PB); $24.99 (HB).

For a full listing of our titles, visit our website: www.dewardpublishing.com

CPSIA information can be obtained at www.ICGtesting.com
Printed in the USA
BVOW04s1713121114

374839BV00002B/155/P

9 780981 970363